Sports Journalism

Based on interviews with leading sports journalists and grounded in the authors' experience and expertise in both the sports journalism industry and sports media research, *Sports Journalism* gives in-depth insight into the editorial and ethical challenges facing sports journalists in a fast-changing media environment.

The book considers how sports journalism's past has shaped its present and explores the future trends and trajectories that the industry could take. The far-reaching consequences of the digital revolution and social media on sports journalists' work are analysed, with prominent sports writers, broadcasters and academics giving their insights. While predominantly focused on the UK sports media industry, the book also provides a global perspective, and includes case studies, research and interviews from around the world. Issues of diversity – or a lack of it – in the industry are put into sharp focus.

Sports Journalism gives both practising sports journalists and aspiring sports journalists vital contextualising information to make them more thoughtful and reflective practitioners.

Tom Bradshaw is Senior Lecturer and Course Leader in Sports Journalism at the University of Gloucestershire, and an award-winning sports journalist. His main research area is media ethics. Alongside his teaching and research, Tom writes for *The Times* and other titles, and broadcasts for the BBC.

Daragh Minogue is Principal Lecturer and Course Leader in Sport Journalism at St Mary's University. His current research focuses on identity, politics and sports media. He contributes to the journalism training programme at Sky Sports News and has received commendations for promoting equality, diversity and inclusion in journalism.

"Sports Journalism analyses the impact on sports journalism of the collision between professional and commercialised elite sport and the digital revolution and is essential reading for sports journalism students, educators and experienced practitioners, all continually grappling with an ever-changing landscape."

Laurie Tucker, *Head of Journalism Training at Sky Sports News*

"Sport journalists are under greater scrutiny than ever before, with the industry needing answers to difficult questions around diversity, gender balance and collusion on its sports desks. Tom Bradshaw and Daragh Minogue have provided the essential guide for any trainee reporters tackling the issues that go beyond the back page."

Owen Evans, *University of Brighton*

"Tom Bradshaw and Daragh Minogue have crafted a brilliantly well-researched, uber-contemporary, rip-roaring read that is crammed full of excellent case studies and thought-provoking content. If, like me, you have an insatiable thirst for sports journalism knowledge in this constantly adapting, technology-embracing, fast-paced era, you will find the time invested in this book very worthwhile."

Will Cope, *Southampton Solent University*

"What this book doesn't tell you about sports journalism in the digital age isn't worth knowing. Tom Bradshaw and Daragh Minogue provide a comprehensive guide to the media, tracing the history of an era of often startling change and pointing to the future in a way that will educate and entertain both current and aspiring journalists. It is the most readable work – students and historians alike will enjoy learning from it, as I certainly did."

Patrick Barclay, *chairman of the Football Writers' Association from 2016 to 2019, former Sports Writer of The Year and author*

"From the outset the book raises the very real dichotomy of opportunities and challenges posed by the shifting sands of sports journalism, underpinned throughout with crucial ethical considerations. From the digital revolution that has transformed the role of the sports journalist, to the implications for journalist-source relationships in the wake of an increasing reliance on PR and communications personnel, the book builds on previous academic work with fresh input from the authors and primary case studies to bring us right up to date. The position of sports journalism in wider contemporary debates is tackled superbly and in-depth with salient chapters on areas including race and representation, coverage of women in sport and LGBT and disability; topics that transcend sports journalism but are also now integral to the development of the vocation and socio-political discussion generally. From students to scholars, to practising sports journalists and those invested in the sports media industries, this book is essential reading to obtain an informed understanding of the past, present and future of sports journalism and the growing significance of its place in the cultural fabric of society."

David Randles, *University of Chester*

Media Skills

Edited by Richard Keeble, Lincoln University

The *Media Skills* series provides a concise and thorough introduction to a rapidly changing media landscape. Each book is written by media and journalism lecturers or experienced professionals and is a key resource for a particular industry. Offering helpful advice and information and using practical examples from print, broadcast and digital media, as well as discussing ethical and regulatory issues, *Media Skills* books are essential guides for students and media professionals.

For more information about this series, please visit:
www.routledge.com/Media-Skills/book-series/SE0372

Sports Journalism

The State of Play

Tom Bradshaw and Daragh Minogue

Routledge
Taylor & Francis Group

LONDON AND NEW YORK

First published 2020
by Routledge
2 Park Square, Milton Park, Abingdon, Oxon OX14 4RN

and by Routledge
52 Vanderbilt Avenue, New York, NY 10017

Routledge is an imprint of the Taylor & Francis Group, an informa business

British Library Cataloguing-in-Publication Data
A catalogue record for this book is available from the British Library

Library of Congress Cataloging-in-Publication Data
Names: Bradshaw, Tom, 1979– author. | Minogue, Daragh, author.
Title: Sports journalism : the state of play / Tom Bradshaw and Daragh Minogue.
Description: London ; New York : Routledge, 2019. | Series: Media skills |
Includes bibliographical references and index.
Identifiers: LCCN 2019015149 (print) | LCCN 2019019028 (ebook) |
ISBN 9780429505409 (ebook) | ISBN 9781138583511 (hardback : alk. paper) |
ISBN 9781138583528 (pbk. : alk. paper) | ISBN 9780429505409 (ebk.)
Subjects: LCSH: Sports journalism–Great Britain. | Sports journalism.
Classification: LCC PN4784.S6 (ebook) |
LCC PN4784.S6 B73 2019 (print) | DDC 070.4/49796–dc23
LC record available at https://lccn.loc.gov/2019015149

ISBN: 978-1-138-58351-1 (hbk)
ISBN: 978-1-138-58352-8 (pbk)
ISBN: 978-0-429-50540-9 (ebk)

Typeset in Goudy
by Newgen Publishing UK

Contents

Preface

Elite sport is, according to a leading figure in the analysis of sports journalism, "one of the most enduring and media-saturated forms of contemporary popular culture" (Boyle, 2017: 495). Put another way, top-level sport now secures so much media coverage that sport is a central aspect of what it means to be a human being alive in the early decades of the third millennium. It has been argued that sport now trumps – or at least rivals – music, film and other forms of contemporary mainstream culture as *the* most powerful means of global inter-connection. As another writer on sports journalism has claimed, sport is now "the common currency, allowing generations and nations and cultures to trade and connect. In terms of newsprint, airtime and net space, sport is now the dominant language of twenty-first-century culture, West and East" (Steen, 2014: 22). Yet if sport and the media coverage of it are so omnipresent in early-twenty-first-century human culture, then that surely leaves sports journalists with something of a responsibility. If sport is, indeed, the global common currency, then – to continue the financial metaphor – sports journalists are on the trading floor either pushing its stock value up or pulling it down depending on what they are broadcasting and publishing. To complicate matters, while sport itself may well be a prominent, or even the pre-eminent, facet of contemporary popular culture, sports journalism itself is an industry that has gone through – and is continuing to experience – a significant culture shock following the technological changes brought about by the digital revolution.

Sport often dominates trending lists on social media, and sports journalists – along with their colleagues in the rest of the media – have had to adjust to the challenges and opportunities that digitisation has presented. They have had to rethink their relationship with their audience; a relationship that is now far more interactive than it once was and which – for better or worse – puts social media at the heart of their work. The sports media ecosystem has been disrupted by the big beasts of tech but also stimulated and enlivened by far-reaching changes in digital technology that have transformed the way that sports journalism is both produced and consumed. Sports journalists who have refused to adapt to this new digital habitat – or who have been slow to do so – have found themselves running the risk of terminal irrelevance, or even extinction. Many of the traditional activities and rhythms of the sports journalist's routine have been challenged and, in some cases, superseded as increasingly sophisticated pieces of audience analysis software have allowed real-time data to inform editorial decisions about what audiences are reading and what they want. Rather than guessing at where their audience's interests lie, sports editors can now mine reams of analytics, with many media companies now employing tech-savvy, number crunchers (some of them journalists or ex-journalists) to do just that. This has led to one of the staples of sports journalism – the match report – being put under scrutiny; yet it has also led to more resources being put into real-time coverage, such as live blogs.

Yet amid all the discontinuities that at times can seem collectively to constitute something bordering on a sense of existential crisis for sports journalism, there are threads of continuity: the need for compelling and engaging storytelling; the willingness to speak truth to power when necessary, and the related quality of being brave enough to ask the awkward questions; the need to be independent-minded and to resist too cosy a relationship with those about whom one is reporting. The conclusion of two sports media academics a decade ago that "in short, sports journalism should be about reporting, enquiring, explaining and at times holding to account sports on behalf of the fans" (Boyle & Haynes, 2009: 183) is in some ways both reassuringly simple and reassuringly still the case today, notwithstanding the technological upheavals that have continued apace.

The fine sports journalists of the past still have plenty to tell us about what the sports journalists of the future should aspire to be, as this book hopes to illustrate. And there are, of course, many superb writers and broadcasters today displaying many of the enduringly important qualities of the successful sports journalist: perseverance, courage, a thick skin, single-mindedness and a mastery of language. Also, there is a louder acknowledgement within the industry that sports journalism needs to do more to shake off its image as a bastion of white, heterosexual masculinity. Moreover, there is a growing need in the digital age for sports journalists to appreciate the powerful role they can potentially play in framing and shaping social and political issues. A number of journalists have shared their thoughts on these and other key topics in this book, and it is hoped that their ideas – and maybe even some of ours – will serve to stimulate reflection on the state of sports journalism as it is today, and the direction it could go in the future.

Acknowledgements

Thanks are due to all the journalists who gave up their time to be interviewed for this book and to all our academic colleagues and friends in the sports media who provided advice and guidance along the way. We would particularly like to thank Sky Sports News' Laurie Tucker, and Paul Wiltshire of the University of Gloucestershire for his perceptive comments on an early draft of Chapter 5. We are also indebted to Professor Richard Keeble and the rest of the committee of the Institute of Communication Ethics without whom this project would not have got off the ground.

Many of the themes and issues we raise in the following chapters have emerged from discussions with our students and graduates. We thank them for contributing to our reflections on the sports media and for providing the inspiration for us to write what we hope will be a useful textbook for the next generation of sports journalists.

Finally, and most importantly, we would like to thank our families for the unconditional support and love they provide. This is for Pam, Martin, Tabitha, Viola and Rufus Bradshaw, and Laura, Kitty and Eliza Minogue.

Part I
Key debates in sports journalism

What does it mean to be a sports journalist in today's digital environment? What are the pressures that influence the content that sports journalists produce? The definition of what it is to be a contemporary sports journalist and how this differs from the past are considered in this opening section. The balance that should be struck between sports journalism that informs and sports journalism that entertains is also examined, as we consider the question of what the proper focus of sports journalists' work should be. The wider contexts – technological, historical and political – of sports journalism are analysed, as is the sports media's often complex relationship with the individuals, teams and organisations they cover. This opening part of the book also considers legal and ethical issues facing the contemporary sports journalist, particularly those arising in the digital era. Case studies and interviews with prominent sports journalists bring into focus the central issues facing the industry, and also highlight the key attributes that successful sports journalists need.

The changing role of the sports journalist

Sportswriting is up there with restaurant reviewing and film censorship as the best excuse for a job on earth. You're waited on hand and foot, you get the best seat in the house for free, you're indulging your hobby and you get paid for it. It shouldn't be called work at all. It should be called professional loafing.

(Simon Hughes, 2006: 4)

Sports journalists now regularly cover issues that shine a light on some of the key ethical questions in broader society. Over the last year sports writers have covered stories about race and sex discrimination, corruption, gambling, drugs, abuse and mental health. The industry needs journalists equipped to handle these questions.

(Andy Cairns, 2018: 11–12)

Is sports journalism a form of "professional loafing"? You must be kidding. When the British sports writer and broadcaster Simon Hughes, a journalist best known for his work covering cricket (and also for his tongue-in-cheek style), published the words at the top of this chapter, he was writing in the year that Twitter was founded. Since that year – 2006 – sports journalism, as with so many branches of the media and wider industry, has been transformed by the digital revolution. Audiences' thirst for real-time updates, for on-demand content and for social media-driven visual material has fundamentally changed not only what sports journalists have to do but also the speed at which they have to do it. The news cycle is now 24/7; every moment of every day is a moment when a sports news item could be published online. And as the number of digital platforms on which content can be published has increased, so too have sports journalists' workloads. Reflecting on the demands made of him during the 2017 British and Irish Lions tour of New Zealand, one highly experienced national sports writer in the UK media put it well during an interview with the authors, capturing the demands but also the exhilaration:

It was unbelievably busy. Morning, noon and night you're at it. And it was fantastic – what a great experience and it was a wonderful thing to cover. But you wouldn't ever work much harder than that six weeks without a day off. It's become much more demanding, the volume is higher. It's becoming increasingly hard to remember what it was like before digital.

Sports journalists might still get the best seats in the house when they are covering live games or tournaments from a stadium, but for every sports journalist there in person, there are likely to be dozens more working remotely producing a live text commentary and combing through social media feeds about the event. And those who are there in the flesh won't be sitting in the press box with their feet up, unhurriedly pondering the opening line to their 950-word report – or indeed doing anything else approximating loafing. With workloads greater than ever, sports journalists covering live events will more often than not be running on adrenaline rather than the complimentary food and drink available in a stadium's media room. As well as the written match reports, spoken commentary, live text commentary and post-match interviews that need to be delivered, sports journalists are involved in delivering an array of social media content – photos and videos via Instagram, Snapchat stories, WhatsApp Broadcast Lists, Twitter updates. These social media platforms will evolve – some will wither, like the short-form video app Vine, and be replaced by others – but one thing that is undoubtedly here to stay is the real-time, 24/7 news cycle that the digital era has heralded.

Phones used to be merely deployed to "phone in" articles to the sports desk – a process whereby reporters would verbally deliver their piece to a quick-typing copytaker at the other end of the line. Now, phones fulfil a fundamentally different role. Smartphones enable reporters on the ground to deliver a huge range of material in real time. Mobile Journalism, or MoJo as it is often referred to, is a facet of modern media that every sports journalist must be comfortable with (Lambert, 2018). Digital technology has changed not only what audiences want and how sports journalism is consumed but has also fundamentally altered how sports journalism is produced and what is required of the sports journalist. This should give sports journalists cause for pause and reflection. Whether you are a student sports journalist, a trainee sports journalist, an experienced sports reporter who has been on the circuit for a lengthy stretch, or the sports editor of a large media outlet who thinks they have seen it all, the digital era poses a raft of questions about where sports journalists' *focus* should be at a time when there is so much other sports content produced by so many people: by bloggers, vloggers, tweeters, fan TV sites and directly by clubs themselves. There are also questions about the *threats* and *opportunities* posed by the never-offline culture within which sports journalists now operate.

Sports journalism is not just about covering live events and groin strains, however. It is also about capturing the personalities behind sport, and investigating the broader issues that underpin how sport is run and governed. Moreover, it requires that those doing such reporting do so in an even-handed and accurate manner. The second quote at the top of this chapter is from Andy Cairns, the executive editor of Sky Sports News. Cairns' words neatly capture the *breadth* of issues that he now expects his sports journalists to be comfortable reporting on, and the list of issues is extensive: political protest, discrimination, mental health, cheating. Covering such issues requires a host of skills and attitudes from reporters, not least perseverance, sensitivity, a knowledge of the law as it affects the media, objectivity and, often, courage. Contemporary sports journalists, therefore, need not only an appreciation of how the explosion in digital technology has affected their practice, but they also need to be attuned to the wider issues affecting sport and society, and how to report on these with rigour and integrity. There is clear evidence that a good number of sports journalists are doing just this. In 2018, for example, a committee of Members of Parliament in the United Kingdom who were investigating doping in sport praised the investigative work of some sports journalists. The politicians highlighted the journalists' diligence in helping expose questionable practices in cycling and athletics, including failings by cycling's Team Sky (Digital, Culture, Media and Sport Committee, 2018). Elsewhere in 2018, journalists on *The Sunday Times* Insight Team, George Arbuthnott and Jonathan Calvert, produced award-winning pieces investigating dubious practices in Qatar's bid to host the 2022 FIFA World Cup, and the pair also shone a light on drug doping at the 2014 Sochi Winter Olympics. Their coverage of the latter involved a blend of fine investigative reporting and superb writing, one article beginning with the arrestingly vivid opening sentence of "The snow was glistening white, but the race was dirty" (Arbuthnott et al., 2018). Elsewhere in 2018, the investigative work of Martha Kelner and Sean Ingle at *The Guardian* won them an award for revealing an adverse drug test by the four-time Tour de France winner Chris Froome (Guardian Sport, 2018). The test found a larger than permitted amount of the asthma drug salbutamol in his system, but Froome was subsequently cleared of any wrongdoing by cycling's governing body, the Union Cycliste Internationale (UCI).

As the preceding paragraph illustrates, sports journalism can – and should – have a depth to it that goes beyond the merry-go-round of match reports and press conference coverage. But despite this, sports journalism has often been perceived as a frivolous – or at least less serious – form of journalism than other forms of writing and reporting (Boyle, Rowe and Whannel, 2010; Humphries, 2003; Rowe 2005, 2007). The sports desk has from time to time been labelled the "toy department of the news media" and its members "cheerleaders" or "fans with typewriters." Some have argued that such name-calling "reveals the extent to which the low professional status of sports journalism corresponds to an elite disdain for sport as corporeally-based popular culture among many intellectuals and arbiters of cultural taste" (Boyle, Rowe and Whannel, 2010: 246). While such criticism of sports journalism can be based on both ignorance and an element of snootiness from other branches of journalism, it is important that sports journalists resist – as far as their significant time pressures allow – skating along the surface with their coverage. The need for originality and depth is vital, as the examples above – and the examples in the next chapter from the history of sports journalism – illustrate.

Digital technology and its impact on the sports media

The growth in digital technology has brought about a new paradigm – or framework – within which Western society communicates and interacts (Castells 2000, 2004), and this has given rise to what has been called *networked media sport*, "a term capturing the movement away from broadcast and print media towards digitized content distributed via networked communications technologies" (Hutchins and Rowe, 2012: 46). In simpler language, online and social media content has moved increasingly centre stage, while more traditional forms of media – particularly paper-based ones – have, as a general rule (and with important exceptions, which will be explored), been fading. The growth of digital technology has also enabled individuals to set up their own media outlets: their own Twitter accounts, their own blogs, their own platforms. The networked society has, therefore, arguably undermined the privileged status of many traditional news organisations (or "legacy" organisations, as news outlets that had an existence before the digital revolution are now sometimes referred to). There are more voices than ever to be heard, and those voices are just a few taps or clicks away. As the "media sport economy" has shifted from the scarcity of the analogue era to the plenitude of the digital era (Rowe and Hutchins, 2013: 2), sports journalism has, in many respects, become a more chaotic activity, with journalists scrambling to be the first with news online, scrambling to attract more and more unique visitors to their websites, and scrambling to be heard above the never-ending din of social media. A distinguished trio of sports media researchers has posed the question of whether this vast quantity of sports content in the digital age has led to more superficial coverage rather than deeper analysis: "Is the sheer volume of sports journalism content saturating cultural space and impeding critical reflection?" (Boyle, Rowe and Whannel, 2010: 247). In other words, is the permanently-on, 24/7 sports news cycle leaving sports journalists chasing their tails at the expense of providing a more considered, reflective view of sport? And is that consequently leaving audiences with poorer content?

In some respects, these are unsettling times for sports journalists. More is being asked of sports journalists across more platforms than ever before, yet the number of sports journalists working for traditional titles – particularly newspapers and their associated websites – has been in steady decline. As readers have migrated from paid-for print content to often free digital content, legacy media companies have struggled to generate sufficient revenue from online advertising to stay in the black. In this new digital era, traditional media companies have experimented with different business models, including paywalls, subscription packages, micro-payments per article and reader donations, yet none has proved a rock-solid model. This uncertainty over revenue and business viability has had an impact on sports journalists' roles, and even on their sense of professional identity. Raymond Boyle has contended that "as the funding of journalism moves centre stage as a driver in shaping the new trajectories of journalism, those working in sports also have had to adapt and re-invent themselves" (Boyle, 2017: 494). Put another way, the uncertain commercial environment brought about by the digital revolution has required media outlets to rethink what content they produce. And that has in turn required sports journalists themselves to refocus, adjust and redefine.

Indeed, the increase in both the number and prominence of non-professional sports content producers – untrained bloggers, vloggers and fan TV sites – has arguably undermined trained sports journalists. The round-the-clock, interactive media ecosystem generated by the rise of digital technology has, it could be argued, blurred the professional identity of sports journalists, due to a more visibly active audience which is itself producing content (Fenton and Witschge, 2011). The emergence of terms such as "citizen journalist," "prosumers," "blogger" and "user-generated content" – all of which refer to a greater or lesser degree to the production of media content by non-professionals – suggests that the line between journalist and audience is now significantly less distinct than it once was (Harcup, 2015; Knight and Cook, 2015). Practitioners within the mainstream sports media have found themselves operating within an online habitat that contains a significant – and growing – number of non-professional content producers, and as a consequence have been forced to re-examine their professional worth and their relationship with their audiences (Boyle and Haynes, 2013; McEnnis 2013, 2015, 2017). To some researchers, the rise of social media has served to pose an existential question to sports journalists. This question has been stated as follows: "Are new media, user-generated content and 'citizen sports journalism' contributing to the de-professionalization of sports journalism?" (Boyle, Rowe and Whannel, 2010; 247). Pursuing a similar line of thought, it has been suggested that the growth of social media platforms through which the "audience" can interact among themselves and with journalists has rendered the traditional, institutional media obsolete in its ability to develop, build and influence audiences (Rowe and Hutchins, 2014).

While this might overstate the decline in influence of the traditional media, it is undoubtedly the case that the growth of Twitter and other channels of digital communication mean that traditional media organisations no longer filter or control the flow of sports information like they used to do. Journalists' loosening grip over the flow of sports content has been accentuated by the growing number of people working in – and the growing amount of content produced by – the sports media relations sector (Gibbs and Haynes, 2013). Those working in sports media relations, or sports public relations, include the media managers and press officers at sports clubs and sports governing bodies, whose job it is to convey information about those clubs and bodies in as positive a way as possible. Such press officers and media managers now produce a huge variety of content about their clubs, ranging from videos on the club's official Instagram feed to articles on the club website. Many clubs also have their own television brands, such as Manchester United's MUTV. Digital technology has, therefore, given clubs significant control over what is read and watched about them, thereby arguably diluting sports journalists' prominence. The traditional "sports media hierarchy," according to which sports journalists distributed content to their audiences in a top-down fashion, has been flattened: "What was once a one-way mode of communication […] is now a two-way mode of communication that represents a form of departure from traditional models" (Gibbs and Haynes, 2013: 405–406). Another complicating factor is the emergence of bogus Twitter accounts purveying misinformation, for example about football transfers (Corcoran, 2014).

It is important, though, to appreciate the upsides of the digital revolution for sports journalism. In many respects, it has made the role of the sports journalist more varied, more challenging and more exciting. There is the need to be multiskilled and to push oneself to embrace new technologies, and there is scope to become a brand in one's own right with an audience that exceeds the size of even one's employer. *The Times'* Henry Winter is one such example, with his enormous Twitter following arguably giving him greater power and voice than *The Times* itself, for which he is the chief football writer. In 2019, Winter had 1.25 million Twitter followers; *The Times'* official feed @TimesSport had 109,000. Elsewhere, however, it has been argued that social media has also ushered in an era of self-obsession among some sportswriters, in which the number of followers they gain on their social media accounts becomes an enduring concern. This, Rob Steen argues, fuels a "cult of the personality" in which the social media platform turns the writer into both the publisher and the product (Steen, 2014: 43).

Nevertheless, the use of Twitter and other social media platforms is now an established form of sports journalism practice (English, 2016; Sherwood and Nicholson, 2012), although research is ambivalent about how effectively sports journalists deploy new media technologies (Fondevila-Gascon, Rom-Rodriguez and Santana-Lopez, 2016; Morrison, 2014). It has also acted as a spur to competition between sports journalists (Gibbs and Haynes, 2013). As far back as

2010, academics were suggesting that the use of Twitter and other new media technologies could be occasioning a "paradigm shift" in sport journalism practice, with traditional journalists losing their privileged position as agenda-setters but also being able to interact more directly with their audience and offer more opinion (Sheffer and Schultz, 2010).

When thinking about the impact of digital technology on sports journalists, it is vital to think not merely in terms of the increased range of platforms on which content can be produced and on which audiences can interact with sports journalists. It is also important to think in terms of the behind-the-scenes digital technology that sports editors now have at their disposal that is used to track which content is popular among their audience. As well as using Google Analytics and analytic tools built into social media networks, sports desks use software such as that produced by New York-based company Chartbeat to enable them to track in real time the popularity of each web article. Chartbeat, CrowdTangle, Google Analytics and a host of other technologies give editors a wealth of constantly updating information about each and every piece of web content. The number of people who are currently reading an article, how far most people are scrolling down through that article, how people have come across the article (was it from a link in social media, for example) and whether visitors are then clicking on to other material on the website, are all monitored by the analytics software. Such data can prompt editors to give greater or less prominence to a particular story on a web page, and can also inform their future decisions about what stories to cover – and which ones to overlook. Many modern newsrooms have the real-time data from such software displayed on large screens on their walls. Again, the software will evolve, but analytics is a facet of journalism that is here to stay, and an appreciation of how to make the most of the data it provides is now a part of sports journalism. But sports journalists need to be attuned, too, to the dangers of chasing eyeballs and merely pursuing populist content, as the following case study illustrates.

Case study: Steve Marshall, assistant editor, BBC Sport

How social media and audience analytics have changed my role and the work of those in my team

Steve Marshall has been with the BBC since 2007. Based at the corporation's Birmingham office, he began as a sub-editor, editing sports reporters' work and checking it for accuracy and completeness before publishing it online. He now runs a team of 17 sports journalists, with each journalist providing online multimedia content for the English regions and the BBC Sport website. While all write digital content, the team of journalists has also been trained in mobile journalism skills (MoJo) to self-shoot and self-edit video packages.

Marshall says changes in digital technology have triggered a shift in what audiences want – and therefore in what sports reporters produce. In particular, live text commentaries – in which journalists provide real-time, blow-by-blow accounts of a match or event – have begun to take priority over match reports that are written after the final whistle.

"As the audience has moved away from desktop computers to more mobile devices to get their sport, the thirst for content has become even more immediate," says Marshall. "We now find there is more demand for live coverage than there is for a traditional match report on a website. So we've put more emphasis on doing our live text content – it's become a huge part of what we do. The audience we get for that is enormous. The appetite for a match report in the traditional sense isn't there so much, so we've switched the resource from that to the live text coverage that is serving us so well."

Marshall splits his reporters into those working on breaking sports news and those covering live sport, but there is also the expectation that they will come up with their own ideas for stories and innovative ways in which to cover them. Marshall places an emphasis on originality.

"When there isn't any live sport on, the reporters have got the chance to focus on some original journalism, and the focus is on them to generate some ideas," he says. "There's so much spoon-fed material these days and it's very easy to get sucked into that. As an editor, I don't want my staff to be stuck behind a desk from 9–5 or whenever their shift is, which is what journalism increasingly seems to have become. You can become a "churnalist" rather than a journalist, and because you're going from story to story, you sometimes don't question what you're doing quite so much. You're just producing. What I'm really interested in is original journalism – really good human interest stories or ones that other people aren't telling. A good example of that was when two journalists on my team did a project on the anatomy of a pregnant athlete and we ran that to coincide with the birth of Serena Williams's first child. It's about challenging people to come up with those ideas that are a little bit out of the ordinary."

Data that Marshall and other editors get through audience analytics is prompting them to review when they publish material and how they go about presenting it. A key focus is to get visitors to the website to then tap or click through to more content once they have read an initial article.

However, while Marshall obviously wants audience figures to increase, he is also mindful of the need for the BBC – as a publicly funded organisation – to deliver content that caters for the full spectrum of sporting interests. So, rather than simply producing football content that he and other editors know will pull in high unique visitor numbers, the BBC takes a broader view.

"I think there's a danger with analytics that you can end up producing populist content," explains Marshall. "We could probably fill our home page with Manchester United stories but then as the BBC we have to offer something more. Look at the back pages of the newspapers these days and they are dominated by Premier League, Premier League, Premier League, and it's largely just a few clubs. As the BBC we have to make sure we're serving different audiences because everybody's a licence-fee payer, and we need to try and reach people we don't currently reach at the moment.

"One of the benefits of analytics is that it does help us focus content a bit more. Unless it's a really big story now, we set a word count limit of 300 words because analytics tell us that by about six paragraphs people are bailing out. Your analytics will tell you that only a very small proportion of your readers get to the bottom of a story or feature. So, for long-form content, you have to ensure the content is pretty compelling to keep the audience involved.

"Increasingly, the audience is predominantly on mobile. In 2012, desktop was the most popular platform and generally your peak audience would be around midday and 2 p.m. when people were at work having a look online at lunchtime. These days there's not a day that goes by when mobile isn't the biggest platform. And rather than there being one peak, you've now got three – you've got peaks as people commute to work between 6–9 a.m., another peak on mobile as people are going home from work, and then another one between 9:30 p.m.–11 p.m. and that's arguably the biggest peak of the day before people go to bed. It's making us think a bit more about when we publish more timeless content – do we publish in the morning or hold it back for the evening peaks?

"People snack on content a lot, dipping in and out – mobile phones have changed the way people get their content and increasingly the focus is around shorter, sharper news stories and we're limiting word counts. Increasingly, we'll try and break the long form stuff up into little snack-sized pieces that people can either read or skip over. Or it's presenting it in different ways, perhaps putting statistical information in mobile-friendly bullet points rather than in traditional written journalism."

In order to capture and retain a younger audience, BBC Sport Online reporters are also incorporating social media into their digital storytelling, for example by embedding tweets or using short-form video with captions and emojis. Social media platforms are also used to try and drive traffic to the BBC website, with BBC Sport also using its social media presence to try and counter the spread of misleading, fake news.

"A couple of years ago our journalism at the BBC was pretty straight-laced," continues Marshall. "Social media and the way that things are presented sometimes can change the way you might approach a story. Rather than telling the story in a traditional paragraph-by-paragraph way, social media sometimes means we tell the story in a way that's a bit lighter.

"We try and make the most of what we can with social media, which can be difficult when it comes to things like Facebook algorithms and how Facebook delivers news, which are changing all the time. We still have to regard social media giants as important as that's where a lot of people are finding their news these days, but because they are third parties, they want to drive their own agenda – and their agenda may well not be your agenda as a journalist. At a time when there's a lot of battles against fake news, if we're not serving social platforms how do people, particularly younger audiences, find the real news when fake news is being served to them?"

The digital age – new working practices, new rivals

Sky Sports News editor Andy Cairns oversees a team of around 200 sports journalists producing sports news across Sky's TV and online platforms. As such, he is well positioned to provide a detailed account of how changes in the digital landscape have affected the role of the sports journalist. Cairns believes the digital era has prompted changes in sports journalists' working practices and forced a redefinition of who mainstream media organisations' rivals are. The growth of digital platforms means sports journalists have to produce output faster than ever before, he says, and when this is coupled with staff cutbacks, it can mean that the modern sports journalist is acting under significant time constraints and significant pressure. "As many newsrooms run with fewer staff it's very often an inexperienced journalist who will have to make that on-the-spot instant decision on their own," he says (Cairns, 2018: 8), adding: "Rolling news puts huge pressures on journalists and means we rarely have time to stand back and look at the bigger picture" (Cairns, 2018: 11).

The quest for eyeballs on a story can also trump the pursuit of truth, with established outlets facing "increasing competition from media organisations with a more cavalier attitude to the truth and to fact-checking, for whom the number of clicks is more important" (Cairns, 2018: 10). In addition, the arrival of non-traditional outlets online has given rise to new ethical challenges that undermined even once sacrosanct journalistic principles, such as the need to have two independent sources corroborating a claim before it is released into the public domain. Cairns is worth quoting at length on this point, as he captures issues about sports journalism ethics and professional self-identity that arise in tandem in the new digital media ecosystem:

> We know where we stand with traditional rivals. But there's a disturbing ground occupied by news and gossip sites, sometimes with significant twitter followings, where different rules apply. They will run stories without checking, will present opinion as fact and run stories that are just wrong. They're popular and they present a problem for traditional news organisations in the battle for viewers and readers. We've had to respond. Most news organisations followed the two sources rule for any story. With the pace of news and increased competition that's not workable now, especially as the second source may be trying to break the news themselves on their own website or twitter feed. So we have a series of checks. Each story is different but our first consideration for story sources who don't want to be named is to challenge whether they are in a position to know for certain. We also consider our relationship with them and how reliable and trustworthy a contact they are. Then we consider why they are telling us. Any doubt and we keep checking and checking. There's no science to this and we have a fantastic contact base and good systems for quickly standing up and, just as importantly, knocking down stories.
>
> (2018: 10)

The proliferation of rumour on social media has also changed the caution exercised by traditional sports broadcasters and outlets. Sky Sports News has established a news team whose task, alongside breaking exclusive stories, is to verify the rumours that originate on social media. Significantly, Sky will now broadcast material that remains unsubstantiated rumour, a situation that Cairns describes as follows:

> The challenge comes when a rumour gathers significant momentum on social media. We can't ignore it so we tell our viewers that this is a rumour we know is gaining traction, that we are checking to verify and that we will update as soon as we can. It's not where we were a few years ago, where we waited to confirm a story before putting it to air, but it's honest with our audience.
>
> (2018: 10–11)

In essence, new technology has given rise to new rivals, and to compete with these new rivals, Sky Sports News has had to adapt its editorial processes. And these adaptations have in turn given rise to modified – and in some cases, more complex – working practices for sports journalists. Yet underpinning these changes is a commitment to accuracy and transparency. So, while the sports desk adapts its activities to cater for technological changes, the fundamental principles sustaining the outlet's approach remain – or should remain – intact.

The changing role of the sportswriter

Rob Steen, a distinguished sports writer specialising in cricket as well as a sports media academic, has vividly sketched out the virtues of sport – and, indirectly, the virtues of documenting it as a journalist: "The miraculous variety of games devised around the possibilities generated by balls of differing sizes; the indestructible buzz of a close contest or a victory against the odds; the dignity sport alone lent to patriotism; the operatic nature of its plotlines; what it taught me about politics and geography and history; how it brought together mutually mistrustful races and buried, however fleetingly, their social and economic differences" (2014: 3–4). Sports writing is, he argues, "for the juvenile at heart, the fun-lovers and the thrill-seekers, the romantics and the idealists" (2014: 9). But it is also, increasingly, for the statisticians – or at least those who like their stats.

Stats and figures have always been an integral part of the appeal of some sports – baseball, cricket and horse racing being the obvious examples. For some aficionados of these sports, the percentages and the ratios are all part of the fun in what represents a curious marriage of an admiration for strenuous physical activity and mathematics. While cricket has its maiden overs, dot balls and strike rates, baseball has its caught stealing percentage, slugging percentage, walks and hits per innings pitched (WHIP), and – almost poetically – groundout-to-flyout ratio. As the official Major League Baseball website states, "For more than a century, statistics have been a staple of the game of baseball […] they are ubiquitous in baseball writing and mass media" (mlb.com, n.d.). Statistics have long been ubiquitous for cricket enthusiasts, too, ever since the *Wisden Cricketers' Almanack* was first published in 1864. It is still published annually now, while the *ESPNcricinfo* website goes into enough microscopic statistical detail to keep even the most numbers-obsessed sports fan happy. Horse racing, meanwhile, is a sport that would mean little without the daily supply of figures containing runners' and riders' recent form and odds.

Sports writers have always made use of statistical data, even if it was as basic as the win-loss split in previous encounters between the two teams at hand. But what has changed is the sheer quantity of data available. Digital and GPS technology means a welter of data is collected from top-flight matches and sporting occasions, but much of the data is still gathered by human beings watching matches and manually recording what occurs. Companies which collate, analyse and distribute this data have flourished in the digital era, and become central to many sports fans' – and sports journalists' – experience of watching and covering live sport. Opta is one example, with the London-based company delivering increasingly sophisticated statistics and data, and presenting it in engaging, eye-catching graphics. Significantly, there is an emphasis on not just gathering data on what has happened, but on predicting what will happen in the future. Opta's World Cup predictor model, for example, delivered projections on the outcome of the 2018 FIFA World Cup. The real-time data acquired and produced by Opta is used by clients to deliver up-to-the-minute insight into a sporting encounter. During half-time of England's quarter-final with Sweden, for example, BBC host Gary Lineker cited Opta data as the basis for analysing pivotal moments from the game. Opta charges media companies from across the world to use its expertise in information gathering, but Opta's own activities are essentially journalistic – telling the stories of sport in as compelling a manner as possible.

The growth of casual and increasingly varied forms of betting and gambling has also brought the use of statistics into the foreground in the digital milieu. With many young audiences now having betting apps and sports news apps positioned alongside one another on their smartphone home screens, getting odds and detailed match information at the tap of a thumb has become increasingly important for such an audience demographic. This has had the knock-on effect of sports writing often developing an increasingly commercial aspect. The football website squawka.com, for example, represents the fusion of analytical writing and "tipster" sports journalism. Such tips-based pieces appear under the title of "prediction" pieces. It is no coincidence that such sites can contain significant amounts of advertising from betting companies, and that certain features of the site are sponsored by betting companies. For example, a podcast broadcast by Squawka at the midpoint of the 2018 FIFA World Cup, The Squawka Talker's World Cup 2018 group stage review, was not only sponsored by a betting company, but a spokesman from the betting firm was part of the panel of pundits (Jennings, 2018). Before the debate got underway, the representative of the betting firm was invited by the host to describe the "flagship offer" that the company was running "which Squawka listeners might be interested in." Cue the bookie to talk about his "Ten Steps to Ten Million" offer. Such instances of the intertwining of sports journalism and betting are becoming more frequent, and reflect shifts in UK society in which more sophisticated forms of gambling have become more prevalent. This is reflected in television advertising content, too. During the course of the 2018 FIFA World Cup, the British television station ITV ran almost 90 minutes of gambling adverts from the start of the competition until England's semi-final elimination by Croatia, meaning that 17% of ad breaks were taken up with gambling advertisements. This prompted concerns from the charity GambleAware that children were being overexposed to content that promoted gambling (Duncan, Davies and Sweney, 2018), concerns which led to online gambling companies agreeing to a voluntary ban on advertising during live sporting events – a so-called whistle-to-whistle ban (Davies and Sweney, 2018).

Opinion in sports journalism

Comment and punditry are now essential ingredients in the daily diet of sports journalism. Not only that, but the distinction between factual pieces and comment pieces is blurring. This position is not a new one. In his seminal 2006 text *Sports Journalism: Context and Issues*, Raymond Boyle quoted the then-*Daily Mail* sportswriter Paul Hayward – currently chief sports writer at *The Daily Telegraph*. "Sports journalism now is more emphatic and dramatic than it was in the past," wrote Hayward in a 2005 piece. "It's about comment, analysis, reaction and reflection" (Boyle, 2006a: 78). The growth of digital technology has arguably stimulated this growth in subjective output, in which the expression of opinion by sports journalists is not only permitted by audiences but is expected. In a piece of research that combined an analysis of sports journalists' tweets with interviews with journalists, it was concluded that the emergence of social media had affected sports journalists' match-day working routines so that the incorporation of opinion had become more central to their output – "opinion is part of the online job" (Roberts and Emmons, 2016: 111). In Roberts and Emmons' study, speed of delivery and entertainment were identified by one sports journalist as what a digital-age audience wants:

> I'll send out some fun tweets just to lighten the mood [...] This is the microwave generation – you get everything immediately. Everyone wants to know now. Some want to be entertained, but some want to be informed.
> (2016: 108)

The balance that sports journalists should strive to achieve between informing their audience and entertaining them, touched on in this quote, is an intriguing issue and one to which we will return in later chapters. Another notable point made in the statement above is how modern audiences expect to know immediately – and thanks to social media, live text commentary and other forms of digital media, they can and do know immediately. Audiences don't have to wait until the following day's newspaper to read what Player X said in his post-match interview, because in all likelihood some journalists will have delivered snippets of it via social media. This speed at which the news is spread has arguably made sports journalists' work more opinion-heavy. Many sports journalists recognise that, in the era of instant updates on mobile phones, they will no longer be the first with a quote or a news angle. So, instead, what they focus on is providing the best analysis, the best colour, the most striking opinion couched in the most striking words.

Steen argues that sports journalists are deceiving themselves if they believe they can do the role totally dispassionately, contending that "every piece of writing, every piece of journalism, is slanted or shaded in some way and hence opinionated" (2014: 17). This is a position with which many would disagree, and is connected to the wider – and long-running – issue about the possibility of true objectivity in journalism. We will return to this topic when we consider issues of sports journalism ethics later. However, from the outset of this book it is important for sports journalists to reflect on their own – and others' – work and consider the extent to which personal emphases and biases potentially appear in published or broadcast material.

Case study: Sam Peters

Sports journalism can change attitudes, force those in positions of power to change policies and potentially even save lives. Sam Peters is a campaigning British sports journalist who knows this better than most.

Peters' tenacious work investigating concussion in rugby has led to the game introducing new protocols designed to improve player safety.

Peters is a well-travelled sports journalist who has worked for a range of national newspapers in the United Kingdom, ranging from red-top tabloids such as the *News of the World* to broadsheet titles including *The Sunday Times*. He has covered many sporting events with distinction and written many interview pieces, but the facet of his sports journalism that has gained him the most recognition is his investigation into concussion and its potential association with dementia.

As an experienced sports reporter, Peters had developed specialisms in cricket and rugby. And it was while reporting on rugby matches weekend after weekend in 2012 that he began to feel increasingly uneasy about the prevalence of concussion that he was witnessing.

Concerned that governing bodies in the game were not taking sufficient steps to recognise and address the possible association between concussion and early onset dementia, Peters resolved in the autumn of 2012 to start campaigning for change in the way concussion was assessed and treated. His reading of what was happening in the NFL in the United States, where a concussion class-action lawsuit was filed in 2011, persuaded him that rugby could also be sitting on a similarly huge medical and legal time-bomb.

Peters embarked on a programme of rigorous research. He interviewed medical experts, waded through scientific reports and sounded out players with whom he had built up good relationships over his years covering the Premiership rugby circuit.

Once his initial research was assembled, *The Mail on Sunday*, which Peters was working for at the time, launched its concussion campaign. Its agenda was to urge rugby's governing bodies to address issues around concussion in greater depth and protect players from the long-term dangers that multiple concussions could trigger. Week after week, Peters and other members of the paper's sports department produced pieces which began to command the attention of the game's administrators at the Rugby Football Union and World Rugby. The campaign gained the backing of neurosurgeons, neuropathologists and Members of Parliament, and has since helped lead to a raft of changes in the way that concussion is assessed during matches and the way players are cared for once a concussion has been diagnosed.

Peters led the campaign, which his sports editor at *The Mail on Sunday*, Alison Kervin, subsequently called "a real jewel," and in recognition of his campaigning work Peters was shortlisted for the Sports Journalist of the Year Award at the 2014 British Journalism Awards.

Explaining what had prompted him to turn his attention to concussion, Peters explains that he had been in search of a more demanding professional challenge than the usual sports journalistic beat of attending matches and writing up pieces from press conferences.

"There was a point after I'd done it for maybe a decade or so that I felt I wasn't getting enough of a challenge from just going to press conferences and essentially just rehashing similar stories to my colleagues in terms of stuff that people had said. 'This person said this today' and those kind of quotes-driven stories aren't always that interesting, and I felt I needed a bit more of a challenge and mental stimulus.

"I was drawn to the concussion stuff because I felt it was more challenging, basically, and I felt more engaged. I had been writing what I felt was some pretty bland quotes stuff before that, but then that was what was being demanded of me."

Once he had decided to investigate the issue of concussion and campaign for change at the highest level, Peters says that perseverance was key. His writings have caused some controversy, with Peters publicly clashing with

Steve Diamond, the Sale Sharks director of rugby, after Diamond took exception to a piece that Peters had published. And Peters admits that winning some of his fellow sports journalists round to what he was doing took some time in the early days of his campaigning.

"I'm not scared of a challenge. Once I get my teeth into something I'm pretty determined and I don't like feeling like I haven't given it a proper crack. I felt there was so much I was seeing in that concussion stuff and it demanded quite a lot of staying power and a fairly thick skin.

"When I started writing about it, I think quite a lot of people thought I'd get bored of it and it would just go away. But when I kept going back to it, and kept going back to it, the penny dropped. Most people, even if they initially thought I was completely bonkers writing about it, now probably think there was something in it and acknowledge that it was quite an important thing to do."

Based on his experiences of the campaign, Peters believes that sports journalism can be a real force for positive change in the sports that he loves. He is also respectful and grateful for the heightened platform that working for the mainstream media has given him when agitating for change.

"Having some staying power and the courage of your convictions is important if you really firmly believe there's something going wrong or there's something that needs changing," says Peters. "You've got a really privileged position if you can write for a national newspaper to effectively bring about change. You've got to convince people of your argument."

Bloggers, citizen journalists and opinion

Published opinion is no longer the domain just of professional journalists. Every single person with an Internet-enabled device and a social media account can publish their opinions on sporting matters. Most of it is likely to be unremarkable; some of it is likely to be illiterate; some is likely to be offensive; a fair amount of content will manage to pull off all three. But some of it is perceptive, well-phrased and engagingly packaged. The question then arises of how such thoughtful – if unpaid – bloggers and citizen journalists fit into the new media ecosystem. Should they be viewed as journalists, as articulate audience members or as something hovering in between? McEnnis (2017) has explored the extent to which bloggers have arguably disrupted sports journalists' work and his broad conclusion, based on interviews with journalists, is that UK sports journalists do not regard fan bloggers as endangering their professional distinctiveness. Journalists regarded their occupational status as being protected through the media accreditation they gain to professional sporting events, and the access they have to professional resources. The question arises, however, about just how long many mainstream journalists will continue to receive such accreditations ahead of popular bloggers/influencers who can boast loyal, young audiences. Moreover, given a pattern of continuing cutbacks within the mainstream sports media industry, the significance of the resources at the disposal of many mainstream journalists is now questionable.

Hutchins and Rowe argue that digitisation and the growth of content from non-professional sources has given rise to a state of competition between professional sports journalists and bloggers. The changes brought about by the growth of digital are "impacting upon the very idea of sports news, changing the amount and immediacy of discussion between journalists and their audiences, and placing demands upon journalists both to observe and, occasionally, to compete with independent bloggers and commentators" (Hutchins and Rowe, 2012: 126). The sports journalist in the digital age, therefore, has more noise to cut through in order to be heard. However, as McEnnis has pointed out, the sports journalist now has more means at their disposal than ever before in order to be heard, such as podcasting, live streaming and social media (2013). Journalists' sense of what sets them apart from citizen journalists has also been explored by Fenton and Witschge. Their findings suggested that "for journalists the main difference lies in perception of professional ethics and values," in particular the provision of accurate information that is in the public interest and which complies with the law, as opposed to the more opinion-based content which journalists regard as citizen journalists' primary output (Fenton and Witschge, 2011: 149). Professional ethics in sports journalism will be discussed in depth in Chapter 4.

Ex-pros and sports journalists' workloads

A number of professional sportspeople have not only moved into sports journalism following the end of their sporting careers but have done so with significant success (Dunphy, 1987; Hughes 2005; Kimmage 2007). However, the volume of the migration from sports field to sports studio/sports page has alarmed some, with Mihir Bose, a former BBC Sport editor, concerned that it has given rise to cliché-ridden content that only serves to increase the public's cynicism about the quality of sports media material (Bose, 2012). The platoons of ex-pros fulfilling such jobs complicates the role of the contemporary sports journalist further still. The modern sports journalist is arguably fighting on two fronts: on one front there are the shots being fired from the blogosphere by citizen journalists, while on the other is the heavy artillery at the disposal of household-name ex-pros.

However, while job opportunities are undermined due to the number of ex-sportspeople being employed in the sports media, there is evidence that the workload and stress on sports journalists is increasing. Interview-based research among sports journalists in the United States found that, due to the pressure imposed by the 24/7 news cycle, the notion of a sports journalist being off-duty was oxymoronic (McGuire and Murray, 2016: 63). The conclusion was that a significant number of sports journalists "feel a sense of inequity with their present job regarding workload and compensation" (McGuire and Murray, 2016: 67).

The role of the sports journalist – amid the change, are there constants?

If the end of the preceding section is a touch gloomy, then that is because it reflects some of the harsh realities of an industry that has been buffeted by the rough winds that the digital revolution has whipped up. The rhythm of sports journalists' working life can be relentless in the digital era – with phones buzzing with notifications, and with social media feeds updating all the time, it can be hard to switch off. However, amid the grind there remains the "buzz" that comes from publishing an exclusive story that has taken you weeks to stand up, or from filing a breathless match report just two minutes after the final whistle, or from seeing a carefully researched interview piece go live, or from grabbing the player-of-the-match in the mixed zone for that TV interview you have been sweating over. These are the moments that trigger the buzz that continue to make sports journalism an exciting – even addictive – job for its practitioners. Indeed, while the rise of digital technology has, in some respects, fundamentally affected the role of the sports journalist, in other respects the more things have changed, the more they have stayed the same. Stuart James, a former professional footballer who is now a football journalist for *The Guardian*, told us that traditional journalistic qualities such as independence of mind, the ability to work under pressure, a willingness to dig out stories for oneself and diligence are as important now as they ever were. Asked what qualities he wishes to see in a young, aspiring journalist, James says:

> First of all, I'd want someone to be really proactive. I think some people still expect things to come to them and I'd want somebody to be putting themselves out there. It's such a competitive industry if you're going to make yourself stand out that means being proactive and thinking beyond

the obvious. You need an inquisitive mind, questioning things and not just accepting what somebody says to you – you should be thinking, why is that happening, how's that happening, should I be reading between the lines here? You've obviously got to be diligent and hard-working and flexible with your approach – you need to be ready to drop everything because that's how sports news reporting happens. You might need to be anywhere at any time. You want sports journalists to be able to cope under pressure because meeting deadlines is everything. It can be very stressful, so having that clarity of thought when something changes everything that you were writing about is important – it's the ability to clear your mind and paint pictures with words even though you're feeling stressed and under pressure. It comes with practice to an extent, but I also think you've got to be a certain type of person to embrace that situation and thrive in it, because it's a buzz as well.

(interview with the authors, 2018)

As well as sports journalism continuing to contain a heady blend of stress and excitement, James argues that the rise of social media has forced sports journalists to raise their game because it has meant that their work is under continual scrutiny. Audiences will voice their opinions on the content they read, and those opinions can often be critical and expressed in a forthright – and even plain rude – manner. Such vociferous criticism requires sports journalists to have sufficient fortitude to brush off any online negativity. And away from the troll-inhabited forum of criticism that social media can become, James is always mindful of the breadth of travelling and experience that his role as a sports journalist has given him. He adds:

As a sports journalist you probably need a thick skin because of the scrutiny you come under from outside. It's not like other jobs where the only people who get to see your work are your employers and fellow employees. With sports journalism everyone sees your work every day – it's posted there on social media and they all get a chance to go through it. You've got to be able to deal with the negativity that will come at some time. There are many characteristics and facets to the job, but it's a brilliant one as well. I think of the places that I've been to through my work that I otherwise wouldn't have had the opportunity to go to, and I still enjoy that sense of satisfaction that continues to come from writing a longer piece and knowing the work that's gone into it, and feeling the sense of pride that you've done the best you can with it and other people are enjoying it. You always want to tell something a bit different and hope that someone finds out something new from what you write.

(ibid.)

Amid the multiplicity of technology-driven demands that are now placed on sports journalists, the role in some ways is the same as ever, regardless of what platform one is working on: to always offer "something new." And if sports journalists stick to this as a principle underpinning their role, then the role is likely to continue to provide a buzz amid the grind.

Questions for discussion

What are the essential skills and mindset needed by the contemporary sports journalist and how, if at all, do they differ from the skills and mindset that a sports journalist needed 25 years ago?

In a social media age, how firm do you believe the distinction is between sports journalist and amateur sports blogger? What sets the two roles apart?

"The massive growth in fan-generated content on social media has made sports journalists more important than ever now, not less." Do you agree or disagree with this statement? Why?

"Sports news organisations are dead as brands. It is individual sports journalists who are the brands now." What do you think is meant by this statement, and do you agree?

2
The history of sports journalism
Continuity and discontinuity

Providing a brief history of sports journalism from the Georgian era through to the twenty-first century, this chapter focuses on the continuities and discontinuities of sports coverage through the decades and centuries. Seminal pieces from the history of sports journalism are highlighted, ranging from William Hazlitt's 'The Fight' through to groundbreaking pieces from the twentieth century. The symbiotic relationship between the growth of certain sports and the growth of the media is explored.

Sports journalists rarely look backwards. Once the live blog is wrapped up, once the match report is filed and once the post-match interviews are done, it is usually a case of being straight on to the next assignment – the next press conference, the next match, the next interview. With some notable exceptions around anniversaries of major events and obituaries, sports journalism is more often than not looking ahead rather than back. Sports editors will, rightly, frequently ask their reporters how they are "going to take the story on." What's the follow-up? What's the next angle on the issue? Can you get to the press conference this afternoon in Brighton, Bath, Barcelona? What other stories have you got? In the digital age of almost unbroken connectivity, the sports journalist is "always on" (Boyle and Haynes, 2009: 179), and that condition of being perpetually connected usually translates to being in a state where it is always a case of moving on to the next story.

But amid the against-the-clock demands of the sports desk and the breathless charge to the next assignment, it is important for sports journalists to be able to see the wider picture and put individual events in their broader context. Managerial sackings and television deals occur frequently, but how does the one that is happening today differ to the ones that occurred in the recent – or slightly more distant – past? The sports media can sometimes be justifiably accused of hyping up the sports events that they themselves are broadcasting, but is this tactic of hype-generation anything new? The Roman thinker Cicero quipped that to be ignorant of history was to condemn oneself to be trapped in a state of eternal childhood. This is arguably particularly true of journalists, with the caveat that journalists also run the risk of trapping their audience in a state of perpetual infancy too if their material is not informed by a historical perspective.

The media has at times exerted a powerful influence on the way that sport is played, bringing about changes in not only the superficial spectacle of sport but also to the very rules and formats of certain competitions and games. This was particularly evident when television was establishing itself in the West in the late 1950s and throughout the 1960s, with the United States, and then the United Kingdom witnessing the game-changing power of "the box." In 1958, for example, golf's PGA Championship switched from being match play to stroke play in response to TV executives wanting more players to be in front of the cameras for the deciding round. Two years later the American Football League was formed with a mission to be TV-friendly – with this objective in mind, players' names were printed on shirts, a countdown clock was introduced and the two-point conversion was added to the regulations. On the other side of the pond, cricket in England responded to a drop in attendance by starting a one-day competition that was deemed more likely to pull in high television audiences. The relationship between television and sport was mutually benefi-cial. While television raised the profile of sport and enabled it to reach a wider audience, sport was able to propel the growth of a new technology. Indeed, some in the television industry have argued that television would never have been the success that it was in its early years without sport. "Television got off the ground because of sports," said Harry Coyle, a pioneering baseball director for the National Broadcasting Company. "When we put on the World Series in 1947, heavyweight fights, the Army-Navy football game, the sales of television sets just spurted" (Collins, 2013: 114).

Television is not the only medium to have significantly influenced the shape of sport. Earlier, newspapers had a far-reaching influence. In 1915, the first Japanese national college baseball side was organised by the country's leading daily newspaper, and when the Japan Baseball League held its inaugural season, more than half the teams were owned by newspaper companies. The historian Tony Collins, in his engaging and at times gleefully provocative history of sport, has also highlighted the particularly close connection between the print industry and cycling in the late nineteenth century, going so far as to assert that "the development of professional cycling owed its entire existence to the alliance between the French newspaper industry and cycle manufacturers" (2013: 58). When the paper L'Auto experienced financial troubles in 1903, it reacted by starting its own cycle race, the Tour de France. The yellow jersey worn by the race leader – le maillot jaune – was styled on the vivid yellow news-paper that L'Auto was printed on. When today the race leader pulls on the famous yellow jersey, he is unwittingly acting as a symbol of the close relationship between the newspaper industry and sport. In Britain, too, newspaper titles have started their own competitions and trophies in certain sports in order to cement their reputation as the place to go in order to get the news about those very same sports. Darts provides one such example. In 1938, in an effort to steal a march over its Sunday newspaper rivals, *The People* launched the Lord Lonsdale Trophy (Holt, 1989: 192).

Collins has articulated a powerful argument for the "symbiotic, mutually interdependent" relationship between the media and sport (2013: 5). By considering the emergence of revenue-generating newspapers in England in the eighteenth and early nineteenth centuries in parallel with the emergence of more systematically organised sporting activities, he has argued that print capitalism and sport in Georgian England emerged simultaneously and remained in a long, firm embrace. This relationship between the print media and sport was mutually beneficial. "Sport would not and could not have been commercialised or codified without the simultaneous development of newspapers and magazines. This would become an iron law of sport [...] The press was both the driver of commercial sport and also its beneficiary" (Collins, 2013: 5–6). Newspapers would not only report on who won what races, matches or fights, but they would also arbitrate on disputed outcomes and thereby play a significant role in codifying sports. Prominent among the force for codification were nineteenth-century sports newspapers such as *Bell's Life in London* and *The Field*. This formalisation of exercise through uniformly accepted rules also facilitated the development of betting, which required all participants to have a shared understanding of how a game – and, thereby, a bet – could be settled. The print media, therefore, helped *games* – in the sense of loosely organised physical activities – become something more organised and commercial: modern *sport*. "Print capitalism provided the electrical charge that was to animate the culture of mass spectator sport" (Collins, 2013: 56). Through the articles they ran, newspapers helped provide publicity and drive the public to attend sporting events that charged an admission fee. And as literacy rates climbed in the final third of the nineteenth century there was a huge increase in the sales of popular newspapers, with sport providing a reliable supply of material to newspaper editors. Considering the development of sport in the Georgian era, Collins argues in a Marxist vein that sport – assisted by newspapers and magazines – reflected back on society the capitalist values that were beginning to underpin it. Sport, with its striving participants and its winners and losers, was a metaphor for life in the emerging capitalist economic order. "Before the commercialisation of sport in the 18th century the idea of commonly agreed, national written laws governing the playing of sport did not exist [...] and formal equality before the law were essential for the smooth transaction of business, just as they were for the regulation of gambling and the playing of games" (Collins, 2013: 6).

Sport and newspapers, therefore, fed off one another, and this interdependency between sport and the media would be reinforced in another guise in the 1950s and 1960s when television began to assert itself as a powerful new medium. So while the technology would change, the interdependency between sports and the media would persist.

However, before the birth of television, the early 1900s saw sports journalists begin to forge a mainstream professional identity of their own. They began to distinguish themselves from other newspaper writers, with the coverage of cricket an important element of this process in the United Kingdom. At the start of the twentieth century, "sports writers themselves were emerging as a specialist breed of journalist." Following on from the microscopic attention to detail shown in John Wisden's *Cricketers' Almanac*, first published in 1864, the "more elaborate prose on cricket emerged in the 1920s and 1930s through the writings of Neville Cardus, of the *Manchester Guardian*" (Boyle and Haynes, 2009: 26). Cardus' elaborate and evocative style sought to elevate sports writing into an almost romantic art form, and while his writings might at times look over-florid to the modern eye and ear, he set the pattern for a tradition of cultured, literary prose that still persists in some corners of the British media. In working-class titles of that era, sport also began to carve out its own increasingly popular space. Boyle and Haynes quote the thoughts from 1936 of Trevor Wignall, a sports journalist from the *Daily Express*:

> Football had a place of its own in newspapers, and even Test cricket was regarded as something that should not be mixed with politics or a readable murder. Sport, as this is composed, is probably the biggest thing in the land. It occupies the thoughts, and empties the pockets, of countless millions.
> (Wignall, 1936, in Boyle and Haynes, 2009: 26–27)

Association football, or soccer, was therefore not only mainstream in British culture in the interwar years, but also its popularity was being echoed and reinforced by the power of the press. However, it was soccer very much on the terms dictated by the Football Association – terms which led to the marginalisation of the women's game. In the years after the First World War, women's football was hugely popular in the United Kingdom, attracting crowds in the tens of thousands. However, the post-war golden age of women's football was short-lived. In 1921, the Football Association – run by men – effectively shut down women's football by instating a ban on women playing on its grounds. It reasoned that the game was not suited to women, and also expressed concerns that, in an amateur era, not all of the substantial gate receipts were going to charity (Wollaston, 2017). The prohibition remained in place for half a century, and we can only speculate at the different trajectory sport – and perhaps society more generally – would have taken had women's football not been artificially held back in such a way. Rugby, too, is a sport where the growth of the women's game was curtailed by social attitudes. In 1891, a tour to New Zealand by a women's team was cancelled following a public outcry, and the women's game in its modern incarnation only began to take shape at British and French universities in the 1960s (De Montford University, 2017).

Today, in Western Europe at least, soccer is by a considerable stretch the most popular sport and the sport that receives the most media coverage. Indeed, operating from the premise that "the media dominates our lives. Sport dominates the media. Football dominates the sports media," journalism lecturer and sports journalist Roger Domeneghetti has argued that "the history of the football media is the history of the media" (2017: xv). He characterises modern football and the modern media as being locked in a marriage which has been mutually sustaining. "While the press helped popularise football, football helped make newspapers a mass-market product. Newsreels brought moving footage of the game to the masses and radio brought live coverage into their homes; football as a key selling point of both" (ibid.).

Other historians of sport, however, have argued that the relationship is not so close. Holt, for example, argues that

> the press have played a major part in popularizing spectator sport and sustaining interest in it, but it is misleading to think of professional football, for example, as having been created or manufactured by the media. The press reflected the living culture of the people; it could influence opinion and reinforce existing attitudes but it did not create new forms of entertainment and rarely attempted to alter the habits or loyalties of its readership.
>
> (1989: 307)

While much sports culture in the early decades of the twenty-first century is focused on soccer, we should resist the error of *presentism* – the fallacy of assuming that because something is predominant now, then it must have always been like that. Association football and rugby football were not formally codified until the latter part of the nineteenth century, with earlier forms of "football" being a mixture of what we would now call soccer and rugby, and with the rules of the game differing from region to region and even from school to school (Collins, 2015). Much of the early newspaper articles about sport focus on fighting: or to give it its more refined-sounding name, pugilism. In the mid-eighteenth century, prize fighting was an activity adored by a number of those towards the pinnacle of the British aristocracy. Huge stakes were wagered on the outcome of fights. The Duke of Cumberland placed a £10,000 bet on a leading pugilist of the era, Jack Broughton, in one contest in 1750. In 1786, wagers of up to £40,000 were reportedly made. Among those placing the biggest bets were the Prince of Wales and the Duke of York. As the eighteenth century turned into the nineteenth, the deeds of pugilists were being reported in the new weekly newspapers that had been launched, including *Bell's Weekly Messenger*, the *Sporting Magazine* and the *Weekly Dispatch* (Holt, 1989: 20–21). Pierce Egan was among the leading sports writers documenting this era of Regency fighting and fast living, with his *Boxiana* recording the lives of famous pugilists. Some of the leading prose stylists and thinkers of the day turned their attention to sport, too. William Hazlitt, for example, whose interests as a writer were primarily political and aesthetic, wrote an essay called *The Fight* (1822) which vividly conjured up the frenzy, excitement and goriness of a Berkshire prize fight. In so doing, Hazlitt became the first in what was to become a long line of distinguished writers who, although best known for other forms of writing, turned their lens to sport with brilliant effect. Chief among his successors in the twentieth century was the American novelist Norman Mailer, who was inspired by Hazlitt's *The Fight* to produce a book of the same name documenting the 1974 bout between Muhammad Ali and George Foreman.

Also following in the tradition was Hunter S. Thompson, the countercultural writer best known for recording the illicit drugs culture and seedier side of 1960s America. Thompson's best-known piece of sports journalism was a magazine piece headlined "The Kentucky Derby Is Decadent and Depraved" (1970), but his sports output extended beyond that. With his characteristic undertow of satire, literary vigour and sense of the absurd, Thompson once recalled a time when he was churning out sports articles at a furious pace:

> Not necessarily because I believed all that sports bullshit, but because sportwriting was the only thing I could do that anybody was willing to pay for. And none of the people I wrote about seemed to give a hoot in hell what kind of lunatic gibberish I wrote about, just as long as it *moved*. They wanted Action, Color, Speed, Violence […] At one point, in Florida, I was writing variations on the same demented themes for three competing papers at the same time, under three different names. I was a sports columnist for one paper in the morning, sports editor for another in the afternoon, and at night I worked for a pro wrestling promoter, writing incredibly twisted "press releases" that I would plant, the next day, in both papers.
> (Collision, 2013; italics in original)

The history of sports writing, then, is one where it has at times broken out of the sports ghetto and taken strides across the terrain of mainstream culture. Dipping into the archives of sports content also illustrates how media organisations' approach to certain sports has altered. As we have seen, fighting and racing were the staples of much early content. Early sporting papers such as *Bell's Life in London* mainly contained articles about forthcoming or recently concluded prize-fights and horse races. By the mid-1880s, the racing-focused paper *Sporting Life* had a circulation of 300,000 (Holt, 1989: 307). *The Times*, while providing substantial coverage of cricket, deemed the 1914 FA Cup Final between Liverpool and Burnley "of comparatively little interest except to the Lancashire working classes" (Holt 1989, 308).

In Victorian England, the growth of sport and the growth of the media were intertwined. As newspapers gave more coverage to certain sports, so interest in those sports grew. And as interest in those sports grew, so did the desire from audiences for more newspaper content about those sports. As one sports historian has observed: "*The Times* featured 19 different sports in 1874 and 27 by 1901 […] Numbers of sporting clubs, governing bodies and other institutions grew rapidly. Older sports had had local and regional variants. Now, in all sports, new rules were increasingly recorded, standardised and regularly modified to suit players' and spectators' needs. By 1901 the new sports had become institutionalised, codified and international in scope. The number of participants grew" (Huggins, 2004: 6).

Before the nineteenth century, information about sport was primarily conveyed orally, but by the final decade of the century newspapers were playing a central role in fuelling the late Victorian appetite for sport as more and more newsprint was dedicated to it. In so doing, it has been argued, the media shaped in a profound way what sport meant and signified to Victorians. "Many first came across sport not by playing or watching but through media coverage […] At the same time they (the media) aided the construction of a sporting reality dominated by the interests, values and ideological needs of the middle classes" (Huggins, 2004: 141). And without the oxygen of publicity provided by the press, events such as the Grand National and the FA Cup Final would not have become such central events on the British national calendar. Indeed, association football's rise to prominence in the 1870s would not have been accomplished were it not for the media. Crowds at football matches were relatively low at the time, but grew as match reports appeared more frequently and the popular press stoked the fires of local rivalries.

The extent of the impact that the press had on the shaping of the Victorian sporting world is illustrated through the early years of the weekly newspaper *Bell's Life in London and Sporting Chronicle*, which was first published in 1822. Its editor from 1824 was Vincent Dowling and he became a key figure in the administration of sport. He arbitrated on sporting disputes, gave expert evidence to a Parliamentary committee on betting and gaming, and was viewed as "a guardian of the interest and honour of the early Victorian sporting world" (Huggins, 2004: 145). Sports newspapers became forums where rules were codified and disputes settled.

The emergence and the growth of "the specials" – the Saturday evening sporting newspapers that reported on the results and performances of local clubs – was swift during the late Victorian era. In the 1880s there were just four such titles, in the 1890s there were 18, and "after 1900 they were ubiquitous" (Holt, 1989: 307). In Glasgow alone, three newspapers competed for sports fans' eyeballs on a Saturday night – the *Evening Times* on pink paper, the green *Evening Citizen*, and the *Evening News*, which was printed on white paper. Readers would wait keenly for the papers to come rolling off the printing presses and reading one or the other of the titles became something of a Saturday ritual, much like listening to the final scores being read out became a radio and television habit a century later.

The printing presses were a powerful driver of sporting culture, and it is important to note the significant role that technology has played – and continues to play – in the evolution of sports journalism. Sports journalism operates within the context of historical and social settings, and technological change is one facet of that. Just as the growth in digital technology has affected the reach and nature of twenty-first-century sports journalism, so did the technological and social changes of the nineteen century enable the sports media to reach new audiences back then. The growth of railways and the invention of the electric telegraph during the 1830s and 1840s enabled newspapers and information to be more effectively distributed, while the abolition of taxes on newspapers in the 1850s, increased literacy levels and higher real-term wages led to higher circulations. Improved printing techniques and picture reproduction also made newspapers more aesthetically pleasing as products (Huggins, 2004: 143–144).

Profile of sports newspaper publisher and editor-in-chief David Emery

"We are niche. We are providing a service you can't really get anywhere else [...] People are grateful and willing to pay for it."

In an era when the growth of digital has seen newspapers suffer sharp declines in sales and in some instances close, sports media entrepreneur David Emery is bucking the trend by continuing to put print products at the heart of his business model.

After three decades working for the sports departments of national newspapers, Emery, a former sports editor of the *Daily Express*, embarked on a new venture by starting his own group of weekly sports titles.

Greenways Publishing, of which he is editor-in-chief and managing director, now has a stable of titles including *The Rugby Paper*, *The Non-League Paper*, *The Football League Paper* and *The Cricket Paper*, as well as a portfolio of sports magazines.

Emery believes the unique selling point of his titles lies in the depth they go into covering their respective niches. Many of the titles cover not only a sport's elite game but go right down to the grass roots too.

"We are niche," Emery told the authors. "We are providing a service you can't really get anywhere else unless you are willing to trawl through dozens and dozens of websites. The papers that have worked are those that contain content that you can't get elsewhere.

"You perhaps can't fight the nationals in terms of their Premier League football content or even their Premiership rugby content – that's what those national papers provide – but you can cover other areas of those sports."

Emery gives the example of his title *The Rugby Paper*, which comes out every Sunday and is available both as a printed product and through digital subscription. It covers everything from international rugby to local club rugby, providing coverage through a network of freelance reporters and some big-name columnists.

"*The Rugby Paper* is strong. We are not just dealing with the Premiership. We go down the leagues. The more you can mine into information and the minutiae of results and put it in one product the better. People are grateful and willing to pay for it," explains Emery.

The digital-subscription version of the paper is available from midnight, with the printed paper distributed nationwide each Sunday morning.

"I can't see *The Rugby Paper* going digital-only for years, if at all," he says. "I think it would be a distress signal if we went online-only."

Emery believes a key element to his titles' success lies in the deliberate policy of not giving too much content away for free on their websites – a policy that contrasts to what many newspapers have done. He will publish a smattering of articles on the free-to-access websites, but only with a view to enticing readers to then sign up for the digital subscription version or to buy the print version.

"We self-embargo ourselves," he explains. "We will put some of the major columns up on the website on a Wednesday after they have first appeared on the Sunday.

"I'm old school. I don't want to chew away at our paying readership by putting too much online for free. I like to use the Internet as a come-on, so that you feed the readers through. Otherwise you end up cannibalising your own product."

Emery, a former head of sport at Express Newspapers, believes many national newspapers in the United Kingdom could merge or become online-only titles.

"It's complex. The big beasts in the jungle are really suffering – their circulation is crashing by alarming amounts. There has been a squeezing of sports departments, with a number of them carrying the same reports that appear in other newspapers."

For Emery, it is essential for him that Greenways Publishing keeps the print and digital aspects of his sports media business working in harmony.

"I love newspapers – I love the way you can chuck them on the floor and return to them over and over again, without having to wait for an Internet connection. But I'm no reluctant on-liner, and I know how important it's also been to the business that we've built social media followings on Twitter and Facebook."

Despite evolving technology, Emery believes young reporters can still learn a huge amount from the attributes and news-gathering ability of veteran reporters, such as Peter Jackson, whom Emery snapped up after Jackson retired as rugby correspondent at the *Daily Mail*, where he had forged a reputation as a sports journalist who regularly broke exclusive stories.

"I still think newspapers sell on news. Peter comes up with news each week and it helps set the agenda – that's a newshound doing his stuff.

"Sports journalists today still need those same qualities: inquisitiveness and the ability to be self-starting.

"You can have some features, some team news and some personality pieces in your papers, and it's important that you have some good columnists. But you also want to be breaking stories if you can."

A recurring theme in this book is the often symbiotic relationship between the sports media and the gambling industry, and it is an issue that has manifested itself in various ways since the emergence of the sports print media in Georgian times. Indeed, as the press began to become more prominent in the Victorian era, social reformers become concerned that poorer members of society were at increasing risk of making bets they could ill-afford.

> What frightened Victorian reformers was not so much the ruin of the aris-
> tocracy as the fact that the railway, the telegraph, and the popular press
> would combine to cause an enormous increase in betting. Instead of going
> to the races once or twice a year, or gambling on the occasional prize-fight
> or athletic contest, improved communications would permit a whole new
> industry to arise which would encourage and profit from habitual gambling.
>
> (Holt, 1989: 180)

Intriguingly, similar concerns are being voiced in the United Kingdom more than a century and a half later following another revolution in communications – this time digital. The prominence of advertisements promoting gambling firms, betting apps on mobile phones and sports articles that focus on betting tips and odds has prompted concerns to be voiced about the ubiquity and dangers of a culture imbued with betting (Sweney and Duncan, 2018). A study by Darragh McGee, of the University of Bath, which monitored the behaviour of football supporters aged between 18 and 35 concluded that young men in the United Kingdom strongly associated their support of football with gambling – a phenomenon referred to as the "gamblification" of watching football (Conn, 2019). The research was first reported by *The Guardian*'s David Conn, a sports journalist with an interest in the relationship between money and football. Breaking the story, he wrote that the research had found that some young men "can no longer watch a football match unless they have multiple bets; com-monly they have up to 25 accounts with online gambling companies, and their football conversations with mates are all about betting, rather than the game" (Conn, ibid.). History, then, tells us that technology influences sport as a spec-tator experience and also influences the way in which the media packages and mediates sport to the public. In so doing, it in some ways reshapes the very essence of those sports themselves.

Profile: Jimmy Cannon

When Jimmy Cannon (1909–1973) died, his obituary in *The New York Times* described him as "an artisan of the language" (Anderson, 1973). Literary panache was an essential quality for sports journalists working in the mid-twentieth century in the United States. Knowing your sport and being able to report accurately on it wasn't enough; you had to be able to coin a phrase too, and have style and swagger dripping off each metaphor.

When hired by *The New York Journal-American* in 1959, Cannon was reported to be the highest-paid sports writer in the land on a salary of

$1,000 a week. His columns became syndicated in that year, meaning they were printed in multiple newspapers across the United States. The impact this had was felt not just by readers but by other sportswriters too, who from Boston to Los Angeles now sought to unpick his style and emulate it. "Now his punchy, breezy, streets-of-New York prose could be read by sports fans from coast to coast; more important, it could be read by sportswriters, who latched onto the Cannon style as if it had been handed down from Heaven" (Yardley, 1978).

Significantly, his obituary in *The New York Times* credited him with being "perhaps the first sportswriter [to be] aware of the sociological impact of the black athlete. Of Joe Louis, the former world heavyweight boxing champion, he once wrote: 'He's a credit to his race – the human race'" (Anderson, 1973). Boxing may have given rise to one of Cannon's best-known lines, but he had an ambivalent attitude to the sport, being simultaneously appalled and attracted by it. He criticised boxing as being the barbaric "red-light district" of sport, but revelled in covering it. Like many of the finest sports writers, he was a careful observer of character and found the circus of hangers-on in boxing to be a compelling subject of study. A review in *Sports Illustrated* of his collected works, published in 1978, five years after his death, highlighted this passage in which Cannon turned his pen on the dubious, hypocritical ways of fight managers:

> The fight manager wouldn't fight to defend his mother. He has never participated in a crime of violence but he lives by the code of the underworld. He imitates mob guys in his dress, speech and manners. He accuses all inefficient pugs of being yellow; he has been a coward in all the important matters of his life. He is cranky and profane when he talks to the kids he manages but is servile when addressing the gangster whom he considers his benefactor. He has cheated many people but he describes himself as a legitimate guy at every opportunity.
> (Cannon, 1978 *Nobody Asked Me, But ... The World of Jimmy Cannon*, quoted in Yardley, 1978)

While some have thought his style too sentimental in places (Yardley, 1978), no less a writer than the novelist Ernest Hemingway was a fan. Paying tribute to Cannon, Hemingway said: "He's an excellent sportswriter and he's also a very good writer aside from sports [...] I don't know anybody who takes his job more seriously or with more confidence. He's able to convey the quality of the athlete and the feeling, the excitement, of the event" (Anderson, 1973).

Reflecting on his career as a sportswriter and how it compared with the more "serious" work done by news reporters at the front section of newspapers, Cannon reflected: "The people who write the pieces up front in the paper consider this a wasted life. It's true that I have solved little of my country's dilemma, but the statesmen also have failed. I like my life because it's a pleasant life. I function in glad places."

Questions for discussion

"The sports media once helped define the rules of sport, but in the twenty-first century sports journalists are powerless in influencing how sports are governed." Do you regard this statement as true or false? What examples can you provide in support of your answer?

Is it the case that sport and the sports media have a relationship of mutual dependence? If so, what examples can you give of that interdependence?

3
Sports journalism, nationalism and politics

Introduction

Ever since George Orwell stated his famously misanthropic view that international sport is "mimic warfare" that encourages "orgies of hatred," there has been fierce debate about the extent to which the sports media promotes nationalism and xenophobia (Orwell, 1945). Orwell's critics, which would include many sports journalists, contend that sport, on the contrary, plays a vital role in promoting harmonious relations between people and nations, and that international sport today is mostly carnivalesque entertainment, producing nothing more than "90 minute patriots" (Bairner, 2015). Analysis would suggest that sport can be both Orwellian and carnivalesque in the senses defined above, because it is fundamentally malleable, open to political manipulation as well as commercial exploitation (Houlihan, 2015: 187).

In recent times, sport has become a vehicle for destabilising traditional "national" sporting identities as the globalised sports media beam the NFL, the NBA, the EPL, La Liga and the Champions League into homes all over the world. Premier League Productions, for example, broadcasts to over 185 territories, where the English Premier League is often much more popular than domestic football (Flanagan, 2016). There is also the related issue of whether the decline of local journalism has led to a decline in the reinforcement of local identities and a sense of community (Hutton, 2018). For decades, local newspapers would help define the issues that were important to a community, including the fortunes of local sports teams. The twin motors of digitisation and globalisation have arguably undermined the ability of the local press to cultivate that sense of community. The relationship between national identity and the sports media therefore needs to be considered in the context of globalisation. We also offer some thoughts on the ethical challenges sports journalists need to consider when they cover international sport.

Broadcasting the nation

If sport is important in forging a sense of cultural or national identity, then how the media portrays those sports has a direct bearing on the shaping of those identities. Indeed, specific sporting events – and the coverage of them – can be said to constitute rituals through which a nation views and defines itself. In England, major sporting events such as the FA Cup Final, the Grand National, Wimbledon, the Boat Race, and Test matches are, Whannel argues, "a significant part of the cultural history of the nation, and forms part of the fabric of 'Englishness', contributing to a sense of national identity" (2002: 3).

Those words were written at the start of the century, and already some of the events that Whannel regarded as helping constitute national identity could be challenged. The FA Cup, for example, has simultaneously slipped down managers' priority lists and withered as a national spectacle. Test cricket, too, has had a diminishing impact on the English national psyche, with the five-day format largely superseded – for good or ill – by limited overs matches. Furthermore, the fact that some of these sporting spectacles argu-ably no longer contribute to defining "Englishness" can with some justifica-tion be explained through reference to the media. Ever since the rights to live Test cricket were snapped up by Sky Sports in 2006, there has barely been a live innings screened on free-to-air television in the United Kingdom. This has led to concerns that a generation of schoolchildren are growing up with restricted access to watching the great players of what was once the national summer sport. It is a not such a big step to see this as having a neces-sarily negative impact on the quality of young players, which, in turn, could diminish cricket's prominence in public life still further. The sports media, then, don't just help define national identity; they can also erode those things that used to constitute such an identity.

When it comes to covering international sporting events involving Britain's national teams, the big four sports broadcasters – BBC, ITV, Sky Sports and BT Sport – have traditionally been patriotic rather than nationalistic. In other words, they reflect pride in the nation's sporting achievements without pro-moting a sense of superiority towards other nations. This is consistent with the dominant values of British society but also the culture of British broadcasting, which places huge value on impartiality and balance, a necessary requirement in a multinational nation state where England, Scotland, Wales and Northern Ireland compete against each other on a regular basis.

The broadcasters have traditionally favoured the popular "national" sports of football, rugby and cricket, but patriotism frequently helps many minority sports gain an audience, particularly during the Olympics. As the national broadcaster for the Olympic Games, the BBC is the designated cheerleader-in-chief for Team GB, creating some of the most iconic sporting memories in recent British history. On these occasions, sport can play a pivotal role in defining what it means to be British. Indeed, during London 2012, the BBC's coverage helped demolish the negative media coverage and pessimism in the run-up to the Games and lift the nation's spirits. The opening ceremony, directed by award-winning film-maker Danny Boyle, showcased "Britishness" in all its rich complexity, presenting a vision of Britain to the 900 million viewers worldwide that was multicultural, innovative, diverse and inclusive (Thomas and Antony, 2015). The opening and closing ceremonies still rank as the eighth and ninth most viewed events in British broadcasting history (BARB, 2012).

While patriotism underpins broadcasters' approach to international sport, national stereotyping is still a feature of sports commentary. Indeed, pundits and commentators will often ascribe traditional national stereotypes to international teams, most notably in football. For example, we still hear Germany described as "ruthlessly efficient," and African teams are often "physically strong" but "tactically naive." Various iterations of Brazilian "flair," Dutch "individualism" and Italian or Argentinian "cunning" are routinely employed (Lavric et al., 2008; Sims, 2014). The stereotyping extends to the representation of foreign managers and players in English football, where they have always occupied an uneasy "insider/outsider" status in the national game. A notable negative stereotype applied to foreign players is their tendency to dive, feign injury and cheat. Despite Opta statistics proving some years ago that they don't dive any more than English players do, these ideas still circulate in football punditry and popular culture (Brown, 2012; Eurosport, 2014). The so-called spygate scandal, involving Marcelo Bielsa, the Argentinian manager of Leeds United, took on a rather predictable moral tone in some news outlets that equated his actions (spying on another team's training sessions) with something only foreigners would do (*The Debate*, January 17, 2019).

While British sports broadcasters occupy an influential position in "mediating" national identity, the digital revolution appears to be disrupting it in uneven and uncertain ways. The spectacular growth of e-sports and fan-based media, such as Copa90, AFTV and Hashtag Utd, are creating new interconnected global sporting cultures where fans and their audiences appear to be less concerned about national sporting allegiances. These developments suggest there could be a cultural shift that poses significant challenges for mainstream sports broadcasters and the international sporting competitions they have traditionally focused on.

Sport and the tabloid nation

Studies of the sports media and national identity still tend to focus on the tabloid press due to their reputation for banging the drums of tribalism, especially during football tournaments (Domeneghetti, 2017). Arguably the most extreme example of this was the *Daily Mirror's* "ACHTUNG SURRENDER!" headline in 1996 on the morning England were due to play Germany in the semi-finals of the European finals. It included the subheading "For you Fritz, ze Euro 96 Championship Is Over." The British Foreign Office issued a rebuke at the time stating: "It's right to be patriotic. But we don't think that sporting events like this should be made a reason for antagonism against other countries" (Thomsen, 1996).

What are the acceptable limits of tribalism and partisanship that are inherent in supporting a team or national side? And does the sports media have a duty to ensure the fires of nationalism aren't irresponsibly stoked? There is no doubt that the tabloids push these boundaries. On the morning of England's last 16 match against Colombia in the 2018 World Cup, *The Sun* newspaper published the front-page headline "Go Kane!", a punning reference to England's captain, Harry Kane, that alluded to Colombia's links to the cocaine trade. Alongside a photo of Kane clenching his fists and pulling a facial expression reminiscent of a roar – while draped in a flag of St George – the full headline read: "As 3 Lions face nation that gave the world Shakira, great coffee and er, other stuff, we say GO KANE!" While not triggering anything approximating a full-blown diplomatic incident, the front page was criticised by the Colombian ambassador to the United Kingdom, Nestor Osorio Londono. "It's rather sad that they use such a festive and friendly environment as the World Cup to target a country and continue to stigmatise it with a completely unrelated issue." Colombian media were displeased, too, with the website of Colombian broadcaster Caracol TV saying the front page had "caused great upset." Was *The Sun* legitimately entertaining its readers in the build-up to a major international match, or was it not only crassly caricaturing a nation but also perpetrating that caricature by attempting a joke based on a bloody trade that has caused misery across the nation? In response that same day, *The Sun* said they hoped the piece would boost the Colombian coffee industry and said the front page was "suitably light-hearted considering the context" (Waterson, 2018).

The game turned out to be anything but light-hearted, with England squeezing home via a penalty shoot-out after Colombia had deployed what many saw as cynical, physical tactics. The *Telegraph* referred with some understatement to the South American side's "tactile approach to marking" (*Daily Telegraph*, 2018). The absence of light-heartedness prompted *The Sun* to continue the "Go Kane" spat. In the following day's paper, the newspaper ran an item headed

"Colombia – An Apology." Composed of undiluted irony, it read: "The front page of yesterday's *Sun* may have given the impression that Colombia is well known for its cocaine trade. This was unfair on the Colombian people, who are far more embarrassed by the way their cheating, fouling, play-acting, mean-spirited national football team played last night. We are happy to set the record straight." This small piece captured three facets of British tabloid sports journalism: the presence of mind always to do a follow-up story when the opportunity presents itself; an attempted dose of humour; and an underlying twang of jingoism. Not that everyone found the humour amusing, even fellow British sports journalists. "It wasn't particularly funny, their apology [...] was even less funny," said Nick Harris, *The Mail on Sunday*'s chief sports correspondent. "I can see why he [the ambassador] wasn't very amused and you can see why a lot of people would be unimpressed by sections of our tabloid media, with sort of lame jokes. If it had been funny fair enough, it wasn't" (The Media Show, BBC Radio 4, 2018).

The "Old Firm": sectarianism and the sports media

There are some sporting contests, such as Boca Juniors versus River Plate, or Pakistan versus India that are so volatile they rarely need the sports media to stoke the flames of tribalism. One of the oldest and most intense football rivalries in the world can be found in the city of Glasgow, Scotland. Its two clubs, Rangers and Celtic, collectively known as the "Old Firm," reflect the traditional religious divide between Protestants and Catholics in Scotland, but the rivalry can only be fully understood with reference to Irish political history too. Established in 1872, Glasgow Rangers became associated with nativist Protestantism. Celtic was formed in 1887, attracting support from the large Irish Catholic minority, mostly migrant workers from Ireland. They are the dominant forces in Scottish football. Between them, they have won the Scottish League title more than 100 times. The scorecard currently reads Rangers 54 titles, Celtic 50 titles. During that period they have played each other over 400 times.

Sectarianism is often defined in simple terms as discrimination and hatred based on ideas of inferiority and superiority between different groups (Nil by Mouth, 2018). It is mostly commonly used with reference to religion (e.g. divisions between Shia and Sunni Muslims or between Catholics and Protestants), but this doesn't mean that sectarianism in Scotland is easy to understand. For example, when Neil Lennon was managing Hibernian, he claimed it was essentially a form of racism (see Chapter 7). The sectarian conflict in Scotland and Ireland can be traced back to the Battle of the Boyne, in 1690, when the Dutch-born Protestant King William of Orange defeated the army of the Catholic King James II. The victory is still celebrated every year by the Protestant Orange Order, mostly in Northern Ireland, but also in the west of Scotland. Sectarianism in Scotland, therefore, may be rooted in religion, but it is also intimately linked to Northern Irish politics (loyalists v republicans), ethno-national identity (British Scots v Irish Scots) and the ideological divisions in Scotland between conservatives, socialists and more recently Scottish nationalists (Bradley, 2014).

The strong religious identification of Rangers and Celtic did not fully develop until the twentieth century when large numbers of people, Catholic and Protestant, migrated from Ireland to the west of Scotland to work in the shipyards and industrial towns around Glasgow before the First World War. In the aftermath of the war, discrimination towards the Catholic minority grew and became institutionalised throughout Scottish society with the Church of Scotland instigating much of the anti-Irish Catholic propaganda. In 1923, they published a notorious pamphlet, *The Menace of the Irish Race to Our Scottish Nationality*. Catholics were excluded from most professions and routinely demonised in the media as untrustworthy, disloyal Papists, criminals, hooligans and supporters of Irish rebellion – the Fenians and the Irish Republican Army (IRA). Rangers Football Club had a no-Catholics employment policy and did not sign their first Catholic player until 1989. Matches between Rangers and Celtic often resulted in violence and disorder. While sectarianism in Scottish society was declining, the tribal divisions around the two clubs persisted, fuelled in particular by the violent conflict in Northern Ireland (1968–1998). When Celtic fans sang songs supporting a united Ireland or the IRA, it would usually provoke a hostile reaction from Rangers fans and the media.

The murder in 1995 of Mark Scott, a Celtic fan, resulted in the formation of the anti-sectarianism charity Nil By Mouth, and both clubs made various attempts to clamp down on fans singing provocative and controversial songs. The Scottish government launched numerous anti-sectarian initiatives under the banner of "Scotland's Shame." Over the last 30 years, secularisation, social mixing, interfaith marriage and the peace process in Ireland have seen sectarianism virtually disappear in Scottish society (Bruce, 2011; Devine, 2018), but it has not died out completely in Scottish football culture. Often individual players will become targets for abuse. When Aiden McGeady, a third-generation Irish footballer who played for Celtic (2004–2010), chose to represent Ireland, he was abused by fans from Rangers and other Scottish clubs. The abuse was given legitimacy in a number of Scottish newspapers. One *Daily Record* sports writer used it to express his antagonism towards Irish-Scots.

> It's time all Scottish Celtic fans got over their obsession with Ireland. The fact that Glasgow sports shops sell as many Ireland football tops as Scotland football tops is both pathetic and ultimately unhelpful. (McKie, 2005)

A series of ugly incidents at matches between Rangers and Celtic in 2011 prompted the Scottish government to pass anti-sectarian laws in 2012. The Offensive Behaviour at Football and Threatening Communications Act, however, was deemed so controversial and ill-conceived that the legislation was repealed in 2018. Since then it appears that sectarian incidents at football matches may be on the increase again. Kilmarnock manager Steve Clarke, who is Catholic, was visibly upset during a press conference, recounting how Rangers fans had targeted him with sectarian chants of "sad Fenian bastard" (Ralston, 2019). Graham Spiers, a Scottish sports journalist and life-long Rangers fan, blames the club for not tackling the problem:

> The club, tragically in my view, has allowed the bigotry issues to relapse. The songs are coming back. *The Billy Boys*, the bigoted anthem that caused all the uproar with UEFA back in 2006 and that Rangers back then tackled, has made an inglorious and full-blown comeback.
>
> (Spiers, 2019)

What is particularly relevant for sports reporters is Spiers' belief that the clubs "want a mute and compliant media" and have banned journalists (including himself) for criticising the club for not doing enough to tackle the issue. It was media pressure on the clubs, Spiers (2019) argues, that forced them to act in 2006, but since then the press in Scotland has failed in its duty to report sectarianism. On a topic as complex and divisive as sectarianism, his views are disputed by critics of the media who accuse journalists of sensationalism, and by some fans who argue the problem is exaggerated (Devine, 2018).

Sky Sports, which currently owns the Scottish Premier League broadcasting rights in the United Kingdom, is keen to capture the intensity of Old Firm encounters, but they have become increasingly cautious not to amplify the hatred. Ofcom, the United Kingdom's communications regulator, dictates that live broadcasts of sporting events should use a short time delay to avoid broadcasting foul and abusive language. In the case of Old Firm derbies, broadcasters often need to dampen the sound of songs and chanting coming from the terraces too. This policy, necessary under Ofcom rules, may give the impression to many viewers that the problem has gone away, but it hasn't. Spiers, with some resignation, concludes that Scottish football will never be rid of sectarianism (*The Times*, February 23, 2019). If his prediction proves to be correct, sports journalists cannot simply continue to celebrate the Old Firm without a critical appreciation of its history, the harmful effects of bigotry and the damage it is doing to the reputation of Scotland and Scottish football.

"Representing" the nation

Aiden McGeady's story illustrates that eligibility is one of the most contentious issues in international sport that divides sports journalists and fans alike. It resurfaces frequently, especially when high-profile sport stars express strong views on the subject. In 2013, the Arsenal and England midfielder Jack Wilshere argued that "foreigners" should not play for England, stating that: "If you live in England for five years it doesn't make you English." It provoked a strong reaction on Twitter from South Africa-born England cricketer Kevin Pietersen, who asked: "Interested to know how you define foreigner…? Would that include me, Strauss, Trott, Prior, Justin Rose, Froome, Mo Farah?" (Scott-Elliot, 2013). Pietersen has an English mother and qualified to play for England after living in the country for four years. The sports media gave Wilshere's comments extensive coverage with some sports commentary ignoring the political context (Sky Sports, October 10, 2013). It was controversial precisely because it was at odds with British government policy as well as Fédération Internationale de Football Association (FIFA) rules on eligibility. Wilshere's remarks were specifically in response to speculation that Adnan Januzaj (then playing for Manchester United) could possibly qualify for England under residency rules. At the time, Januzaj could have qualified for at least six countries. Born in Belgium shortly after his parents fled the war in Kosovo, he could have opted for Kosovo, Serbia or Croatia, from his mother's ancestry; Albania, his parents' birthplace; Turkey, the homeland of his father's parents; or England, where he had played since he was a teenager (Berkowitz, et al., 2018). His case was unusual, but many athletes and players qualify to play for more than one country. He has actually ended up playing for Belgium.

Sports journalists, quite rightly, regard the issue of eligibility in international sport as a legitimate issue for scrutiny and debate, but the negative media coverage directed towards athletes with mixed or dual heritage, especially in the current political climate, needs to be critically examined. Athletes and players who have represented one country but later switch to another usually attract the most attention because they are unusual and highly emotive. The pejorative term "plastic Brit" gained widespread currency in the press in the run-up to the London 2012 Olympics as a number of foreign-based and foreign-born athletes were selected to represent Great Britain. Some reporters saw the Team GB decision to select foreign-born athletes, such as Tiffany Porter, as a ruthless strategy designed to win medals at all costs and argued that it went against the Olympic spirit. Porter had grown up in the United States, but had held dual nationality since birth thanks to her British-born mother. Neil Wilson, who has covered 19 summer and winter Olympics, wrote: "There's no way I'll be standing for National Anthem when 'Plastic Brit' Porter wins gold" (Wilson,

2012). The *Daily Mail* ran with the "plastic Brit" theme for months, with one headline stating: "Team GB have 61 plastic Brits" (Sportsmail Reporter, 2012). This figure was achieved by counting all the foreign-born athletes including Mo Farah, and the *Daily Mail* never actually clarified what they meant by "plastic Brit." Another *Mail* reporter, John McEvoy, asked Tiffany Porter at a press conference if she could sing a few lines of "God Save the Queen" to demonstrate her British credentials (Kelly, 2012). Jessica Ennis-Hill and other teammates came to her defence and the UK Sport performance director called the "plastic Brit" campaign "unpleasantly xenophobic" (Gibson, 2012a)

Academics who study national identity describe this process as "othering" – the impulse to put people and groups into binary opposite categories of "them" and "us." This is how nationalists seek cohesion, "through discourses of inclusion and exclusion" (Thomas and Antony, 2015). "Othering" relies to a great extent on stereotyping, a process which "reduces, essentializes, naturalizes and fixes difference" (Hall, 2003: 258). Sport naturally lends itself to binary opposites, and it seems some sports journalists find it difficult to avoid them. However, the "plastic Brit" tag has rarely reappeared in sports media discourse since. Arguably the success of Team GB at London 2012 was the main reason as a third of the team's medal winners were either foreign born or had foreign-born parents.

A more recent example that has caused a lot of controversy on both sides of the Irish Sea is Declan Rice's decision to switch from playing football for the Republic of Ireland to England. Eni Aluko's comments in *The Guardian* on this case should be read in conjunction with Martin Samuel's column in the *Daily Mail*. Drawing on her own mixed national identity, Aluko (2019) wrote: "I don't think people fully appreciate how difficult it can be to have two nationalities in football and the kind of stigma that can come with it" (*The Guardian*, February 14, 2019). In contrast, Samuel (2019) uses the Rice case to accuse the Football Association of Ireland of acting like "predators" intent on "gaming the system" to groom second- and third-generation Irish players at an early age. It is a strongly worded column that also recycles the old "plastic paddy" trope that was popular in the tabloids in the 1980s. In many ways, Aluko and Samuel represent the main fault line in the sports media on this issue.

"The sports media and politics don't mix"

It has been argued that sport is a powerful engine for positive political transformation. "As a cultural phenomenon, as an agent of change, it is without equal," contends Steen, arguing that the collapse of systematic racial segregation in South Africa would not have occurred without the pressures exerted by sport (2014: 5–6). And if sport can bring about change, then a case can be made for the media that cover sport being an accelerant or retardant for such change. At the international level, sport continues to be used for "soft power" diplomacy between nations, often leading to positive outcomes, but it is also vulnerable to political exploitation. Indeed, the extent to which political leaders will go to use sport for their own purposes was highlighted once again during the FIFA World Cup Finals in 2018. In the build-up to the tournament, it seemed that sports reporters were having to cover politics rather than the football. The British foreign secretary's claims that Russian president Vladimir Putin would exploit the tournament the same way Adolf Hitler used the 1936 Olympics for propaganda purposes received extensive coverage in the sports media, and Mohamed Salah's unhappiness at the way Chechen leader Ramzan Kadyrov used him and his Egyptian teammates to stage-manage positive publicity for his brutal regime was also widely reported (Sky Sports, June 13, 2018).

Putin and the French president Emmanuel Macron unsurprisingly gained positive publicity from the tournament following France's victory, but most sports journalists covering the tournament generally agreed that Croatia's president, Kolinda Grabar-Kitarovićher, was the real "political" star of the World Cup. Aided by her country's unexpected journey to the final, she delivered a public relations masterclass by attending all their games, paying for her own tickets, wearing Croatia's distinctive checked strip and socialising with the fans in the stands rather than the political elites. Mediatoolkit, a Zagreb-based analytics company, found that there was "25 per cent more focus on her in news stories about the final than any of the players on the pitch, including Golden Ball winner Luka Modrić" (Hajdari, 2018).

These examples illustrate that the range of topics sports journalists have to cover has broadened. Traditionally, sports journalists were not expected to write political news stories, but the industry has changed and professional boundaries have blurred (Boyle, 2006a: 163). However, it has been argued by some that sports journalists have for a long time fulfilled a role that has made much sports content politically disengaged. American sports journalist David Zirin, author of *Game Over: How Politics Has Turned the Sports World Upside Down*, attributes the astonishing commercial success of sporting brands such as the NFL and NBA over the past 30 years to them making their product and players "explicitly apolitical." The sports media, he argues, are largely complicit in this enterprise, leaving little scope for investigative or critical journalism (Zirin, 2013: 3). The wider commercial interests of news organisations and sports media companies can act as a powerful constraint on sports reporters. When stories started to emerge about alleged doping at Team Sky, for example, some newspaper journalists, such as the *Daily Mail*'s Matt Lawton, questioned why Sky Sports News appeared to be ignoring the story (*Twitter* @Matt_Lawton_DM, March 17, 2017). This leads us to the question about how sports news is *manufactured*: how is it gathered and what makes editors run certain stories in preference to others? To that question we turn in the next chapter.

Issues for discussion

"Sports journalists can help bring about positive political and social change." To what extent do you agree, and why? Give examples.

"A sports journalist should focus on the on-field action and leave politics to the politics reporters." Do you believe this to be a sensible division of labour for journalists?

4
Defining sports news

Facts about sport versus sports news

What is it that elevates certain *facts* about sport into sports *news*? Why does Player X's injury receive news coverage, while Player Y's does not? Both are facts, yet one fact is regarded – for whatever reason – as more *newsworthy* than another, and will, therefore, go on to be included within an article, a social media update or a broadcast. The other fact, meanwhile, remains unpublished, unread and, therefore, potentially unknown. Perhaps one way of considering the distinction between facts and news is the following: while all news is fact (or at least should be, notwithstanding the era of *fake news*), not all facts are news. There are millions of statements of sporting fact that could be made every day, but not all of those facts constitute news.

Every day, a sports journalist or sports editor encounters a welter of facts about the sport or sports they cover. However, only some of those facts will become news, in the sense that only some will go on to be selected for a website or programme. A fundamental point to recognise here – and it can be something that journalists themselves forget amid the hurly-burly of the 24/7 news cycle – is that sports news (like all news) is not something that is somehow preordained or self-selecting. Rather, it is the outcome of a complicated chain of human decisions and human processes. Moreover, in today's social media-dominated news culture, it is not just journalists who make decisions about what is newsworthy – fans can do so too, through the publication or sharing of content on social media platforms and blogs, or through comments they may make online about a certain piece that a journalist has produced. Think about the last time you retweeted or shared a social media post about information relating to sport. Indirectly, you were making a decision about the level of interest – or newsworthiness – of a certain nugget of content. In that moment, you yourself had become part of the many-headed beast of early twenty-first-century digital culture which determines what the sports news *is*. While sports journalists continue to form a group distinct from their audience, they are no longer handing down news to their audience from on high. In some instances – many instances – non-journalists are making decisions about what constitutes sports news. Content in many instances has become increasingly "fan-led" in the digital age; editors and reporters are constantly trying to anticipate what content is going to stimulate response and engagement from the supporters of a particular sport or club. The concept of fan-led content will be discussed in more detail later in this chapter.

The following somewhat crude scenario illustrates the complicated and changing factors at play in what elevates *facts about sport* into *sports news*. For a moment, put yourself in the shoes of the duty sports editor of a media outlet that publishes both online content and a printed newspaper. On a specified day, you have six reporters at your disposal. A year ago, you had nine reporters, but cutbacks mean you have fewer journalists to cover the same number of clubs and events, meaning you have to be more selective in deciding where to send your reporters. You make the decision – perhaps following a conference with the editor-in-chief of your organisation, and also having viewed your rivals' most recent content – that you want each of the reporters to attend press conferences at certain sports clubs around the country. That very decision in itself starts to set a boundary for what is going to constitute the news for your media organisation, and, by extension, its audience or readership. The decision to deploy your reporters to certain clubs *excludes* other clubs. Perhaps you make some of those deployments on grounds of the geographical proximity of some clubs compared with others. Most of your staff are based in London, say, so you focus on clubs in the Greater London area, both for reasons of accessibility and to keep travelling expense costs down. Your reporters will then interview certain coaches and players rather than other coaches and players, again *narrowing the voices or sources of information* that will make it into your media organisation's output. Another complicating factor here is that each sports club's media department will, in most cases, decide which players or coaches are available to be interviewed at a press conference, so these media departments themselves also influence the voices that will be heard and – indirectly – the news that will be produced by sports journalists and consumed by sports supporters. Upon completing their interviews, each journalist will make a decision about what they think is the best "angle" or "top line" for a story. They will usually discuss this with you, the sports editor, over the phone, and what will emerge through this conversation is the way in which each story is going to be *treated*. What quotes are juiciest? What information needs to be put online immediately? What quotes or information can perhaps be held back for a story at a later date? What angles are rival outlets likely to take on the same interview? You will also consider what focus is likely to go down best with your organisation's target audience (Andrews, 2014: 17). From this discussion will emerge the emphasis or *line* for each piece. Your reporters will then write their article, file their stories with you, and as duty editor you will then review their copy to make sure you are happy with it. This could involve you "re-nosing" a story – by which is meant giving it what you think is a more compelling, newsworthy introduction – and other forms of editing; maybe you will remove certain quotes because you think the piece is too long. The piece may well be put through another colleague's hands, a subeditor, before it is published underneath a headline that the subeditor has chosen. By the time the sports news is published, the sequence of human interactions that have gone into it mean that, in a significant sense, the news has been constructed or *manufactured* (Shoemaker and Reese, 1996: 3; Harcup, 2015: 42). It has not simply fallen from the heavens and landed on a mobile screen, tablet or newspaper. Instead, decisions involving resources, logistics, access to interviewees, the target audience and subjective decisions about newsworthiness have all gone into the process. What emerges is not inevitable. Instead, it is the result of a complex web of decisions.

This process of whittling down facts until what emerges is the "news" is called *gatekeeping* (White, 1950; Harcup, 2015: 44–45). On this model, it is journalists – and specifically editors – who decide when to "open" the gate to let through certain facts into wider public awareness. By deciding to publish or broadcast certain material, some facts become news while others remain metaphorically stuck behind the gate and therefore unknown to the audience.

There are numerous factors that *influence* what gets included in the sports news and the sports media more widely. Media content, as one influential text has put it, is "shaped, pounded, constrained, encouraged by a multitude of forces" (Shoemaker and Reese, 1996: ix). These forces arguably include the routines that journalists and news organisations have around their work (such as having to work with the press officers of sports clubs to secure access to sports stars), and the sometimes unconscious yielding to market forces (the desire of journalists to produce what they think is going to sell and what they think might keep advertisers happy).

But let us return again to our scenario. Imagine once again that you are back in our fictitious newsroom, wearing the shoes of the duty sports editor. Whilst trawling through TweetDeck or another platform that enables you to keep track of what is emerging or trending on social media, you come across videos that appear to have been posted by a golf fan of a big-name golfer stumbling out of a nightclub in Atlanta, Georgia, the day before the Masters is due to start. You speak to your social media editor, who is working next to you on the sports desk, and after some time spent verifying the provenance of the footage, she confirms that they seem to be genuine. Social media is abuzz with comments about the videos, which have gone viral. You immediately phone your golf correspondent and discuss how you are best going to cover the story and *throw it forward* (i.e. develop the story in an original way). All of a sudden, as a sports news organisation you are playing catch-up to content that has originally been captured and published by a non-journalist. Rather than playing gatekeeper, you are, instead, frantically sprinting after facts that have been released into the wild by a member of the public via social media.

This is just one example of how the digital revolution has radically altered the ecosystem within which sports journalists – and journalists generally – gather and distribute sports news (Knight and Cook, 2015). The growth of Twitter and other channels of digital communication means that traditional media organisations no longer filter and control the flow of sports information with as much control as they once did, and in that sense they have lost their privileged position of determining what constitutes sports news. Moreover, new digital communication channels mean sports clubs and sports stars can communicate directly with their fans without having to use journalists as an intermediary. And fans, of course, can produce their own content too via blogs and social media accounts. This has sometimes been referred to as the "democratisation" of news, and sports media academics have attempted to capture this by saying that the traditional "sports media hierarchy," according to which sports journalists distributed content to their audiences in a top-down fashion, has been "flattened" (Gibbs and Haynes, 2013).

As described above, media departments of sports clubs and sports organisations seek to control the flow of information surrounding their club or organisation. Those clubs' athletes have often received media training in order to help them bat away tricky questions in face-to-face and phone interviews, and it is often claimed that sports stars' interviews are full of platitudes – or, to put it more directly, plain dull. The media departments of sports clubs seek to deliver positive messages via social media platforms, but social media can also be fertile ground for stories when athletes "go rogue" and post their own sincerely held views on social media, possibly in the heat of the moment. This combing of social media platforms for nuggets of information which could form the basis of a story is termed "information accident reporting" by Hutchins and Rowe, according to which reporters wait to pounce on crumbs that drop from the table. It is worth quoting their thoughts in detail, as it captures well the convoluted and changing way in which "sports news" can emerge:

> Sports journalists search for information accidents, while athletes, publicists and sports organisations seek to avoid them. This is a strategic media game played in a round-the-clock digital sport and news environment. Journalists comb through voluminous messages on Twitter, Facebook, and blogs searching for content that may provide the basis – no matter how

slim – for a story that would otherwise go unreported. This is a digital search for disagreements and disclosures that elicit responses from the subject of stories. It is also an example of an almost ineradicable schism that exists between the individual right and ability of sportspeople to express themselves publicly, and the determination of leagues and clubs to exercise tight control over media comment and self-expression in order to keep unwanted stories out of the news [...] Information accident reporting by journalists is producing numerous stories of uneven news value, including claims of personal animosity between teammates and opponents, athlete outrage at official decisions, complaints about playing conditions, and serious matters such as the adequacy of security arrangements at tournaments.

(Hutchins and Rowe, 2012: 90)

An early example of this was Samoa rugby player Eliota Fuimaono-Sapolu's extraordinary use of Twitter in 2011. The comments made by Fuimaono-Sapolu on the social media platform gave sports journalists plenty to write about, and also earned him punishment from World Rugby (then the International Rugby Board) and the Rugby Football Union. During that year's Rugby World Cup, the Samoan took to Twitter to accuse a referee of bias and racism, and described Samoa's tournament schedule as having similarities to slavery, apartheid and the Holocaust. Following a league match between his club, Gloucester, and Premiership rivals Saracens, he then used his Twitter account to accuse opponent Owen Farrell of "FAKE toughness you p**** s***." A season earlier, Fuiamaono-Sapolu had also abused Farrell following a match with a less-than-tasteful critique of his play: "Farrell put more bombs (high kicks) on us than the U.S. did on Osama Bin Laden. Genocide" (Gallagher, 2011). Writing stories based on such tasteless and abusive outbursts is a legitimate activity for sports journalists. In Fuimaono-Sapolu's case, reporting on his comments and the fallout from them was in the public interest as his remarks had a bearing on the standing in which rugby is held by the wider public. However, journalists should be wary of becoming hooked on being drip-fed content via social media, as addictive as it might be. It is a largely passive form of sports newsgathering, and it should not trump more active, traditional newsgathering techniques such as getting out and about and looking people in the eye rather than looking at their tweets on a screen.

So, we might tentatively suggest, then, that while sports news is still *selected and shaped* to an extent by editors and journalists, it is also increasingly selected and shaped by audiences and sports clubs. It is also shaped by sports stars themselves, who can take to the social media platform of their choice to communicate directly with thousands – sometimes millions – of fans. (This can be horrifically misguided and self-defeating, of course. One example was American swimmer Ryan Lochte posting an incriminating photo of himself receiving an intravenous drip in May 2018. Having seen the photo on Lochte's Instagram account, the US Anti-Doping Agency investigated and discovered that the 12-time Olympic medallist had taken an amount of Vitamin B that exceeded permitted levels and banned him from competing for 14 months.) In an interactive, social-media driven era, it can be the "audience" itself or sports stars themselves who drive the news agenda by making certain facts go viral.

Profile – David Walsh

David Walsh, chief sports writer for *The Sunday Times*, is best known for his fearless investigative work exposing the cheating of American cyclist Lance Armstrong. His 13-year investigation culminated in Armstrong being stripped of all seven of his Tour de France titles for doping, and Walsh receiving a number of awards for the quality of his journalism. But the road to those awards was as bumpy as the cobbled streets around the Champs-Élysées, with Walsh being sued for libel by Armstrong. When Walsh received a lifetime achievement award in 2013 for the quality of his journalism, the man presenting him the prize – former Olympic rower Sir Matthew Pinsent – said: "David Walsh led a fight for the very soul of sport. This award is for a man who put his life on hold in search of a truth" (*Sunday Times*, Sport p4, May 5, 2013).

Good journalism is fearless in its pursuit of the truth, and Walsh's work to expose Armstrong as a fraud can be held up as one of the great pieces of long-term, investigative sports journalism. In an article he produced for *Sports Illustrated*, Walsh described the battles he encountered during the course of his investigation. He wrote: "How to prove what you knew, that was the challenge. He (Armstrong) called me 'the worst journalist in the world', referred to me as 'the little fucking troll' […] and, of course, he sued me. That lawsuit now seems as close as you can get to an 'Oscar' in our game. It's been a good journey because the truth was never hard to find in this story. You only had to be interested in looking" (Tinley, 2012). The final sentence here is salutary. Sports journalists – like any journalists – need to look beyond the surface of things; to be prepared to see the deeper issues at play. And to then cover those issues with doggedness and integrity.

Walsh has at times turned his fire on fellow sports journalists as well as on cheating sports stars. Too many sports journalists, he has argued, have been content to stay away from heavy, complex issues such as doping for fear of alienating contacts and jeopardising access to sources. His account of his years exposing Armstrong's drug-taking, *Seven Deadly Sins: My Pursuit of Lance Armstrong* (2012), is an important book, and contains withering assessments of some journalists, whom he effectively accuses of backing off from the big story.

His recollections of covering the 1999 Tour – the first of Armstrong's seven Tour wins – contain some particularly direct criticisms. The press tent, he writes, is "crammed to dangerous levels with sycophants and time servers," while journalists are part of the "confederacy of cheerleaders" who protect Armstrong, along with administrators at the Union Cycliste Internationale (Walsh, 2012: 88).

Walsh has contended that any attempt to produce sports journalism that does not comply with the imperative of honestly pursuing the truth, regardless of professional cost, is not worth the paper it is written on. This position is conveyed by Walsh in both his own account of his pursuit of Armstrong (Walsh, 2012), and also in an interview given to the BBC's HARDtalk programme: "As a journalist you're thinking, if this is the greatest fraud, and you believe it's the greatest fraud, you have an absolute responsibility to go after it and reveal him to be a fraud" (HARDtalk, 2017: 3.42–3.51). The key term here is "absolute responsibility"; the sports journalist's unconditional duty is to attempt to expose the truth. In another interview, Walsh expresses it another way by saying he would have felt "a fake" if he had scaled back his investigation of Armstrong for fear of jeopardising interview access (Bailey, 2015).

However, Walsh, an Irish journalist based in England, has at times had his own professional integrity questioned (McKay, 2010). Such questioning has focused on his acceptance of an offer to live and travel with Team Sky in 2013, an experience which he used as the basis for a number of articles and a book. By being "embedded" with a cycling team in such a way, it was suggested that Walsh was in danger of surrendering the journalistic independence that he had shown through his tenacious coverage of Armstrong, and instead becoming the mouthpiece for an organisation that he should have been reporting on critically (BBC, 2017). Four years later – long after the embedding project with Team Sky was over, and after allegations around Team Sky's medical policies had emerged – Walsh concluded that he had after all been used. Interviewed by Stephen Sackur for the BBC's HARDtalk show, Walsh said he had been "duped" by Team Sky's director, Dave Brailsford (HARDtalk, 2017).

Walsh's decision to accept the offer to live with Team Sky as a means of gaining journalistic access raises a number of areas for ethical enquiry. One is around whether embedding of this nature is ever ethically justifiable by a sports journalist, or whether it inherently runs the risk of being equivalent to – or close to – cheerleading or collusion. The second, more general, area is around the long-standing question about the distance that should ideally exist between sports journalists and the people and teams they are reporting on. Should sports journalists, for example, share a flight with a team they are covering? Should they have a beer with them? If so, how many? Walsh has argued that his time with Team Sky did not involve him breaking his ethical principles (Walsh, 2013), while also conceding – as the "dupe" claim suggests – that he was to an extent manipulated (HARDtalk, 2017).

Walsh's career is an informative case study in the ethical issues confronting sports journalists, and his relentless work covering Armstrong is an example of what young sports journalists should aspire to. Walsh himself regards his pursuit of Armstrong as not only career defining but also life defining. "I know that when I'm on my deathbed and somebody asks: did you ever do anything as a journalist you were proud of, I would say only one thing: Lance Armstrong" (Pugh, 2012a). And while his pursuit of Armstrong had its pressures and frustrations and was at times all consuming, Walsh has said it was professionally invigorating. As he told the BBC's HARDtalk programme: "I never saw it as a sacrifice [...] My feeling all the time was this was the most fun I was ever going to have as a journalist [...] It wasn't horrible, I never felt more journalistically alive as I was during those years" (HARDtalk, 2017: 9.40–10.04).

It is not only through social media channels that sports stars can seek to convey their thoughts and perspectives directly. *The Players' Tribune* (www.theplayerstribune.com), for example, is a sports news website with a difference: all the content is written exclusively under the name of sports stars themselves. While columns written under the byline of a high-profile sportsperson are not new and have indeed been a staple of British newspapers for a number of decades, to *only* have content by them represents a point of departure. The Players' Tribune project was founded in 2014 by a former baseball star, New York Yankees shortstop Derek Jeter, in conjunction with sports marketing businessman Jaymee Messler. Their aim was to give professional athletes a platform on which they could publish their own stories. Initially, athletes were even given journalistic job titles, with the Boston Red Sox's David Ortiz, for example, the editor-at-large (Barshad, 2018). Stories began to be broken on the site, notably when Kobe Bryant announced his retirement from basketball via a poem on the website called "Dear Basketball" (Bryant, 2015). The content on the site is ghostwritten by experienced writers, but the final say on what is published rests with the sports star whose name is at the top of the article. During an interview in 2018, the company's chief executive, Jeff Levick, formerly of music streaming service Spotify, described the website as a platform for "athlete-generated content," prompting the journalist who interviewed him to comment: "The site gives its subjects final approval of their own coverage. Normally, this would be a journalistic sin, were it not for an elegant and cynical workaround: giving the subject the byline" (Barshad, 2018).

Is this journalism, or is it anti-journalism? To some working in the sports media, the concept of so-called athlete-generated content being mentioned in the same breath as journalism is enough to send a chill down the spine. The presence of a site such as *The Players' Tribune* is arguably another aspect of the modern sports media landscape that suggests sports journalists have lost their role as the custodians and purveyors of sports news. According to this line of thinking, a site such as *The Players' Tribune* is just another way in which highly paid and highly marketed sports stars get the chance to burnish their own carefully crafted public image even further. In an extended piece in *The New York Times* reflecting on the website, journalist Amos Barshad put it like this: "Perhaps *The Players' Tribune* can be best understood as an effort by athletes to seize that most precious contemporary commodity – the narrative" (Barshad, 2018). However, this is arguably a form of professional surrender by journalists. Journalism should, on one traditional school of thinking, be independent and as objective as possible, which means not peddling the lines that sports stars want you to peddle. Perhaps the presence of sites such as *The Players' Tribune* indirectly serves as a call to arms for sports journalists to be more active and independent than ever. Rather than taking the remarks of players in heavily ghostwritten columns at face value, sports journalists should provide a critique of those sports stars and the issues they raise. Instead of making sports journalists obsolete, there is a strong case for arguing that *The Players' Tribune* makes independent, rigorous sports news reporting more important than ever; otherwise, we run the risk of sports stars' choreographed statements becoming the dominant sports news.

Sourcing and selecting stories

Where do sports journalists get their stories from? As with news journalists, it can be helpful to make the initial broad distinction of "on-diary" and "off-diary" stories (Andrews, 2014: 23). On-diary stories are those which are literally on the sports desk's diary: match fixtures, athletics meetings, mid-week press conferences, the date of an impending World Anti-Doping Agency media briefing. Off-diary, in contrast, refers to stories that reporters are able to gather at times when they do not have specific diary events to attend at the sports desk's command. So, this could mean meeting up with a sports club executive over coffee to get background information about a hot topic, or ringing around contacts to see if they are aware of any simmering stories that could be coming to the boil. Or it might mean making contact with the author of an interesting comment you have spotted on Twitter and seeing if they would be happy to speak over the phone. More recently, Kozman has referred to the "story channel" when attempting to classify the origin of sports stories, breaking the channels down into "routine" (stories arising from a reporter's "beat" – or specialism – and which are primarily scheduled events, such as press conferences and post-match interviews) and "non-routine," which she describes as "mainly based on original, creative reporting" (Kozman, 2017: 52). So, gathering quotes from a manager at a press conference in order to write a preview for a forthcoming match would fall under the category of "routine." Spending time investigating allegations of doping within a particular sport, by contrast, would be non-routine. Another form of non-routine sports journalism is what is sometimes referred to as *participatory journalism*. This is where a sports journalist, in order to gain first-hand insight into a sport, actually takes part in that sport, perhaps by training with a particular club or even competing. Arguably the best exponent of this form of journalism was the mid-to-late-twentieth-century American writer George Plimpton. Plimpton wrote about a range of sporting experiences, including a three-round exhibition bout he had with the then-world light-heavyweight champion Archie Moore, and a stint as a rookie quarterback with the Detroit Lions during the team's summer training camp (Homberger, 2003). This form of sports journalism is unorthodox and unusual, and might be inadvisable for those more accustomed to availing themselves of the pre-match hospitality in media centres. But it is a good anti-dote to desk- and screen-bound sports journalists sitting in air-conditioned newsrooms merely scrolling through social media feeds in the hope of finding something newsy.

Making the news

This chapter began by posing a fundamental question about sports media: what elevates certain facts about sport into sports news? Even more fundamentally it can be asked, what is news? Since a groundbreaking study in the mid-1960s by two Norwegian academics (Galtung and Ruge, 1965), it has been hypothesised that there are a certain number of *news values* that journalists wittingly or unwittingly apply to information when deciding whether it is newsworthy or not. Journalists can in some instances be dismissive of academics' attempts to provide an analysis of the factors that make certain facts newsworthy, suggesting that judgements about what constitutes news are resistant to categorisation, and that a decision about what is newsworthy is self-evident or intuitive – a "gut feeling" – rather than the application (conscious or otherwise) of so-called news values (Schultz, 2007). Nevertheless, as practising sports journalists it is worthwhile for us to consider the prevailing factors that Galtung and Ruge, and more recently Harcup and O'Neill (2001, 2017), have sought to identify as making information *newsworthy*, not least because it makes us more reflective about our professional practice and some of the activities we perhaps do unthinkingly.

Among the factors that Harcup and O'Neill (2017) identify as making a piece of information – or story – more likely to get published by mainstream British newspapers are *the power elite, relevance, bad news, good news, surprise, celebrity, exclusivity* and *conflict*. This is by no means an exhaustive list of the factors they identify, and it is important to note that their content analysis did not look at the papers' sports news pages but only the news pages. However, it is useful to consider whether and how they apply in a sports context. *The power elite* criterion states that a story is more likely to get published if it is about powerful individuals or organisations. In sport, we may think here of how a story about the International Olympic Committee or the head of FIFA is more likely to be selected than a story about less powerful people and institutions. *Relevance* refers to "stories about groups or nations perceived to be influential with, or culturally or historically familiar to, the audience." In this regard, we may think of how British sports media audiences are more likely to be interested in sports from the United States given the ties between the two nations than, say, sports from South East Asia. This makes stories about American sport more likely to be selected to appear in British news outlets than articles about Vietnamese sport. *Bad news, good news, surprise* and *celebrity* are self-explanatory criteria, while *exclusivity* refers to whether the story the outlet has is unique to it. If it is – if no other news organisation has it – then the exclusive nature of the story bolsters its news value and makes it more likely to be selected for publication. An exclusive interview with a baseball star just banned for a doping offence would be an example here. *Conflict* refers to controversies, arguments and break-ups. If a footballer falls out with the manager of his club and the pair comes to fisticuffs on the training ground, then that conflict makes the story newsworthy.

In their more recent study (2017), Harcup and O'Neill considered how news values had evolved in the digital age since their original study (2001). In the wake of the changes in news consumption brought about by the digital revolution, they concluded that *shareability* (stories that are likely to trigger sharing on social media) and the amount of *audio-visual* material available to illustrate a story were now key news values. In terms of defining shareability more precisely, they admit the term is nebulous but suggest that a necessary condition of shareability is that it provokes some form of an emotional response, such as anger or amusement. In providing an updated list of news values, they conclude that in order to be selected, "news stories must generally satisfy one and prefer-ably more" of their criteria (Harcup and O'Neill, 2017: 1482).

A point that can be drawn from this is that the factors or variables that make something news are not set in tablets of stone. While there are some constant factors, decisions about what is news vary from place to place and time to time. As technology changes, arguably so does the definition of what is newsworthy. A generation brought up snacking on a diet of memes, GIFs and podcasts on their mobile phones is likely to digest – and want – a different menu of content to those of an earlier generation brought up with the routines of newspaper reading and regular bulletin watching. News, as one media academic puts it, is "defined by a shifting set of practices, informal and often implicit agreements about proper conduct, style, and form […] those practices are in flux; mul-tiple, debatable, and open for reconsideration" (Baym, 2010: 375). Moreover, packaging information as "the news" is a way of taming the world of events; of bringing order to the chaos of information that surrounds us. As Baym adds, "News has always been a particular kind of narrative art, one that arranges the events of the phenomenal world into neatly defined stories – dramatic tales rich with heroes and villains, conflict and suspense" (2010: 375). And the act of reporting on something is arguably in and of itself an act that distorts the thing that is reported. By reading or watching a particular report, the audience's perceptions of the world shift, and shift according to the emphasis and focus that the report has. "Reality is necessarily manipulated when events and people are relocated into news or prime-time stories. The media can impose their own logic on assembled materials in a number of ways, including emphasizing behaviours and people and stereotyping" (Shoemaker and Reese, 1996: 37).

When he wrote the words quoted in the preceding paragraph, Baym was concerned with news stories generally, not just sports news stories. However, sport is an area of human life and popular culture that is arguably without rival when it comes to "dramatic tales rich with heroes and villains, conflict and suspense." It is an arena of life that provides the full array of characters and emotions. As such, it arguably provides journalists with one of the richest seams from which to mine engaging stories and news. As one sports-journalist-turned-academic has put it, "With its daily dose of breath-taking winners and gallant losers, trailblazers and exemplars, cheats and leeches, what more could a writer possibly wish for in a subject?" (Steen, 2014: 2).

Yet lurking beneath all of this is another question: What should be the proper subject matter of sports journalism? Is it the weekly staples of match previews, interview-based profiles, match reports and match analysis? Or should it be deeper, more "significant" content – content like investigations into corruption at governing bodies, or investigations into doping within elite sport? One answer is that sports journalism can be both. This is the view of Nick Harris, the chief sports correspondent at UK title the *Mail on Sunday*. Speaking on The Media Show, a weekly BBC Radio 4 programme that is essential listening for students of the media in the United Kingdom, Harris argued that the role is multifaceted, and that sports news comes in different guises. "As in any branch of media, people have their specialisms, so you have people who are focused on a particular patch and particular clubs, they'll be doing day-to-day news, transfer news, injury news, covering matches, that kind of thing," he said. "I happen to specialise in investigative journalism, so I'm doing, you know, investigative work. It's not everybody's job to cover everything and actually I think you find, increasingly, a general football reporter has to know a bit more than they used to know about football finance and football economics and football business, and given the amount of corruption in club ownership and issues like that, more reporters are covering more different topics in more depth" (The Media Show, BBC Radio 4, 2018).

Not all journalists who produce sports news take Harris' broad view. The investigative journalist Andrew Jennings, for example, argues that UK sports journalists are too concerned with the merry-go-round of press conferences and matches to really get under the skin of sport and thereby tackle the big questions. Jennings, who has published books and presented BBC investigations into FIFA corruption, has repeated his indictment of sports journalists over a number of years. In a 2010 interview with the industry magazine the *Press Gazette* headlined "Andrew Jennings: We have world's worst sports reporters," he was quoted as saying:

> Why haven't our reporters spent all this time turning them (FIFA) over? There are some very good reporters around but they don't seem to work in sports news […] It's time editors started looking at the garbage that you get from sports news reporters. They are probably the worst in the world, they won't check, they won't research and they won't cultivate the sources that you need to get the documents that reveal what is really going on.
> (Ponsford, 2010)

Jennings turned the guns on his journalist peers once again in another *Press Gazette* interview, this time in 2015. While acknowledging the strong reporting done by *The Sunday Times*' Insight team, which won the 2015 Paul Foot Award for its investigations into Qatar's bid to host the 2022 World Cup, Jennings saw little else to praise in the way the UK media had covered corruption at FIFA, and also allowed himself a swipe at two institutions of British journalism, the BBC and *The Guardian*:

> Let's be clear: in the UK, the only journalism has been me and my colleagues at *Panorama* and our friends at Insight […] The BBC needs to examine its catastrophically bad reporting of FIFA corruption […] When did *Guardian Sport* ever break a story?
> (Turvill, 2015)

For Jennings, the majority of activities conducted by media professionals who call themselves sports journalists are simply not journalism at all. Writing match previews and reports are not, as he sees it, activities deserving of the name journalism.

> This journalism business is easy, you know. You just find some disgraceful, disgustingly corrupt people and you work on it! You have to. That's what we do. The rest of the media gets far too cosy with them. It's wrong.
>
> (Miller, 2015)

A journalist who interviewed Jennings for the *Washington Post* puts it another way. "As other journalists were ball watching – reporting scorelines or writing player profiles – Jennings was digging into the dirty deals underpinning the world's most popular game" (Miller, 2015). This notion of ball-watching is a useful concept and can be elaborated upon to illustrate the different views among sports journalists about just what it is that constitutes sports news. Ball-watching is literally what many sports journalists do; they watch a tennis ball go back and forth over a net, for example, and talk and write about it. Or they watch a ball – usually round, but sometimes oval – be kicked or thrown in a particular way, and talk and write about it. But the claim in Jennings' writing and interviews is that by becoming *too* focused as a sports journalist on where the literal ball is, one figuratively "takes one's eye off the ball." Underlying this would seem to be a tension that confronts every sports journalist. How much time should a sports journalist spend covering what might be termed the superficial activities of a sport (the on-pitch action) and how much time should a sports journalist spend on "digging under the surface" to reveal the "deep" activities (the matters of governance)? Jennings clearly holds literal ball-watchers in a state of contempt, but that is arguably extreme, unfair and simplistic, given the appetite for information about day-to-day action that exists among sports fans. However, what can certainly be taken from Jennings' assault on what passes for sports news is the point that a press corps that becomes too consumed by the treadmill of literal ball-watching runs the risk of becoming one-dimensional and failing to hold those in positions of power to account.

A leading sports journalist of the twentieth century, Hugh McIlvanney, who retired in 2016 after working for a combined total of 53 years on *The Sunday Times* and *The Observer*, described sport as "our magnificent triviality" (Mitchell 2016). On this understanding, sport is trivial in that it does not concern life and death matters in the way that "hard" current affairs news does, but magnificent insofar as it serves as a platform on which skill, athleticism and triumph can be performed, witnessed and exalted. A reporter of Jennings' viewpoint might regard this concept of sport as magnificent triviality as misguided, even dangerous. Indeed, he might argue that such an attitude is what leads to ball-watching and a failure to pay attention to the "serious" or hard issues underpinning sports and its governance. Ball-watching is therefore a useful concept, forcing sports journalists to think hard about just how much match reporting is good for their professional soul.

Case study

James Pearce has one of the most sought-after jobs in British sports journalism, reporting on one of the biggest clubs in the world in one of the most football-obsessed cities in the world.

But since taking on the role of Liverpool FC reporter for the respected daily title the *Liverpool Echo* in 2011, Pearce says the role has changed hugely as the digital era has prompted the *Echo* to further shift its focus from print to www.liverpoolecho.co.uk.

He is active across Instagram, Snapchat and Twitter, using the social media platforms to interact with supporters and engage with a younger audience. On Twitter alone, Pearce has more than 400,000 followers – more than 11 times the paper's daily circulation, which as of August 2018, was officially put at just over 35,000 (Linford, 2018)

Social media represents something of a double-edged sword in Pearce's eyes, and sports journalists need to develop the ability to ignore the personal criticism and abuse that can be directed their way by trolls and aggrieved sports fans.

"Social media represents one of the biggest ways in which sports journalism has changed," he says. "It's such an important part of the job now to interact with fans, primarily on Twitter. On a daily basis you get abuse about various things and you have to have a thick skin to deal with that. With Liverpool being such a big club and having so many supporters, you get accused of having agendas here, there and everywhere. Sometimes fans don't want to believe that something is true and that can prompt a barrage."

When he first began the role, Pearce would have a daily chat with the subeditors – the page designers and copy editors – about how many pages of Liverpool FC content they needed from him that day, and that would determine his workload. Now he admits that he barely gives the printed edition much thought, instead directing his energies into feeding the never-ending appetite for online content.

"What's changed more than anything is the immediacy – having to get stuff out there so quickly. I don't have much to do with the putting together of the printed product now, they make a paper out of what's gone online."

The demands of the digital age – the need to be constantly updating the *Echo* website with multimedia content and to be updating social media – can be onerous.

"It can seem that you very rarely have time to craft something. More often than not you're rattling out something. We now also have video with pretty much every interview we do, and podcasts that I do two or three times a week.

"It's almost a never-ending cycle of getting stuff out there. There's such a thirst for content and it's making sure standards don't slip. I'd rather be second and right with a story than first and wrong."

For Pearce, the nurturing and preservation of strong contacts is vital. He is acutely aware of the balance that needs to be struck between being an independent journalist who won't be cowed by the club, and being dip-lomatic and at times flexible with the club for the sake of preserving its good will.

"In this day and age, a lot of websites have gone down the route of thinking that you don't really need those relationships with clubs – that you're almost better off being able to say exactly what you want when you want. But although it's more difficult, I think it's more rewarding and beneficial to try and tread that tightrope of reporting and commenting objectively but at the same time retaining those relationships. It's helped that Liverpool have usually been pretty good to deal with. They are not that touchy to criticism. People at the club from the board down have always said that if it's fair opinion or factually correct, then it's very rare to get a phone call from the club."

Walking that tightrope can be particularly difficult when the story is a potential exclusive about a player transfer.

"It can be a dilemma when you get information about new signings," says Pearce. "I had information about one signing that I'd got from a source and when I spoke to the club to get it double-sourced I was told it would go down like a lead balloon if I ran the story. The club was also in negoti-ations with another player at the same time and they were concerned the price for that player would go up if the story went out. My response was, ok, so if I sit tight on this for a few days what other stories can I have in return? Sometimes it's a trade-off."

Pearce recalls another occasion in which he had to decide whether to publish a story and incur the club's anger, or hold off in the hope of obtaining the club's favour and gaining the inside track on some other stories. Through his sources, Pearce had gathered that the club could be moving from Melwood, its long-standing training base, to a new site. However, the purchase of the land for the new training facility had not been completed, and the club was concerned that the seller could pull out if the story of the relocation appeared in the media, and the club appeared that they were taking the purchase of the land for granted.

"Sometimes you decide you can't sit on a story because it will come out via another media outlet," says Pearce, who emphasises that it is essential to him that the club's bosses know he is an independent journalist whose first duty is to his readers, not to them. "Sometimes you have to play the long game."

"When I first took the job I was told to regard the role as being like a critical friend – you hold them to account when you need to, but there are times when they need a bit of support."

Pearce says that relationships with managers are inevitably different from manager to manager. He enjoyed a close relationship with Brendan Rodgers, who was Liverpool's manager from 2012 to 2015, but admits that he has not got as close to Rodgers' successor, Jürgen Klopp.

"With Brendan Rodgers I'd have half an hour with him in his office most weeks, and about 50 per cent of what he said was on the record and 50 per cent of it wasn't. I don't think Klopp really sees that distinction between local and national reporter. It's been tough at times. What makes it manageable is that all the journalists covering the club are in the same boat. I'm not aware of any journalist having got his personal mobile number. With Brendan Rodgers, I could text or call him if anything happened during the week. The only one-on-one interviews I get with Klopp are maybe when I go on pre-season camps with the club."

Infotainment and sportainment

Do sports audiences want news, or do they want entertainment? Perhaps they want a hybrid of the two: *infotainment*. A more fundamental question, building on the above discussion of Jennings and ball-watching, could be posed: is sports journalism about news or entertainment? One response is that the two aren't mutually exclusive. Good sports journalism should simultaneously be able to both inform as well as entertain. One example of this is Stephen Jones, *The Sunday Times'* long-serving and multi-award-winning rugby correspondent; a writer whose knowledge of the game is sometimes only exceeded by his ability to stir up (always entertaining) controversy through the publication of colourfully expressed opinion. Providing pleasure to the reader has been the goal of some of the most distinguished sportswriters down the decades in different parts of the globe. The mid-twentieth-century American sports columnist Red Smith, for example, wrote that providing his readers with pleasure and entertainment was to him an important aspect of his journalistic activity (Steen, 2014: 30).

However, if journalism is primarily the gathering and then the dissemination to an audience of information that they were previously unaware of, then sports journalism is primarily about news. But sport audiences of course want to be entertained, and there are times when entertainment now seems to be the primary function of some sports journalism. Entertainment can come in different guises: it can come in the form of an amusing GIF that perhaps ridicules a football player's dive; it could be a provocative piece of punditry issued during a podcast or radio phone-in; or it might be a quiz on football website *Squawka*. The balance between information and entertainment appears to have shifted. As has been observed, for sports journalists "the priority was set in stone long ago: inform, then, if space and/or time permit, entertain. The weight of emphasis, if not completely reversed, has certainly altered" (Steen, 2014: 53). However, is there anything wrong with the news being entertaining – or indeed being entertainment? Indeed, can a meaningful distinction be made between "serious" news and entertaining news? Not all scholars think so. Baym, for example, argues that "the dividing line between news and entertainment is fundamentally porous, if not entirely arbitrary, and difficult to define with any meaningful measure of precision" (2010: 376). A related question is whether it makes sense to speak of sports news as being distinct from other forms of news. The traditional layout and structure of newspapers and television bulletins – with sport on the back pages and towards the end of the bulletin respectively – suggests a clear boundary. But it could be argued that sports news no longer belongs in such ghettos, primarily because the complementary growth of professional sport and celebrity culture has made sport transcend the back pages and the tail-end of bulletins. As a trio of distinguished writers about sports journalism have put it:

> The rise of celebrity culture means that sports stars appear more often in other sections of the media – in fashion shoots, gossip columns, show business, celebrity profiles, chat and game shows. The sheer scale of the sports business has made it a subject for the financial and business sections

of the print media. The intense focus on mega events such as the World Cup and the Olympic Games transcends the narrow boundaries of the sports section. Sport as a subject has found itself spreading beyond the confines of sports journalism and, indeed, beyond the territory of sports journalists themselves.

(Boyle, Rowe and Whannel, 2010: 250)

The type of sports journalism that focuses solely on the daily flow of build-ups to big games, post-match debate and a sprinkling of big-name interviews has been referred to as the "sportainment" model, according to which sports reporting is viewed as effectively being just a branch of entertainment (Hardin, Zhong and Whiteside, 2009: 336). On this understanding, the pejorative description of the sports desk as being the "toy department" of the newsroom is viewed as justified. This perspective on sports journalism arguably takes as its basis the perception that sports journalism itself is close to fandom (McEnnis, 2017), with sports journalists themselves closely associated in interests and outlook to fans themselves. This view of the nature of sports journalism content goes some way to account for how three of the best-known names to have written academically about sports journalism have written that "the sports section is not generally seen as prestigious within the culture of news and journalism" (Boyle, Rowe and Whannel, 2010: 245). Is this a statement that should make the sports journalist feel uncomfortable? Maybe not uncomfortable, but it should certainly make the sports journalist think.

Sportainment and infotainment are concepts that have been used by sports media academics when analysing the nature of sports content in the early twenty-first century. An important additional concept to consider alongside them is one that sports editors themselves have been using, and that is *fan-led*. An experienced regional sports editor working for Reach, a major publisher of sports news in the United Kingdom, gave an articulate and powerful insight into the nature of fan-led content during an interview for this book. Fan-led is arguably an approach that supersedes the more traditional approach of thinking in terms of news values, and is driven by the pressure for sports journalists to generate strong viewing figures for their material. It is also an approach that requires a high level of interaction by sports journalists with supporters, as the following lengthy excerpt from our interview illustrates:

> I think "fan-led" is a term that's used a lot. What do fans want to see? What do they want to read? What's the issue that's winding them up? It can be anything from why a team is wearing a certain colour on a certain day to things about FIFA to things about wrestling. A guy that I used to work with on football is now covering World Wrestling Entertainment for Sky. That's just incredible really when you think about it; it's not really a sport, it's sport entertainment. But news organisations are probably investing a lot more time, money and effort into that than they are in

things like golf and tennis because there's the demand for it. Instead of just chucking stories at people you've now got to almost be part of a conversation with supporters all the time. Live blogs, web chats, Facebook Lives, Periscopes – you can create a lot of content just on fan opinion and what fans are talking about. It's almost like understanding the trending topics about the club you're covering and tailoring your content towards that. As a sports journalist, you have to go straight in and you're expected to produce page views on day one. The best way to do that is interactive fan-led content and to engage with people. So you're the sort of hub of all that, all that chat and all that debate and all those issues – the audience will come to you to find out what you make of it. It can't just be a one-way thing now. With newspapers before digital, the decision to include content would be purely based on what editors thought was a good story – put it in the paper and hope that people want to buy it. Now, you're constantly looking at what people want. There's no hiding place for content that isn't performing.

(2018, interview with the authors)

We can distil two key – and related – features of this fan-led approach to news selection. First, a key factor in determining what constitutes sports news is now what the audience wants, and understanding just what audiences want is done through analysing the viewing figures for each piece of online content. Secondly, the role of the journalist here is akin to stimulating and then presiding over a debate – interaction with supporters is key in order both to get debate going and then sustaining that debate. As such, sports journalism is no longer an aloof activity. The decisions about what to include as sports news are based on real-time viewer figures, and generating positive audience figures is done through high levels of activity and engagement with supporters through social media.

This approach finds a form of echo in the thinking of Steve Marshall of BBC Sport. Marshall appreciates now that the BBC needs to provide a form of content that is attuned to audience-viewing data and which reflects readers' cultural reference points. "One thing that analytics and audience data show is that young people like not just Premier League football but European football and there's been a drive to do more European football. Why do youngsters like European football? Well, probably because they're playing with teams like Real Madrid and Bayern Munich on computer games like FIFA; those teams have become more prominent in their everyday world" (Steve Marshall, 2018 interview with authors). Sports news may still be something that sports journalists select and shape, but there is more focus than ever by the sports desk on understanding – and then tailoring content – to what audiences want. It is perhaps a rather crude formulation, but whereas prior to the digital revolution it was sports journalists who led fans in terms of news selection, it is now fans who – to a significant extent – lead sports journalists.

Celebrity, sensationalism and "soft" news

When making decisions about what stories to publish or broadcast, sports editors are more likely to be interested in a piece if it involves a "big" name (preferably with a large financial figure attached to it – such as a multi-million-pound transfer fee or astronomical weekly wage). Celebrity, as defined by Harcup and O'Neill, is therefore a key consideration when determining a sport story's newsworthiness. Although this might come as no surprise when considering the output of tabloid newspapers – news providers which have long been sustained by a diet of celebrity-propelled content – it is also true of so-called quality newspapers. Indeed, it can be argued that a cult of celebrity dominates in much sports journalism, with cult figures (A-list sports stars) protected by carefully managed media choreography that affords mere mortals (the media and their audiences) just the briefest of glimpses of the glorious athletes. Boyle and Haynes have argued that access to sports stars has been "routinized and sanitized" through processes such as the post-match flash interview, and connect this to what they claim is the superficial focus of much sports journalism content. In a distinctly downbeat assessment of mainstream sports journalism's ability to engage with deep issues, they argue:

> More considered star profiles are commonly based on opinion and sensationalism rather than reflective analysis and long-form interviews are placed and managed by agents and publicists as part of a wider marketing function. In this rather glib, gloomy version of contemporary sports journalism, investigative approaches to sport are increasingly rare. There are exceptions, such as investigations of match-fixing, performance-enhancing drugs, corruption in the governance of sport and financial irregularities. The subject competence of sports journalists in some of these areas, including sports finance, is often found wanting, as they step into areas of expertise beyond their comfort zone. So the "bread and butter" of sports journalism remains soft news stories based on quotes from press conferences or press releases, with additional gossip thrown in from a network of sources.
> (Boyle and Haynes, 2013: 207)

In a way, this is Andrew Jennings' perspective redressed and reinforced in academic clothing. What it underscores is the importance of sports journalists reflecting on the type of news they are seeking to gather and publish. Are they satisfied to stay in the realm of sportainment, or do they want to aim for more "reflective" and "investigative approaches" in addition to this?

Uniformity and diversity of sports news

Surf from website to website or browse the back pages, and it is often the case that mainstream sports outlets have very similar output to that of their rivals.

They tend to cover broadly the same set of sports, and will often follow the same angles on certain stories (English, 2014). Based on research of six quality titles and their online output in the United Kingdom, Australia and India, English argues that competition between titles actually leads to uniformity of content. Such standardised content, he contends, "is a major element of contemporary sports journalism coverage in print and online, both through the practice of follow-ups and journalists making news decisions similar to those of their competitors" (English, 2014: 491). One journalist at *The Guardian* "complained that the web, which was supposed to encourage diversity, had 'crushed the variety of tone' and resulted in 'bland' offerings" (English 2014: 485). Paradoxically, then, the Internet – a place with infinite room for content – has arguably fostered a narrowing, or uniformity, of sports news content. This could be connected to Whannel's concept of vortextuality, which he describes as the rapid and constant feeding off each other by the purveyors of digital information (Whannel, 2002: 206).

One of the reasons that a similarity of content can occur between rival publications is that the reporters from the main outlets tend to roam in a *press pack*. At the end of a press conference, they will often *carve up* the interview among themselves and decide what the main angle is, and what content they might hold back for another day. "With a remarkable degree of homogeneity, the mainstream media ape one another each day, relying on the same narrowly articulated understanding of 'news value' to report on a largely identical set of topics" (Baym, 2010: 377). Institutionalised processes of story selection can also inhibit the variety of items that receive coverage. Galtung and Ruge's (1965) analysis of news values highlighted the mainstream Western media's bias towards reporting elite First World countries, elite people and items that fitted in with outlets' production schedules. It could be hypothesised that this paradigm applies to sports journalism output, too. It has been argued that there is a "consensual news value system operating throughout the mainstream media, with only a limited range of opinions permitted, particularly at times of crisis" (Keeble, 2009: 22). Although Keeble is addressing news journalism here, the point can apply to sport too. Sports journalists need to be wary of merely following the pack; sometimes the best sports journalism arises from being the lone wolf who pursues prey that everyone else overlooks for softer targets, or in being the columnist who is prepared to be the only one to voice a contrary and unpopular opinion. As such, a diverse, pluralistic media containing outlets that are prepared to stray from the mainstream perspective can inject important lifeblood into sports journalism and give an added breadth to what constitutes the sports news. In the United States, deadspin.com is an example of such a website, with the site at times using a stridently informal tone to cover stories and address issues that are often overlooked by more traditional media. Such websites are also an antidote to what has been called *churnalism*, which is the lazy repackaging of information that has been issued by a sports club or governing body as news. The recycling of other outlets' content is also churnalism (Davies, 2008), and it is a phenomenon that has been accentuated by the growth of digital media and the consequent ease with which others' content can be found and then copied and pasted. It has been argued that sports journalism is ridden with this form of lazy, complacent churnalism (Boyle and Haynes, 2013: 207), and is it not too controversial a statement to say that all self-respecting sports journalists should seek to gather their own sports news and spurn the churn.

Truth, virality and clickbait

It has been argued by a British newspaper editor that in a "post-truth" culture propelled by social media, the currency of online information is no longer truth but virality (Viner, 2016). In other words, people seek to publish content that will be popular and gain a reaction – go viral – rather than communicate accurate, truthful information. Audience engagement (by which is meant high unique visitor numbers and the sharing of content) becomes the altar on which "good" journalism is potentially sacrificed. On this understanding, what engages people online and prompts them to consume and share content is not its veracity (truthfulness) but its "affective" – or emotional – power (Hermida, 2016). This leads to the propagation – unwittingly, but sometimes wittingly – of misinformation in an era in which "facts become secondary to feeling; expertise and vision to ersatz emotional connection" (Smith, 2016). Truth is in some instances relegated to being an optional extra. In sports news, an example might be the publication of a speculative story about a big-name football transfer, even when the only source for the story is the player's agent who has a vested interest in ramping up demand for his player. The journalist writing such a story might have reservations about its accuracy but might be tempted to publish it anyway on the grounds that the player's profile guarantees that the story will be popular and "get a reaction" and "gain a lot of hits."

Truth is also in danger of being undermined by clickbait, an online phenomenon in which readers are enticed to click through to an article only to find it bears a disappointingly loose connection to how it has been promoted. In an analysis examining the Twitter feeds of 15 major football media outlets between 2010 and 2017, Cable and Mottershead carried out a thorough analysis of clickbait in the UK sports media. They concluded that quality is being undermined as outlets pursue "a never-ending quest for easy content" in which "attractive headlines trump journalistic content" (2018a: 69). Producing clickbait content is, they contend, a short-sighted way of attempting to build an audience base that will return to a site. They suggest that sports desks and sports journalists should provide more interaction with the audience rather than more clickbait content. "If the competition is for eyeballs then surely the way to build a community and audience is to interact and not to churn out unsatisfying yet tasty morsels of clickbait for the audience to gorge themselves on" (Cable and Mottershead, 2018a: 78). The question arises, however, about how dependent the audience has already become on a diet of such tasty morsels, and whether they can be weaned off it.

Case study: reporting sporting tragedies

It has been often been suggested by critics of the profession that the routines and preoccupations of sports journalists make them ill-prepared for reporting hard news stories and tragic events. The evidence suggests otherwise. Consider the pressure David Lacey and his Fleet Street colleagues were under when they had to file their match reports from the 1985 European Cup Final between Liverpool and Juventus. These are the first three paragraphs from Lacey's report from the Heysel stadium:

"Liverpool lost the European Cup to Juventus last night, but the game of football has lost far, far more. In short, it died along with the 47 people trampled to death when a group of mainly Italian supporters stampeded to get away from rioting Liverpool fans and were crushed when first barriers, and then a wall, collapsed.

After the scenes of death, injury and destruction in the Heysel Stadium in Brussels, the result seems irrelevant, the details meaningless. How can a match be anything else when even as the players are winning their tackles, making their passes and producing their shots, the death toll continues to mount?

After the wretched affair had ended with the Juventus team doing a hurried half-lap of honour with the trophy, news came through that all 11 members of the Anderlecht youth team who had taken part in the warm-up game had perished." (Lacey, 1985)

Although it later transpired that the 11 members of the youth team had not died and the final death toll was 39, Lacey's first edition match report remains an important historical document and a reminder of the pressures sports journalists can face when a routine sporting event becomes anything but routine. Some Fleet Street newspapers decided not to publish a match report at all that evening.

The helicopter crash at Leicester City Football Club, October 2018.

Recounting his experience of covering the helicopter crash at Leicester City in October 2018, Rob Dorsett, Midlands Correspondent for Sky Sports News (SSN), explains some of the challenges he and colleagues encountered during the immediate aftermath and the days that followed.

When the helicopter came down outside the King Power Stadium on Saturday, October 27, 2018, killing club chairman Vichai Srivaddhanaprabha, the pilot and three other passengers, Dorsett was still in the press room, having completed the usual post-match interviews and news conferences:

"I'm still typing things up, sending some emails. My cameraman heads out to put his kit away in the car and 10 minutes later, the West Ham press officer says, 'I've just been round the back where our coach was heading off. It looks like the helicopter has come down' […] We all rush round. I'm ringing my cameraman en route. He says, 'Rob. I'm filming it now'. He was in staff car park E; [the helicopter] came down 80 yards away from him and he was angry with himself for not filming it as it crashed."

Dorsett says they "would never have used the footage anyway," but his cameraman, Dan Cox, was able to get shots of the burning wreckage. "By the time I got there, it was eight to ten minutes after it crashed. It was still in flames." He knew "instinctively" that no one had survived, "because you look at the body language of the emergency services and the only people who were rushing were the fire brigade." Before Cox could get their kit set up for live pictures, Dorsett did his first live broadcast over the phone at approximately 8:45pm, 20 minutes after the crash. It wasn't long before SSN made their first key editorial decision – not to show video of the burning wreckage. "We only showed those pictures for two hours before we took the decision that it was too much," recalls Dorsett. Sky News ran the pictures a lot longer than SSN, illustrating that even within the same media organisation, the approach to this story would be different, reflecting the differing priorities between a news channel and a sports news channel.

As no news organisation knew who was on board the helicopter, the story quickly became problematic as speculation and rumour spread rapidly across social media about who had perished in the crash. Dorsett recalls that: "The social media storm that was happening at the time was extraordinary."

"We were keen not to speculate about who might be on board, even though we knew that Vichai, the chairman, had arrived by helicopter, he always leaves by helicopter and he was at the game. We didn't know who else was on board, and I started speaking to people who I knew at the club and it became clear that his son, the VC, was not on board, neither was Jon Rudkin, the director of football, and so I reported that."

The speculation was not, however, confined to social media. A number of news organisations were to come in for a lot of criticism for the way they were reporting the story. The ipaper's football reporter, Sam Cunningham, suggested that "some media outlets reported the Leicester City helicopter crash like it was a transfer story." He was particularly scathing about the BBC's Saturday evening news bulletin which speculated about whether Leicester City manager, Claude Puel, was on board, when they did not know whether he was or not. Cunningham wrote: "Is the public's thirst for details of death so unquenchable and the media – and by this I include traditional and social – so obsessed with breaking the names of the dead that a little patience and accuracy are forgotten?" (inews.co.uk, Monday, October 29, 2018).

Cunningham criticised other media outlets for reporting on Sunday that the chairman's daughter had died. Dorsett recalls he managed to establish very early on from a contact at the club that this was wrong and reported she was not on board. He says: "In hindsight, I'm pretty comfortable that confirming that people were not on board was factual information we could report," but he recognises that even this approach could be viewed critically. "Ethically, I was very conscious by ruling out those that weren't on board, we were also contributing to the speculation, who is on board." He also acknowledges that it was sometimes difficult getting the phraseology right and admits he wasn't always sure if he did. On the Saturday night, he recalls reporting: "You have to say, when you look at those pictures, you have to ask the question, whether anyone could survive a crash like that?" Dorsett concedes that "for a news audience, that's fine, that seems okay, but the [sport] audience we were talking to, who have a relationship with and affection for [Vichai], it is a step too far."

The biggest ethical debate Dorsett had with his colleagues concerned goalkeeper Kasper Schmeichel. On the night of the accident, Schmeichel, the only player left at the club when the helicopter crashed, ran towards the burning wreckage and the police had to restrain him. "In any other circumstances, I had enough information from two sources to run it," but after speaking to his editor about the implications for Leicester's goal-keeper and concerned he would be breaking Schmeichel's confidence, they agreed that "it's not the sort of story where we should be running exclusives."

"So I worked it out this way, where I would ask Claude Puel about it at the [Thursday] press conference [...] I asked him directly [...] As soon as I asked him that question the whole room fell silent. He basically confirmed it. So that was the Thursday and we could run the story. But again, I wonder if I was a news reporter, would I have waited three days to run the story?

The BBC ran into further trouble on the Monday after the crash when their reporter Dan Roan was caught on camera outside the King Power Stadium saying the Leicester city boss had died with his mistress. The recording went viral and Roan quickly apologised on Twitter, but it led to calls from Leicester City fans for Roan to be sacked.

The following day *The Daily Telegraph* reported that Roan was to be reprimanded by his employers. Their BBC source claimed:

"The BBC have taken a dim view of this. They told him at the outset that the main thing he needed to do was to strike the right tone, and then this happens" (*Daily Telegraph*, October 30, 2018).

Dorsett's recollection of the helicopter crash underlines the value of the local sports reporter. When the world's media comes to town they can be invaluable and offer a perspective the newshounds often miss, but despite having a good understanding of Leicester City football club, Dorsett says that even he was taken by surprise by aspects of the story. For example, he had not clearly grasped how close the players were to the owner until he saw how emotional Jamie Vardy, his wife and some other players were when they arrived at the stadium to see the floral tributes. And it was only through interviewing fans that he came to appreciate how close Vichai was to the people of Leicester. This became a feature of a number of Dorsett's reports, which seemed wholly appropriate for a sports audience.

SSN is sometimes criticised for soft pedalling on certain football stories due to its commercial relationships with the clubs, but here, their sports journalists told a tragic story very much with their audience in mind, treating the bereaved and fans with dignity and giving them a voice to express their grief. Was it at the expense of objective reporting? Certainly, it was cautious and the instinct for exclusives was set aside, but Dorsett and SSN captured the truth about how Leicester City Football Club and its fans coped with their tragedy. What emerges is a "journalism of attachment," which is arguably what this story required to counter the sensationalism and speculation, gossip and rumour that was rife elsewhere.

On February 25, 2019, Dorsett won the Sports Journalists' Association Broadcast Journalist of Year Award for his coverage. The judges said: "Rob's work at the Leicester helicopter crash – one of the biggest stories of the year – was quite outstanding. Sensitive, accurate, controlled and dignified, an object lesson in how to report a tragedy" (February 25, 2019).

Spinning and framing stories

By selecting a certain "angle" or "line" to focus on, journalists – sports journalists included – present reality in a certain way. Consciously or unconsciously, the audience is being told that *this* fact is important, or at least more important than others. Stories are "spun" and "framed" in a particular manner, with certain facts and a certain narrative given prominence. Sports journalists need to be aware of this, along with the associated concept of *representation*. Some news organisations can pigeonhole or stereotype certain sportspeople or sports teams, and reinforce that perception with each piece that they do: the Brazilian football team is a team of unparalleled flamboyance and creativity; the golfer Seve Ballesteros was a swashbuckling, fiery Spaniard; football manager José Mourinho is an unpredictable enigma. Sports journalism can, if it is not careful, reduce the participants that it is covering to pantomime villains/goodies, or even examples of lazy stereotypes. One example of this is the British footballer Joey Barton, a professional with a chequered past, including criminal convictions. Somewhat ironically, Barton used a newspaper comment piece to complain about the persona that newspapers and the mainstream press had projected about him:

> After years of interviews, it became clear that no journalist was willing to tell my tale. Anything I said, anything I did, was given an angle to fit in with the bad-boy image [...] I was [an] enigma [...] They projected someone who was not the real me: it was the me that the press wanted to project.
> (Barton 2012, quoted in Boyle and Haynes, 2013: 212)

In this piece for *The Times* of London, Barton explained that such misrepresentation had prompted him to take to Twitter in order to get his own views across without media (mis)-projection. "No longer," he wrote, "would I let journalistic interpretation to [sic] run wild without any accountability" (ibid.). Barton suggests here that sports journalists can be complacent to the point of behaving unethically, and it is to issues of ethics that we turn in the next chapter.

Questions for discussion

"It is a pointless exercise to try and draw up a list of criteria that seeks to capture the different factors that make certain facts about sport newsworthy. The newsworthiness of something is grasped more by instinct than criteria." Do you agree with this perspective on news values? Give examples from your own practice as a sports journalist in justifying your answer.

"Once it used to be the case that sports journalists would determine what sports fans read. Now, in the digital era, it is the case that sports fans determine what stories sports journalists write." Does this perspective on story selection have merit? Can you provide examples from your work as a sports journalist that support both sides of the argument?

Has the infinite space of the Internet paradoxically led to less variety of sports news content from mainstream media organisations?

TASK: Select a tabloid newspaper and a quality newspaper from the same day and compare the stories that they have run in their sports sections. What news values do you detect being at play in the story selections?

Now analyse the stories that appear on the two newspapers' websites. What news values do you believe are behind the story selections here, and do the values differ to those that were used for the printed editions? If there is a difference, what might be the reasons for this?

Listen/watch two different radio/TV stations' sports news bulletins. Again, what news values do the stories exemplify?

Across all the platforms, to what extent is there a uniformity of content – that is, to what extent have the different outlets covered the same stories? What does this uniformity or lack of uniformity tell us about the state of the sports media?

5
Ethics, regulation and law for the sports journalist

This chapter focuses on ethical and legal debates in sports journalism, including: self-censorship among sports journalists; tensions between object-ivity and subjectivity in sports writing; codes of conduct; media regulation in a digital sports media environment; the key legal issues facing sports journalists.

> Ethical journalism is not an oxymoron. Ethical journalism is not only possible, it is essential; not just for journalists' sense of self-worth, but for the health and well-being of society. It requires journalists – wherever they work – to be reflective practitioners, engaged in a constant process of reflection and learning while doing their job. And it requires journalists to be prepared to voice their concerns within the newsroom.
>
> (Harcup, 2007: 144)

Introduction – law, regulation and ethics

A knowledge of media law and an appreciation of the ethical issues that con-front sports journalists is not an optional extra for those working in the industry but is essential. Do you agree with that opening sentence? Some might agree with the first contention of the statement – that a knowledge of media law is essential (if merely for the sake of self-preservation and not landing oneself or one's employer in court) – but disagree that a sports journalist must also be attuned to ethical issues. Are there really, it might even be argued, any major ethical issues that confront sports journalists? One of the purposes of this chapter is to show that such a dismissive line of thinking towards sports journalism ethics is misguided, even dangerous. The role of the sports jour-nalist requires its practitioners to make judgements – about which stories to run, which stories to drop, which people to talk to, which questions to ask, which sources to use – and many of these judgements, as we shall see, contain an ethical dimension. If we are perhaps tempted to think that sports journalism does not contain many ethical decisions or dilemmas, then that is possibly because we as hard-pressed sports journalists are too busy trying to hit deadlines and gather stories to think about *which* stories we are pursuing and the nuances of *how* we go about reporting on them. Amid the hurly-burly of the industry, sports journalists can perhaps lack the time to do the important *reflection* that Harcup refers to in the quote at the top of this chapter.

Journalists are subject to laws that restrict what they can publish or broadcast. While these laws differ from jurisdiction to jurisdiction, the key legal issues that journalists generally need to concern themselves with are the laws around libel (laws that are intended to protect people from having statements made about them that unfairly harm their reputation), laws concerning contempt of court (laws that are intended to ensure that what is published by the media does not unfairly influence the outcome of a judicial process), laws around privacy, and laws concerning copyright. This is far from being an exhaustive list of media law issues as they impinge on sports journalists, and those wanting a comprehensive guide to media law should consult a law textbook relevant to the jurisdiction in which they work (*McNae's Essential Law for Journalists* being a highly regarded standard text in the United Kingdom). However, it is important to note that the toughness of laws as they affect the media differ from country to country. France and the United Kingdom, for example, might be separated by a relatively thin channel of water, but libel laws in the United Kingdom are regarded as being tougher on journalists than libel laws in France – at least historically. Put another way, journalists in France are less likely to be successfully sued for saying something defamatory about a person than journalists publishing the same statement in the United Kingdom. The sports journalist David Walsh discovered this when seeking to expose the cheating of cyclist Lance Armstrong, as we shall see below. Since then, libel laws in the United Kingdom have undergone a change in focus with the introduction of the 2013 Defamation Act. The legislation was brought in to reassert the balance between freedom of expression and protection of reputations in favour of the former over the latter. Now, if a person wants to bring a successful action for defamation, they need to show that the negative statement that was made about them has resulted in "serious harm." The intention of the act was to raise the threshold for successful libel actions, thereby reducing the chances of journalists being sued for publishing contentious content.

The laws that restrict what journalists can publish or broadcast can be either *civil* or *criminal*. If a sports journalist commits a civil wrong (for example, by groundlessly libelling someone), then they can be sued and ordered to pay damages. If a sports journalist breaches criminal law (for example, by committing contempt of court by publishing a statement during the trial of a sports star that leads to the athlete being unable to receive a fair trial), then they will be prosecuted and fined – and potentially even jailed.

Case study

When the English football manager Harry Redknapp stood trial in 2012 for alleged tax evasion, a sports journalist's careless reporting resulted in the judge imposing a Twitter ban. In a tweet, the journalist named a juror in the case, and also reported the evidence of a witness that was given while the jury was not present in the courtroom (Pugh, 2012b). Both of these actions are prohibited under the 1981 Contempt of Court Act, an act which is intended to protect the smooth and fair administration of justice. Following the breaches, the judge at Southwark Crown Court banned both the use of Twitter and of live texting at the trial, and referred the case to the attorney general, the government's chief legal adviser who decides on whether prosecutions should be brought for contempt of court. The incident illustrates the importance of journalists having a sound grasp of what they can and cannot report when covering a court case. Redknapp was cleared of tax evasion.

The law, then, is something that sports journalists literally cannot afford to ignore. Sports journalists, like other subgroups of journalists, also need to consider industry regulators. In the United Kingdom, broadcasters are regulated by the government-approved Office of Communications, Ofcom. Journalists working in television and radio are required to comply with Ofcom's Broadcasting Code. The code covers issues such as fairness, accuracy, privacy, not causing harm and protecting under-18s, and if a broadcaster is found to be in breach of the code, they can be fined or even, in rare cases, have their licence suspended. The situation is different for newspapers and news magazines in the United Kingdom, which have historically been subject to a process of *self-regulation*. Under self-regulation, it is the publishers of newspapers and magazines who voluntarily agree to sign up to a code of practice and who themselves pay the running costs of the regulator. In the United Kingdom, the main press regulator is the Independent Press Standards Organisation (IPSO), the previous regulator – the Press Complaints Commission – having been disbanded after coming in for fierce criticism during the 2011 and 2012 Leveson Inquiry into press standards. IPSO can order a member publication to publish an apology and can also levy a fine. Under the IPSO Editors' Code of Practice, members of IPSO agree to comply with a range of clauses covering accuracy, the public interest, harassment, use of clandestine devices to obtain stories, privacy and other areas. The first code of practice in the United Kingdom was introduced by the National Union of Journalists in 1936 (Sambrook, 2012: 9), and there is increasing debate about whether sports journalism itself needs a code of conduct that is distinct from more generalised codes of journalism practice (Bradshaw and Minogue, 2018). Indeed, two Spanish sports media academics have put forward a bespoke code of conduct for sports journalism which they believe should be applied globally (Ramon-Vegas and Rojas-Torrijos, 2018). They argue that there are two main reasons why a specific code is needed for the sports journalism industry: first, to raise awareness within the industry of the need for sports journalists to be held accountable, and, secondly, to enhance the public's perception of sports journalists' credibility, which they claim has been eroded partly by the collapse of the distinction between content that is factual and content that is opinion. They argue that their ten-point code seeks to "bridge the gap between the ideal and professional practice" (Ramon-Vegas and Rojas-Torrijos, 2018: 23). The code is ambitious in scope, not least the section in Clause 7 (Promotion of positive sports values) which asserts that sports journalists "should contribute to the promotion of positive values, such as [...] international peace and understanding through their coverage of sports events among citizens, with special attention for youth and children" (Ramon-Vegas and Rojas-Torrijos, 2018: 24). While some sports journalists might shudder at the idea of their work having to adhere to what would appear to be political objectives, the final clause of their code consists of a call for a richness of coverage that arguably has a creditable ambition to it.

Xavier Ramon-Vegas and Jose-Luis Rojas-Torrijos have proposed the following code of conduct for sports journalists across the world. Which of the ten clauses do you agree with? Do you believe sports journalism needs its own code of practice and, if so, do you think it would be effective?

1. Public function and right to sports information

Sports journalists should report on all areas of sport. As an essential part of their public-service approach, they should not only concentrate on mainstream disciplines but also give exposure to underrepresented sports that generate news and have a large number of practitioners. This can help broaden the coverage and expand citizens' sporting culture. Media professionals should not report on the private lives of sports people unless the information is relevant to understanding the athletes' performance.

2. Conflict of interest

Sports journalists should avoid taking part in activities that lie outside of their professional realm or in employment that may create conflict of interest. This includes working in the field of public relations (PR) and as advisers for a sportsperson, club or federation, and writing for a team or league publication. Editors and reporters cannot be sources who are assigned to themselves. Behaving professionally entails remaining loyal to the news organisation for which one works.

3. Hospitality from sources and independence

Sports journalists should reject invitations and gifts from teams or promoters that could call into question their working as independent eyewitnesses. Likewise, they should not use their position as journalists to obtain free tickets for any sports event from sources other than those which customarily make passes or tickets available when a performance has a clear bearing on the journalist's job.

4. News gathering and impartiality

Sports journalists should avoid developing a close relationship with sports sources and maintain a critical distance by seeking and using a varied and representative number of arguments and facts on any issue, and presenting them appropriately without bias towards their audiences. They should also avoid misconduct such as "boosterism" and nationalistic or chauvinistic approaches. Impartiality entails being professional rather than behaving like fans.

5. Factual reporting

Sports journalists are committed to truthful and factual reporting. They should establish a clear distinction between facts and their personal opinions about them, as well as between news and advertising or sponsored content. Reinforcing methods of verification is essential to the fight against fake news, the pervasiveness of speculation and rumour in sports content, and to discarding sensationalism and trivialisation in news reporting.

6. Journalistic quality and use of language

Sports journalists are committed to journalistic quality and must, therefore, rely on a correct use of language as their main working tool by which to enhance their stories. Acquiring a vast vocabulary and developing the ability to use suitable words and phrases in referring to any sportsperson are valuable assets towards improving content quality within the field.

7. Promotion of positive sports values

Sports journalists should contribute to the promotion of positive values, such as fair play, non-discrimination and international peace and understanding through their coverage of sports events among citizens, with special attention for youth and children.

8. Violence in sports

Sports journalists must avoid using warlike language, as well as disseminating expressions and images that emphasise or legitimate any form of violence towards individuals or groups of people within or outside sports venues. Sport is not a substitute for war. Thus, journalists must minimise confrontational narratives and warlike imagery.

9. Gender perspective

To counteract the long-standing under-representation of sportswomen, sports journalists should work with greater dedication to promote equality in their reporting by giving female athletes more exposure when their results deserve it. More women should be incorporated as expert sources into the news agenda. Sexist comments and stereotypes should be avoided when referring to them.

10. Sports beyond sports

Sports journalists should go beyond the dramatic action on the field and raise public awareness about relevant contexts that exist behind the play. Sports should be thoroughly explained from their social, financial, cultural and political dimensions. (Ramon-Vegas and Rojas-Torrijos, 2018)

There has been sustained and fierce debate about the impact and efficiency of journalistic codes of conduct. On one understanding, codes aim "to create a collective conscience of a profession" (Keeble, 2009: 16). However, journalistic codes are arguably inadequate by themselves in terms of stimulating ethical behaviour or in limiting/preventing unethical behaviour, and need to be supported by a wider engagement by journalists in matters of ethics as they apply to the industry (Cairns, 2018; Luckhurst and Phippen, 2014). Views on the relevance and importance of codes of conduct differ hugely, from those who perceive them (for different reasons) as redundant, to those who regard them as an important way to build trust in the media. Some contend that codes "all have one thing in common: they are not worth the paper they are written on" (Norris, 2000: 325) because to imagine that a journalist who is chasing a story up against deadline is going to consult a code is "to live in cloud-cuckoo land" (Norris, 2000: 329).

The relevance of traditional codes of journalistic practice in the digital age has been questioned (German, 2011; McEnnis, 2018a). Due to the sheer volume of content that is being produced – much of it by people who would not regard themselves as professional journalists – questions have been raised about whether it is meaningful to talk about regulation in the way that the debate has traditionally been framed.

> How do traditional and historically embedded notions of ethics transpose to digital environments that are not so tightly regulated? [...] The growing complexity of regulation and ethics within different types of sports journalism is a useful indicator of a fragmented professional culture more generally.
>
> (McEnnis, 2018a)

As part of this fragmentation, McEnnis believes that sports media regulation is not a simple concept that means the same thing for one sports journalism outlet as it does to another. In a case study examining the work routines of sports journalists working for Sky Sports News and *The Sun*, he provides an intricate discussion of what regulation means for sports broadcast journalism versus sports print journalism. A central thrust of his paper, informed by his own journalistic experience, is that the routines of TV sports journalists are more influenced by regulatory codes than those of print sports journalists. The spirit that animates the IPSO code, he argues, is the desire of the press industry to be independent from government interference.

Laws and regulations exist in statute books and in published codes of conduct. However, that is not where it ends for sports journalists when it comes to considering the guides and restrictions on their professional practice. Cairns (2018) argues that compliance with the law and adherence to regulation are not enough; there needs to be a deeper understanding and appreciation of ethical nuance by his employees. "Compliance, regulations, code of conduct, while offering some kind of framework, don't go anywhere near covering all the ethical challenges a sports journalist faces in 2018" (Cairns, 2018). This echoes Luckhurst and Phippen's distinction between rules and values. Rules-based systems of journalistic regulation, they argue, foster a culture of "box-ticking" and "evasion," and have repeatedly failed since the 1947 Royal Commission into standards in the press heralded self-regulatory processes. "Rules are too easily regarded as little more than an incentive not to get caught" (Luckhurst and Phippen, 2014: 57). Journalism based on values, by contrast, cultivates a stronger sense of moral awareness among journalists. "Ethics place the power to improve the profession in the hands of practitioners" (Luckhurst and Phippen, 2014: 60).

Ethical values in sports journalism

In the view of Sky Sports News' executive editor Andy Cairns, the Leveson Inquiry's report into press standards in 2012 gave rise to a closer scrutiny of media ethics generally, not just of news journalism ethics (Cairns, 2018). But what are the key ethical values that a sports journalist should possess? A commitment to accuracy, the thorough verification of claims, balance, impartiality and objectivity might be regarded as starting points. However, even some of those might be questioned in a digital social media-driven age where opinion (and therefore the writer's own *subjective* views) is increasingly to the fore. Objectivity, impartiality and detachment are related concepts, although their precise meaning and the nature of their overlap is contested (Bell, 1998; Kieran, 1998; Sambrook, 2012; Schudson, 2001; Ward, 2010). They are regarded as "traditional" journalistic values (Preston, 2009), although it has been argued that the conception of them as somehow timelessly essential to journalistic practice overlooks how they arose in specific historical contexts (Schudson, 2001). For Sambrook, impartiality is defined as "the removal of bias," while objectivity is defined as "a disciplined approach to isolate evidence and facts" (2012: 5). Impartiality has been explored in some depth, at least from a current affairs and news perspective, by Marsh, who defines it a process rather than an outcome (2012). It is not something that is achieved in a single moment, but rather something that is obtained over time in order to ensure that "all the significant voices along all the significant axes are heard – but weighed to reflect their overall significance to the debate" (Marsh, 2012: 77). Considered in a sports journalism context, this might mean that a series of articles about the Taking a Knee protest in American football would need to display a sense of balance and impartiality when taken as a group. So, the first article might only contain interviews with players supportive of the protest, and thus on its own seem highly partial. But if the second article contains quotes only from those who are critical of the protest, and the third and fourth contain a blend of interviews from those on both sides of the debate, then impartiality is achieved.

American sports journalism contains a long tradition of "boosterism" – the partisan support by a regional news organisation of the local home team – and this is an accepted, and even expected, practice. "In the rare cases where an American news organization is designed with a national audience in mind – USA Today – sports reporting operates by an objectivity norm, but ordinarily sports reporters openly favor local teams" (Schudson, 2001: 164). Such boosterism means local teams are "examined from a stance that presumes enthusiastic backing of the team" (ibid.). It is wrong, however, to think that objectivity has long been a prized virtue in the British sports media. The evolution of sports journalism in Victorian Britain was not rooted in a culture of objectivity. One historian has noted that dispassionate observation was rare by reporters due to them often being involved in the sports themselves as secretaries, club administrators and players (Huggins, 2004: 151). Moving forward to the present time, Steen, a sports journalist and sports academic, suggests that objectivity as a sports writer is neither achievable nor necessarily desirable. "For all the impartiality it requires, this (sports writing) is no more a job you can do dispassionately than you can do blindfolded [...] there is no newspaper or magazine editor I know you would hire anyone for such a position who did not have the wherewithal to be one-eyed" (Steen, 2014: 10). He adds that "every piece of writing, every piece of journalism, is slanted or shaded in some way and hence opinionated" (Steen, 2014: 17). Objectivity, then, is perhaps a myth in sports journalism. However, in a so-called post-truth era where fake news can fly around social media platforms far faster than the accurate rebuttals that follow, it is arguably more vital than ever that journalists of all stripes – sports journalists included – are more diligent than at any point in their history in their commitment to fact checking.

In an analysis of the emergence of a post-truth culture, one journalist and media commentator has defined fake news as false content that falls into the bracket of being "easily shareable and discussable stories, posted to social media for jokes, for ideology, for political reasons by groups connected to foreign nations, such as Russia, or – most commonly – to make a bit of money" (Ball, 2017: 1). While false news is nothing new – misinformation has often been purveyed by the media – fake news is distinct from false news in the speed at which it is disseminated (Rajan, 2018). Sports journalism has experienced instances of bogus stories on social media being taken up by the mainstream media and then distributed as though fact. Made-up stories on social media about football transfers, for example, have then been repeated by national newspapers (Corcoran, 2014). So, while it might be an overstatement to insist that sports journalists always need to be detached and neutral, it is not an overstatement to say that sports journalists need to be committed to thorough verification. Without stringent fact-checking processes, the public can be misled and a key function of the media is undermined.

The speed at which sports journalists work in the digital era can also pose ethical issues. A study based on interviews with sports PR professionals in Australia found three areas of concern about the quality of sports content in the 24-hour digital era: that accuracy was a casualty of the speed at which sports journalists were seeking to publish stories; that more content was attempting to be produced with fewer resources; and that there was an increase in complaints (Edmondson, 2018). Following 26 in-depth interviews with sports communication professionals, she concludes that "routine violations of core ethical standards of Australian journalism" are happening as a consequence of the digital 24/7 news cycle (Edmondson, 2018: 54). No doubt a good number of Australian sports journalists would dissent from this conclusion, and the fact the study is based on interviews with PR staff rather than journalists themselves needs to be considered when evaluating the reliability of the conclusion. But it, nevertheless, raises questions about how the digital age is posing fresh ethical issues for sports journalists.

Another key contemporary ethical topic for sports journalists to negotiate arises from the fact that there are now more parties than ever trying to control the flow of information around sport. A range of PR officers and consultants working on behalf of sports stars and teams compete to drive the sports news agenda and to influence the media narrative in their clients' favour. Many clubs and governing bodies employ increasingly large communications teams, while players' agents, sports marketing consultants and other external PR consultants working on behalf of clubs, brands and sports stars all seek to emphasise certain news angles and divert journalists away from others. Such a proliferation of communications officers and the ready-made content that they provide to sports journalists should put sports journalists on their guard. It might be the path of least resistance to use content that is provided via press releases and to do the interviews that are served up on a plate by a star's media manager, but sports journalists should always make sure they are working on their audience's behalf rather than putting themselves at risk of becoming a puppet serving a particular club's or sports star's agenda. As sports content becomes increasingly stage-managed by PR managers who brief players and coaches before interviews, there is the danger that interviews – and the journalism pieces arising from them – become increasingly bland. This dullness is accentuated by more and more sports stars becoming "media trained" in how to bat away difficult questions. This culture, Cairns has argued, has made it harder for people inside sport to speak up when they feel they need to voice concerns about an important issue, which in turn has led to the ethically questionable phenomenon of the increased use of anonymous sources – people who speak to journalists but who are not prepared to be named as the source of the information.

> And this attempt to control information from clubs, agents and governing bodies, has made it harder for those inside sport who want to speak out. Luckily for journalism, there are still people who do want to talk to journalists. And it's led to the growing phenomenon of the anonymous source.
>
> (Cairns, 2018)

This increasing effort from various parties to control the flow of sports media information takes us on to another issue that affects the information that audiences receive: self-censorship by sports journalists. By self-censorship we mean the deliberate withholding of facts from a story, or the dropping of an entire story, or the deliberate decision to not voice an honestly held opinion in an opinion piece. In a moment of self-censorship, a journalist or editor decides to withhold a fact or opinion from the public on a matter of public interest due to one or more pressures. These pressures might not even be acknowledged by the sports journalist to him or herself.

Self-censorship

Clause 3 of the International Federation of Journalists' declaration of principles on the conduct of journalists states that "the journalist shall not suppress essential information." However, there is significant evidence that sports journalists – not unlike political and entertainment journalists – often suppress a wide range of important content.

In his highly regarded book examining issues affecting modern sports journalism practice, Raymond Boyle contends that the closeness of the relationship between sports journalists and many of the teams that they cover means they run the risk of producing content that is "complicit" with those organisations' aims (Boyle, 2006a). Boyle refers to this as the danger of "travelling too close to the circus" and suggests a need for the sports media to put more distance between themselves and those they cover by "run[ning] away from the circus" (2006b). Sugden and Tomlinson (2007) also consider the complicity potentially involved in sports journalists' relationships with both their subjects and sources, arguing that a "collusive dynamic" exists. Elsewhere, Andrews (2014) provides an interesting starting point when considering the issue of the nature of the relationship between sports journalists and their sources. Such a relationship, he says, "is inevitably a close one. They (sports journalists) must never allow it to become incestuous" (2014: 85). What all these writers on sports journalism have explored or hinted at is how a sports journalist can become compromised by having too close a relationship with the sources they use. Such close, cosy relationships can potentially – and without the sports journalist even being aware of it – lead to them asking gentler questions than they might otherwise do, or not addressing certain controversial issues for fear of upsetting a source with whom they have become friendly. Or maybe they might not offer too much criticism after a string of undeniably poor performances, again out of fear of alienating a contact. In other words, the sports journalist might dilute what they publish or even withhold content – and in so doing they are self-censoring.

Allegations of sports journalists self-censoring to the detriment of truth have been made from within the industry as well as from without. Kelvin MacKenzie, a former editor of *The Sun* whose controversial career is stained by his title's appallingly offensive coverage of the Hillsborough stadium disaster, alleged in a *Sun* column that "the real bad boys" during Sam Allardyce's removal as England manager in 2016 following a *Daily Telegraph* exposé were sports journalists. In colourful, unflinching language and under the headline "Sports mafia that's kept Big Sam's secrets safe for years," MacKenzie effectively reasserts Boyle's claims of journalistic complicity with the sports stars they are covering, and asserts that too many sports journalists put the enhancement of their own career trajectory ahead of telling the truth and exposing questionable behaviour. MacKenzie writes:

> They (sports journalists) have been hearing this type of stuff for years and yet have never written a word about it for fear that it will ruin their cosy relationship with players, managers and owners. Can I explain something to them? They are not PRs for the clubs. They are supposed to be disclosing to readers, viewers and listeners what is really going on in football. Better to be banned from the ground than to not do your well-paid job properly. Instead writers (and I have one particular example in mind) spend their entire time hanging around radio studios giving their views about Allardyce and Co but not once disclosing important questionable information they have picked up on the grapevine. Perhaps they are more interested in the books they ghostwrite and the size of their Twitter following than blowing the whistle.
>
> (2016)

Why might sports journalists self-censor? As MacKenzie suggests, it might be for reasons of maintaining a close relationship with certain contacts, or it might be for reasons of career enhancement. The preservation of relationships with contacts is undoubtedly a significant factor. For example, US freelance sports writer David Davis told researchers: "You've got to keep a relationship with these people! Yes, you can say, 'he had an off day,' and this happened and this happened, but you don't want to burn a player so that he'll never talk to you, and it's the same with the coach. That form of relationship, it's so subtle and it's so difficult to explain" (Hardin, Zhong and Whiteside, 2009: 324). As the end of that statement suggests ("it's so subtle and it's so difficult to explain"), the activity of self-censorship is not one that journalists are always able to immediately recognise; it can become so ingrained into what many sports journalists do that it becomes difficult to recognise when it is occurring.

Research has also suggested that some sports journalists – in common with other journalists – now self-censor because they fear the abuse they might receive online if they publish certain stories or opinions. "In the last 15 years, being insulted and harassed online has simply become part of the job for most journalists" (Binns, 2017b). Her conclusion is that journalists, including news, feature and sports journalists, self-censor in light of the new interactive digital framework which enables audiences to insult, criticise and abuse them (Binns, 2017a).

The fear of being sued might also prompt a sports journalist or their editor to self-censor – or, as one sports media researcher has put it, to exercise "discretion" (Sefiha, 2010). Even when sports journalists know something to be true, they on occasion back off from publishing it out of concern that it could trigger a financially ruinous legal action. In a study into the North American cycling magazine *Bikesport* that was based on a number of interviews, one researcher writes:

A fear of legal action can influence what writers investigate. While neither writers nor editors expressly indicated dropping an emerging story for fear of legal action, one writer clearly recognized the ramifications of covering certain stories regardless of their veracity. "There are a million, totally substantiated stories we could write about JT, throw him under the bus for a million reasons, but he's got deep pockets and lots of legal power. This shouldn't affect what gets printed but it does."

(Sefiha 2010: 213)

Sefiha's study was focused on *Bikesport's* coverage of the use of performance-enhancing drugs (PEDs) – an issue of perennial fascination to investigative sports reporters. His paper discusses the extent to which exposing PED use can "severely compromise" a journalist's relationship with sources (2010: 209), and suggests that this can cause hesitancy among journalists in publishing the truth. Sefiha refers to cycling journalist Jeremy Whittle's view of professional cycling as a community that imposes an *omerta* – a Mafia-like code of silence – on those within the community. On this view, cyclists, cycling teams and the journalists who cover the sport form a type of club, and broadcasting to the outside world what goes on inside the club is tantamount to being blackballed from the club. Sefiha highlights the professional dilemma that confronts sports, specifically cycling, journalists in this context: either expose wrongdoing and potentially be ousted from the inner circle so that one can no longer report on the sport effectively on a daily basis from the "inside"; or keep quiet about the wrongdoing so that one preserves source relations and is able to report effectively – that is, with access to sources – from the inside on a day-by-day basis. He summarises the predicament of one sports journalist who dared to publish the truth about a cyclist's use of drugs:

A Belgian investigative sports reporter who also writes about doping indicated that, "After writing that story (which revealed doping practices among a Belgian cycling team) I know that (now) I can't go to the Panaracer (team) bus anymore, probably ever again. I know they won't talk to me." For these and other cycling journalists that have written doping related stories, the loss of reliable sources within the community has seriously compromised their ability to provide daily cycling coverage.

(Sefiha, 2010: 209)

The concept of cycling being a sport in the grip of *omerta* occurs repeatedly in many of the writings by distinguished cycling journalists. Whittle, David Walsh and Paul Kimmage have all used the concept, and it is one that merits further consideration in the context of journalistic self-censorship. "Professional cycling has always exercised an *omerta* and it has played a significant role in the endurance of a drug culture," wrote Walsh in his account of his pursuit of *omerta's* arch-enforcer, Lance Armstrong. "But more than a code of silence is at work here and it is not coincidental that the Sicilian word has become associated with the peloton, because when a rider breaks the code, he can expect a mafia-like response" (Walsh, 2012: 73). When Kimmage, who competed in the Tour de France, retired from professional cycling he published a warts-and-all memoir of his time in the peloton – a book that was effectively a declaration of war on the code of *omerta*. It was the opposite of self-censorship: it was a cyclist-turned-journalist's uncompromisingly honest account of exactly what went on in the peloton and the pressures that cyclists were put under to conform to the PED culture. "The law of silence: it exists not only in the Mafia but also in the peloton," he wrote. "Those who break the law, who talk to the press about the dope problem in the sport are despised. They are branded as having 'crache dans la soupe', they have 'spat in the soup'. In writing this book I have broken the law of silence" (Kimmage, 2007: 229). Kimmage was quick to assert that the *omerta* spread its muffling tentacles not just to the cyclists themselves but also to the media covering the sport. Cycling journalists would deliberately not publish what they knew to be the case about doping and instead write fluffy stories of homage about the leading cyclists of the day. Criticising the French daily sports newspaper *L'Equipe* and the wider French cycling press, Kimmage wrote: "The absence of adequate [doping] controls in France is common knowledge, but rarely highlighted. The papers and magazines know about the problems but choose instead to fill their column inches with portraits of the stars – of present 'greats'" (2007: 244). Kimmage's criticism of fellow journalists could be withering and brutally contemptuous. Returning to cover the Tour de France in 2006, he was depressed by what he perceived as the fawning atmosphere in the media room, regarding the press corps as "mostly fans with typewriters" (Kimmage, 2007: 280). When the announcement was made of the withdrawal from the race of a number of big names due to a doping investigation, he contemptuously described the scenes among the press as "The Muppet Show" (Kimmage, 2007: 281). Through their commitment to exposing some of the unpalatable truths about cycling, both Walsh and Kimmage have attempted to loosen the grip of *omerta*. This is noteworthy not just for those with an interest in cycling. While cycling might, in the recent past at least, have exercised a peculiarly powerful form of *omerta* over those in its inner circle, it would be naive to think similar unofficial codes of silence do not exist in other sports. Sports journalists should be vigilant about this, and where wrongdoing occurs they should take their lead from the likes of Kimmage and be ready to call it out – even if they are 'spitting in the soup'.

Law and sports journalism – "I always think that there is a greater likelihood of sports reporters running into legal problems"

As mentioned in the introduction to this chapter, an awareness and knowledge of the laws affecting what can or cannot be published is not an optional extra for a sports journalist; it is essential. While editors and lawyers can provide guidance, every journalist needs a working knowledge of the laws that potentially restrict what they can safely publish. That said, some sports journalists need to be more sensitive to legal restrictions than others. An investigative sports journalist with a particular interest in exposing corruption, for example, will be confronted with more legal hurdles than a sports journalist who primarily reports on matches. Investigative sports journalists – and investigative journalists generally – often sail close to the legal wind. Indeed, some would say that if you are not sailing close to the wind as a journalist occasionally, then you are being too soft on those in positions of authority. Investigative journalists' work necessarily involves pursuing enquiries and publishing material which powerful people and institutions would prefer journalists steered clear of; and such powerful people will often deploy lawyers in an effort to protect their name and put journalists under pressure. Through years of experience, some investigative journalists acquire an in-depth knowledge of media law. Whatever one's daily focus as a sports journalist, however, an awareness of the key legal issues that form an important part of the backdrop to one's work is vital. Primarily, this means having a decent grasp of libel laws – the laws that protect people (and corporate bodies) from having their reputations unfairly maligned.

While Western democracies generally seek to safeguard freedom of expression, as we saw at the start of this chapter every legal jurisdiction places some limits on what can be published or broadcast. This is not because they are necessarily illiberal, but because modest curtailments of freedom of expression can be essential for the preservation of other legal rights or public goods: the administration of justice, the maintenance of public order and the protection of people's good reputations, for example. To give an illustration, it is a criminal offence in many jurisdictions to incite ethnic hatred, so publishing material that could be reasonably expected to give rise to such hatred is prohibited. There are also automatic lifetime bans on the media identifying the victims and alleged victims of sexual attacks, unless the victim chooses to waive their right to anonymity.

The biggest legal concern for sports journalists is the law of libel, or *defamation*. In essence, to defame someone is to lower that person's reputation through the publication of negative statements about them. So, for example, to write of a baseball league administrator that he is "corrupt," or of a tennis player that she is a "cheat," or of a golfer that he "lied" over the score that he submitted to the tournament scorer, is to defame them. Additionally, to suggest that a club or individual is experiencing financial troubles is also defamatory. In and of themselves, such defamatory statements might not put the person or organisation that publishes them in legal trouble, because they might have a solid defence for making them – the most obvious one being that they can show that they are true. However, if a journalist or outlet making such an assertion does not have a defence (for example, cannot show it to be true), then the statement is a *libel* and the journalist and the outlet that has published it can be ordered to pay very large sums of damages to the aggrieved person in addition to their legal costs. The law of defamation in the United Kingdom is contained in the Defamation Act 2013. It is important to note that defamation is not a *criminal* offence but a *civil* wrong. As such, a sports journalist (or any journalist for that matter) is *sued* for defamation by an individual, rather than being *prosecuted* by the authorities. In some instances, this could mean that people with access to lawyers and the money needed to pay them are more likely to sue than those with fewer resources, an important consideration for sports journalists, as outlined below.

Media law expert Paul Wiltshire, who has trained hundreds of journalists in media law, both in industry and as a university lecturer, believes that sports journalists are potentially more at risk than news journalists of publishing content that gets them into legal trouble. "I always think that there is a greater likelihood of sports reporters running into legal problems because sports journalists perhaps don't have their legal antennae as finely tuned as their counterparts who are involved day to day in court or crime coverage," says Wiltshire, who worked as a deputy editor and in-house trainer for Trinity Mirror (now Reach) before moving into university teaching. "If you're involved in news reporting, you're perhaps more regularly asking yourself, 'what can I say here?' My fear is always that sports journalists are at risk of inadvertently blundering into legal problems" (interview with the authors, 2018).

One news organisation whose sports desk has had to have its legal antennae permanently tuned in is the *Blackpool Gazette* in the north west of England. The publication had to cover a long-running and bitter dispute between Blackpool Football Club and its supporters, who accused the club's now former owners, the Oyston family, of mismanagement. In such a context, Andy Sykes, the *Gazette*'s former deputy editor, says that the football reporter covering the club had to have legal knowledge because he is "just as likely to be covering a protest march or a court case as a football match" (2018). The *Gazette*'s coverage of its local club is an example of how a knowledge of media law – and a willingness by sports journalists to cover off-pitch issues as well as on-pitch performances – can enrich content and arguably inflate the esteem in which sports journalism and the sports media are held. The *Gazette*'s football reporter is Matt Scrafton, and Sykes says:

> Most football reporters try to maintain a distance between on field matters and politics off the pitch so as not to damage relationships with the football side. That has been unavoidable for (Matt) […] as the footballing element has often been the sideshow to more pressing matters. He has to be the voice of the fans and amid the fog of armchair experts via social media, he

has had to find a way of striking a balance between reflecting those views but correcting the sea of misinformation in a respectful manner.

(ibid.)

Sykes was of course writing about one of his own reporters, so his assessment of Scrafton's reporting is naturally likely to be positive. Notwithstanding that, Scrafton's reporting underscores how important it is for credible, trusted sports reporting to be underpinned by a legal knowledge married to journalistic balance.

Many of the participants in the dispute over Blackpool FC were wealthy individuals, and professional sport generally is an industry which has no shortage of owners and participants with very considerable bank balances. Wiltshire also contends that the wealth of many elite sportspeople in the media spotlight increases the risk of legal action being taken against sports journalists. While the average person would probably think twice about pursuing legal action due to the often prohibitive cost of instructing a solicitor, Wiltshire points out that many of the subjects of sports journalists' stories are not constrained by such concerns. "It's an obvious point that many of the people sports journalists could be writing about have access to and the means to fund excellent legal advice. Martin O'Neill's track record in suing over stories alleging he had 'lost the dressing room' – obviously a frequently-used phrase – is a salutary one."

O'Neill, a football manager who has been in charge of both top-flight club sides in England and Scotland, as well as the Republic of Ireland national side, is, indeed, an instructive example. Over the past decade and a half, O'Neill has successfully sued a range of newspapers and websites for defamation. The *Daily Mirror*, Football 365, Independent, BBC, *Daily Record* and *Observer* are all titles that have had to apologise to him and pay him damages (Malone, 2013). What is notable is that O'Neill has successfully sued over types of stories which many would regard as common currency on football websites. As Wiltshire states, "so-and-so has lost the dressing room"-type stories are arguably a staple of the sports journalist's diet of angles on manager stories. Yet O'Neill launched an action for £200,000 against the *Daily Mirror*, citing a range of articles that the newspaper had published during his time at and exit from Aston Villa. The apology which the *Mirror* ran following O'Neill's successful litigation makes for sobering reading for sports journalists, and is worth stating in full:

> On 24 June 2010, we wrongly reported that Martin O'Neill, while manager of Aston Villa, had been secretly interviewed for the position of Liverpool manager, in breach of Premier League rules and his contract.
>
> We accept that no such interview took place.
>
> On 10 and 11 August, following Mr O'Neill's resignation as Aston Villa manager, we published a number of articles claiming that Mr O'Neill had lost the confidence, faith and respect of the dressing room, causing a players' revolt which forced him to resign.

We also alleged that his resignation resulted in general celebration amongst the squad.

We now accept that Mr O'Neill had not lost the dressing room, there was no players' revolt and no general celebration over Mr O'Neill's departure.

We apologise to Mr O'Neill for these false allegations and have agreed to pay him damages for libel and his reasonable legal costs.

(Mirror Football, 2011, updated 2014)

Put bluntly, the O'Neill example illustrates how carefully sports journalists need to tread. Managers and sports stars can – rightly and understandably – be concerned about the preservation of their professional reputations, as a damaged reputation can potentially lead to fewer (or less lucrative) contract offers in the future. In addition, they often have the bank balance to instigate legal action should they feel the need to. O'Neill saw that his reputation as a manager had been besmirched by articles, and by suing for defamation he secured not only an apology but also a substantial sum. Other factors also make the law around defamation a difficult one for journalists. When they are sued for defamation, media organisations can often decide against defending themselves against the claim, even when they think they have a strong defence. This is because of the unpredictability that is often perceived as existing in UK courts' rulings in libel cases. Such unpredictability has led to one media academic referring to the "casino chamber of litigation" that media companies can enter if they decide to contest claims (Crook, 2017). Moreover, because it is up to the sued organisation or individual to show that what they published was true rather than for the aggrieved party to show that it was false, "the dice in most UK media law cases are loaded in favour of claimants with the burden of proof on media defendants" (ibid.).

Defamation laws vary from country to country, and this can lead to multiple legal cases taking place simultaneously in different jurisdictions, and with potentially different outcomes in the different jurisdictions. David Walsh and Pierre Ballester's 2004 book L.A. Confidentiel: Les secrets de Lance Armstrong, for example, triggered much activity among Armstrong's legal team. The book contained what Walsh called "circumstantial evidence" that the Tour de France champion was using performance-enhancing drugs (Sandomir, 2004). Armstrong's French legal team argued that the book be either taken off shelves or that eight passages be removed, due to the defamatory content they contained (Henry, 2004). As well as suing Walsh and Ballester, a former journalist for French sports daily L'Equipe, Armstrong initiated legal proceedings against the book's French publisher, the publishers of L'Express magazine, which had reprinted a ten-page section from the book, and Walsh's employer, The Sunday Times, which published a news report about the book. His lawyers were simultaneously taking legal action in Paris and London.

The case in the United Kingdom went to the High Court and, two years later, Armstrong won, although, in hindsight, it was to turn out to be a case of winning a battle but not the war. The paper's lawyers had argued that the words used in the article had conveyed to the reader nothing more than the presence of reasonable grounds to suspect Armstrong of taking PEDs, rather than an outright statement of him having taken them. The judge, however, indicated in a pretrial hearing that he was persuaded that the meaning of the article – taken in its entirety – implied that the cyclist had taken drugs in order to cheat. This led to a very large amount of money being paid to Armstrong in settlement, and an apology from the newspaper via its lawyers. "*The Sunday Times* has confirmed to Mr Armstrong that it never intended to accuse him of being guilty of taking any performance-enhancing drugs and sincerely apologised for any such impression" (*The Guardian*, 2006). Very swiftly, Armstrong then dropped the defamation actions he had brought in France, claiming that he had been vindicated and had no desire to spend his life in litigation (*USA Today*, 2006). Another interpretation is that, given the difference in defamation laws in France to the United Kingdom, it was far from clear that a French court would rule in Armstrong's favour. So, rather than continue with an uncertain legal action in Paris that could potentially serve to undermine his cause, Armstrong opted to retreat back to Texas and make sanctimonious statements – or, rather, as it turned out, sanctimonious lies.

Ultimate victory went to Walsh and *The Sunday Times*. The book paved the way for Armstrong's activities to be put under more and more scrutiny, on both sides of the Atlantic, and Walsh was courageously undeterred. When, in 2012, the US Anti-Doping Agency issued a report saying it had uncovered "overwhelming evidence" of Armstrong having been the ringleader of a doping programme within his US Postal Service cycling team, *The Sunday Times* announced it would consider taking legal action to both recover the funds it had spent on the case and to pursue Armstrong for fraud (*CNN.com*, 2012).

Sourcing content online and infringing copyright

Parts of this chapter have highlighted how the digital era has posed fresh ethical challenges for sports journalists. Some of these challenges arise from the pervasiveness of social media and the desire for outlets to gain as many clicks on their content as possible. Relatedly, one of the challenges confronting sports journalists in the digital era is to resist the temptation to become a desk-bound social-media-obsessed churnalist. With so much material circulating on social media – and with so many stories breaking on social media – it can be easy to spend the entire working day using social media management dashboards such as TweetDeck or Hootsuite to monitor what stories are brewing or breaking, and to use them as the springboard for one's own work. While there is of course a place for using social media to source stories and to complement traditional newsgathering approaches, unique content will decline unless journalists break out of the social media bubble – and get out of the office. Media law expert Paul Wiltshire views the growth of social media as having posed a new raft of legal and ethical issues for sports journalists. One of them is that journalists might not fact-check as thoroughly as they should do out of a desire to get stories live as quickly as possible. Another is that the quality of writing might decline, again as a consequence of journalists working so quickly. Moreover, the scramble to source images to go alongside stories might result in copyright being infringed. "In terms of journalists sourcing stories, I suppose the fast-paced nature of social media means that less thought and consideration might go into their writing, and the spectre of accuracy versus gaining clicks always potentially looms large," he says. "A bigger issue in sourcing material is likely to be copyright, and ensuring that the right alarm bells ring when journalists want to use pictures sourced from Twitter remains a challenge."

Issues of copyright and copyright infringement surface in various areas of sports journalism, and as new forms of technology emerge, so too do new questions around copyright. For example, what – if any – copyright applies to photos that appear on public social media accounts? Is the photo of Olympic gold medallist X smoking a cigarette outside a nightclub at 3am which appears on the publicly viewable Instagram account belonging to member of the public Y fair game for journalists to download and use in their stories? The starting point here is that the copyright for a photograph rests with the person who took it (who might not be the person who uploaded it), so journalists need to be wary of assuming they can use images just because they are publicly viewable. Certain sites may even assert that they have the copyright to all images that are uploaded onto them. "Publishing photos copied from a social networking site – such as Facebook, Instagram, Flickr, Twitter, or Tumblr – may infringe the copyright in the site, and/or the copyright held by the person who created ('took') the photo, who might not even be aware that someone else has uploaded a copy on to the site" (Dodd and Hanna, 2018: 366). So, while the Internet has been dubbed the "Wild West" of content, it is very far from it being a free-for-all in terms of obtaining images.

While the specifics of copyright vary from jurisdiction to jurisdiction, copyright is intended to control who can copy work that has been created by artistic or intellectual effort. In the United Kingdom, the majority of UK law on copyright derives from the Copyright, Designs and Patents Act 1988 and its amendments. While no editor would expect a journalist or sports journalist to be conversant with every element of such an Act, an awareness is vital to prevent news organisations being served with bills for copyrighted content that they have published.

For sports broadcasters, the copyright infringement defence of *fair dealing* is an important one to be aware of in the Act. Utilised effectively, it can be an important way of ensuring that you can legally use modest amounts of other people's footage when working on bulletins or packages for television. Fair dealing essentially allows an outlet to use a small amount of another organisation's footage when reporting on current events, even if there is no consent from the copyright owner. For a sports journalist, this can be invaluable when covering a major sporting event for which your company does not own the broadcasting rights. Suppose fan violence breaks out at a match, or suppose Manchester United draw 3–3 with their rivals Manchester City, but your outlet does not hold the rights to broadcast the matches. Under the terms of fair dealing, you can use small amounts of footage that have been aired by the rights-holding broadcaster without fear of being successfully sued. So, it is legally acceptable to show a snippet of footage showing the worst of the crowd trouble, or of Manchester City scoring the 89th-minute equalizing goal. However, there are conditions that need to be met in order for the defence of fair dealing to be solid. The broadcaster that is running another organisation's footage needs to credit the original source of the content, and also needs to ensure that it is not taking unfair commercial advantage of the copyright owner by screening more content than is necessary (Dodd and Hanna, 2018: 375). It does, however, remain something of a grey area about how much of someone else's footage you can safely use without overstepping the mark and losing fair dealing as a defence to infringing someone's copyright. What's too long a clip? How many times can the clip be repeated? *McNae's* provides an example of how rival sports broadcasters can take differing views on this. Following the FIFA World Cup in Italy in 1990, the BBC and British Satellite Broadcasting (BSB) went to court over the satellite company's use of BBC footage from the finals. The BBC argued that BSB had infringed its copyright by using an excessive amount of its footage, footage to which it had bought exclusive rights. However, the High Court dismissed the BBC's action, ruling that the satellite company's use of short goal clips which were between 14 and 37 seconds long, and shown up to four times in 24 hours and always with a graphic crediting the BBC, was legal. The use was protected by BSB having the defence of fair dealing when reporting on current events (Dodd and Hanna, 2018: 376).

Final thoughts

Sports journalism is not an ethics-free zone, and changes in digital technology have presented a fresh group of ethical challenges to sports journalists. Law and regulation form the backdrop to sports journalists' work, and it is important for sports journalists to be acquainted with their demands and requirements. However, on top of that, sports journalists need to consider wider ethical decisions that can have significant bearing on editorial policy. The issue of self-censorship among sports journalists highlights this.

Questions:

Media law expert Paul Wiltshire is quoted above as saying, "My fear is always that sports journalists are at risk of inadvertently blundering into legal problems." What legal issues do you think Wiltshire is referring to, and why is a working knowledge of media law important for a sports journalist?

What is the biggest ethical challenge that the growth of social media has posed to sports journalists?

"Sports journalism does not need a code of conduct – in fact, all journalism codes of conduct aren't worth the paper they are written on." Do you agree or disagree with this statement? Why?

Have you ever self-censored when working on a story or opinion piece? If you have, what do you think was the factor that motivated that act of self-censorship?

"Sports journalists can get on fine without ever thinking about ethics." Does this statement have any merit?

6

Sports media relations and complicit sports journalism

Sports clubs and governing bodies are employing an increasing number of people to run their public relations and communications departments as they seek to bypass traditional news outlets and take control of the flow of information themselves. Many of the employees in these roles are trained sports journalists, often referred to as "in-house" journalists. This chapter explores what the rise of club communication departments – with their television stations, multimedia content and multi-platform social media output – means for traditional, independent journalism. Does the growing amount of content produced directly by clubs and governing bodies run the risk of making sports journalists obsolete, or does it make independent sports journalism more important than ever? In particular, this chapter looks at the nature of the relationship between sports journalist and club PR officer. Who is the more powerful figure in the relationship, and how has that power relationship shifted? Who is in charge of the sports news agenda, the journalists or the PRs? The issue of whether sports journalists are at risk of becoming too subservient to the agendas of club media departments is explored, and the importance of sports journalists retaining a distance between the people and organisations they are reporting on is emphasised. A detailed case study casts light on the pressures and demands of running an elite club's communications department.

Crashing the party of "idiot reporters"

The lengthy process that culminated in Sepp Blatter being ousted as FIFA president amid a welter of corruption claims can, with some plausibility, be traced back to a man in hiking boots. It was 2002, and football's world governing body was holding a press conference in Zurich following Blatter's re-election as president. Andrew Jennings, a British investigative reporter who had previously exposed corruption inside the International Olympic Committee, had set his sights on Blatter. Jennings cut an unorthodox figure at the media session – not that that bothered him in the slightest, as he recalled in an interview with the *Washington Post* that was published on June 3, 2015, the day after Blatter resigned:

> I'm surrounded by all these terribly posh reporters in suits and silk ties and buttoned up shirts, for God's sake […] And here's me in me hiking gear. I get the mike and I said, "Herr Blatter, have you ever taken a bribe?" Talk about crashing the party […] Reporters are moving away from me as if I've just let out the biggest smell since bad food. Well, that's what I wanted. Thank you, idiot reporters.
>
> (Miller, 2015)

Calling one's fellow reporters "idiots" might seem a touch extreme. But what Jennings was getting at in his interview was his concern at how sports journalists are too often afraid to ask tricky questions of those in positions of power. Rather than hold the powerful in sport to account, Jennings has argued that many sports journalists are instead preoccupied with not "rocking the boat." Elsewhere, Jennings has skewered sports journalists for having too close a relationship with public relations executives whose job it is to convey positive messages about their clients. Put another way, he is concerned that many sports journalists have – or run the risk of having – too cosy a relationship with those they are supposed to be scrutinising and holding to account. And such cosiness, if it goes unchecked, runs the risk of making reporters complicit in the corruption and wrongdoing that might be being perpetrated, or at least complicit in pedalling the content that a club or governing body wants them to publish.

The allegation that sports journalists have too cosy a relationship with the individuals, clubs and organisations they cover is a recurring one in the academic literature on sports journalism practice (Boyle 2006a, 2006b). Boyle has characterised such cosiness as "running too close to the circus" (2006b). However, for the allegation to be made from within the profession rather than from without, and for it to be made with the vehemence with which Jennings delivers it, gives the claim added weight, and it is an issue that any thoughtful sports journalist should be aware of. Jennings accuses his fellow reporters of professional idiocy, and his suggestion that they are complicit in a mutually sustaining arrangement – or "party" – with FIFA suggests he regards some reporters as being not merely too close to the circus, but as de facto collaborationists in the preservation of the governing status quo.

In a 2012 article for the *British Journalism Review*, Jennings gave his considered view of how close sports journalists should get to what Boyle has referred to as the "circus" of PR professionals and slick media management that orbits modern professional sport. Jennings' answer is: as far away as possible. Jennings laments the diminishing lack of distance between sports reporters and sports

PR managers. In particular, reflecting on the membership list of the Olympic Journalists' Association from 2009, he complains about the inclusion of a number of spin doctors and brand consultants. This, he argues, is symptomatic of a decline in professional detachment among sports journalists, for without that detachment there can be no effective fulfilment of journalists' watchdog function:

> What on earth were *those* people doing in the reporters' club? Whatever happened to journalists' independence, keeping a distance from the people we write about? The membership lists says a lot about what is wrong with sports journalism, the lack of scrutiny and scepticism that is its hallmark [...] That reporters let the media masseurs into their private club is just one symptom of a much bigger problem: lack of scrutiny.
>
> (Jennings, 2012; italics in original)

Jennings' point can be distilled to this: how far can modern sports journalists be trusted to discharge the traditional responsibilities of professional journalists, primarily those of holding powerful organisations and bodies to account?

There is an element of provocation to Jennings' reflective writing about his investigative work but there is no doubting its energy and its efforts to persuade sports journalists to reconsider their working practices. Journalists should not tow the PR-dominated press conference line, he argues, because

> it's so much more fun on the other side. I've had a hoot exposing sports secrets over the years. I got a suspended jail sentence in Switzerland for saying that International Olympic Committee president Juan Antonio Samaranch was corrupt – I'm really proud of that. I'm quite chuffed to have been banned from FIFA press conferences and premises since 2003, when I published a documented story about a big secret bonus Blatter paid himself. Of course, FIFA shouldn't have done that. It's authoritarian, pure censorship. Still, I take it as a compliment.
>
> (ibid.)

While this book is not urging young and aspiring sports journalists to see how many suspended jail sentences they can get under their belts, what this book very much wants to achieve is to get sports journalists thinking carefully about how they go about sourcing their stories and what they think the goal of their work is. Are you, as a sports journalist, too close to the club or clubs that you are reporting on? Does the closeness of those relationships mean that you run the risk of becoming complicit in helping those clubs achieve their own agenda, rather than working as the eyes and ears of the public? Are press conferences the best means of obtaining news about those clubs, or should you as a journalist be pursuing alternative – and more independent – sources of material? One may argue that Jennings has on occasion overstated his case and been too exacting and too critical of his fellow journalists, but the questions raised by his crusade against "professional idiocy" are ones that demand attention, for they get to the heart of what amounts to an existential question for sports journalism: what is its purpose?

Journalistic distance, relationships and the role of sports communication staff

The old adage has it that "a journalist is only as good as their contacts book." In other words, journalism – and sports journalism is no exception – is about acquiring, nurturing and maintaining contacts. If a sports journalist wants to break stories, then a sports journalist needs sources, and if a journalist is to have sources, then they need to develop and sustain relationships with those involved in the sport or sports that they are covering. Club media managers and press officers are likely to be people with whom sports journalists have frequent contact, but they are not sources in the true sense of the word. The job of a club press officer is to convey positive messages about the club at the time that best suits the club's commercial and reputational interests. On occasion – in fact, frequently – such a job will be in conflict with the sports journalist's role of conveying news about a club as soon as they are convinced of its accuracy. This information may be positive or it may be negative, and publishing it may have a detrimental impact on a club. Yet sports journalists, particularly those working for regional outlets who are producing content about the same club day in, day out, generally rely on a strong relationship with a club's media department. As such, they need to preserve that relationship, and therefore need to tread with some wariness when handling stories that could trigger a negative response from a club. The challenge for sports journalists is often to preserve such relationships without becoming too cosy or too beholden to the media department of the clubs that are being covered. Consider the following fictional scenario involving a reporter's relationship with a club. What are the pros and cons of each option at each stage?

Interacting with a club's media officer – mock scenario

Suppose you are a football correspondent on the website Bristol Live, covering Bristol Rovers.

A source inside the club (a non-executive director who you were chatting to after Saturday's game) tells you that the club has a scout/representative in Merseyside who is looking at potential new signings there. During your chat, it's not clear whether the information is on the record or off the record.

Once back in the office, you phone a sports journalist you know on the Liverpool Echo, who tells you that there is a talented 18-year-old member of Everton's academy, Brad Tomshaw, who is rumoured to be on the move because he wants to be nearer to his family in Somerset (which is just south of Bristol). Some separate online research reveals that Tomshaw is a former England U16 player. Do you

1) publish a speculative story linking Tomshaw to Bristol Rovers, without approaching the Bristol Rovers media department or the Everton media department before publication or
2) phone either the media manager or the first-team manager at Bristol Rovers (whose mobile number you have) before deciding whether or not to publish a story?

Assume that you eventually take option 2).

After some thought, you approach the media manager at Bristol Rovers, who tells you that Tomshaw is indeed likely to be joining Rovers, although nothing has been signed yet. He asks you to hold off on running the story until the deal has been done. He then tells you: "Don't worry, we will make sure you have the story as an exclusive. If you publish the story now, then the manager will be very unhappy and he may reduce the opportunities you have to interview him." Do you

1) agree to wait until the club gives you the go-ahead to publish the story or
2) publish the story online immediately, telling the media manager that the story is too big for you to sit on due to the England connection?

Assume that you eventually take option 1).

While speaking to a football agent who is a contact, the agent tells you about Tomshaw's plans to move from Everton to Bristol Rovers. He tells you that you can use the information but not to name him as the source. You still haven't heard back from Bristol Rovers' media department, six days after having first contacted them about the story. Do you

1) publish the story in the next edition, citing an unnamed source or
2) continue to wait until Bristol Rovers confirm the deal is done and dusted before publishing the story?

As this scenario hopefully illustrates, the decision-making process can be a complicated one. The task of simultaneously preserving the relationship with a club while retaining one's journalistic independence can be a tightrope – and it is a tightrope that many sports journalists have had to try and negotiate on a daily basis. If you are too accommodating with a club, then you run the risk of becoming *complicit* with the club, inasmuch as you can become little more than a mouthpiece for the club. Switched-on fans can pick up on this, and this can lead to a loss in credibility. On the other hand, if you burn your bridges with a club, then being "on the outside" can lead to a club no longer providing you with information or tip-offs, and in some instances even banning you from press conferences or from attending matches in the press box. To some extent, tension is inevitable – and if there is never any tension between club and journalist, then the journalist is arguably not doing their job properly. As Mark Douglas, the head of football at *Chronicle Live* in Newcastle, has put it: "Even as the local media landscape changes there is one thing I'm fairly certain will remain constant: the existence of friction between a football club and regional journalists who cover it" (2018). Douglas is more aware of these tensions than most. In 2013, Newcastle United responded to a front-page story in the *Chronicle* about a fan protest against the club's owner, Mike Ashley, by imposing an open-ended ban on the news company's reporters. It followed a lengthy period of sustained criticism by the *Chronicle* of Ashley's ownership. As Douglas pithily puts it: "the tensions that come with an unpopular owner, unhappy fan-base and questioning media make for a volatile mix" (ibid.). The ban had its downsides in that the club could no longer directly interview players and coaches, but Douglas believes it had many benefits as it necessitated devising fresh and innovative ways of covering the club. It is worth quoting his response at length, as it reflects the liberation that can come from being released from having to walk the journalism-PR tightrope described above:

> When the tap of manager and player quotes is turned off, you stop shaping your working week around Wednesday player interviews and a Friday manager press conference and start to see every day as an opportunity to so something new. We turned to an array of columnists to replace player quotes, pushed more fan issues and replaced interviews with analysis – which felt like it chimed with the changing mood of supporters who have become more savvy and no longer interested in players making bland or obvious statements [...] There is also a freedom to being banned which I think led us to become more supporter-led in the way we viewed things. When you are glancing over your shoulder waiting for the next phone call from a club official, it is inevitable there can be a chilling effect.
>
> (Douglas, 2018)

The rift between *Chronicle* and Newcastle United has healed, but how the media company negotiated the ban serves to highlight how it can reinvigorate sports journalists to step away from the weekly merry-go-round of press conferences and instead seek content away from the routine of press-officer-arranged player interviews.

While the *Chronicle Live*–Newcastle United case is an example of a media organisation stubbornly – and admirably – retaining its independence and resisting the pressures from a club or governing body, there are examples of sports organisations and media organisations becoming too closely entwined. In some isolated instances, this has resulted in cases of sports journalists backing off from covering big stories, even stories about corruption. Such instances illustrate how at risk sports journalists can be of becoming complicit in the commercial objectives of the organisations and individuals they should be holding to account on behalf of the public. Such allegations of complicity between sports governing bodies and the media are often made in connection with media companies that hold the rights to broadcast particular sports. The reasoning here is simple: because a company has paid many millions – or even billions – of pounds or dollars for the right to televise a certain event or league, they have a vested interest in that event or league retaining its integrity, for fear of the sporting public turning off the screen if a corruption scandal, doping controversy or similar emerged. Therefore, the media company holding the broadcast rights is likely to steer clear of asking the difficult questions or pursuing investigative journalism into the sport for fear of undermining their own product. One such allegation in South America – that Grupo Globo, the broadcast rights holder for major footballing events in Brazil, had avoided reporting on corruption allegations against Ricardo Teixeira, the head of the Brazilian Football Confederation – led to supporters using social media to launch a campaign, #ForaRicardoTeixeira ("Get Out Ricardo Teixeira"). It has been argued that the campaign was a factor that led Teixeira to resign in 2012 (Vimieiro, 2017).

The danger of sports journalists surrendering – consciously or unconsciously – their independence, and instead producing content that serves the purposes of others is an issue that has commanded a significant amount of attention among sports journalism academics. As one distinguished sports media academic has written: "The expansion of the sports industry and the range of commercial and political stakeholders involved also means that rigorous, uncomplicit journalism is required in this area as never before. This represents a major ethical challenge for contemporary sports journalism" (Boyle, 2006a: 5). The Jennings and Teixeira examples discussed above suggest that the danger of complicity remains a key issue to which sports journalists need to be attuned.

The academic literature on the topic also suggests that sports journalists can fall into line with a club's wishes in order to preserve their relationship with press officers and thereby access to players. One example cited by researchers is American sports journalists' failure to report on steroid abuse in Major League Baseball; reporters knew of the abuse but did not cover it – a prima facie example of complicity. "Reporters may shy away from writing critical stories in fear of losing access to the athletes" (Hardin, Zhong and Whiteside 2009: 324).

What can sports journalists do to ensure they retain their integrity in such matters? How can they report and broadcast in a manner that ensures their independence is not compromised? How can they be confident that they are serving their audience's requirements rather than serving the agenda of those they are reporting on? One answer to this is to stress the importance of journalists retaining sufficient *distance* from those teams and people who are the focus of their reporting. Distance in this sense means the ability – or the conscious decision – not to become too close or attached to those about whom one is writing or broadcasting. It means retaining adequate *detachment* from the people and issues one is reporting on. So, in an obvious sense, that might mean a local journalist not becoming a drinking buddy with the head coach of the team that she reports on. Or it might mean not being so much of a fan of a team that your judgement about that team is obscured and compromised by your support. So, while distance in the sense being discussed does not necessarily mean physical distance, a case can be made for the health of independent sports journalism being undermined by journalists literally spending too much time in close proximity to the teams and people they are reporting on, perhaps by travelling with them to matches and/or staying in the same hotels as the teams.

Cycling journalist Jeremy Whittle has brilliantly and candidly captured the cocoon-like environment that can build around reporters and those whom they are supposed to be reporting on objectively. Whittle has described how living, working and travelling alongside cyclists made the boundary between journalist and the professional sports people he was reporting on seem blurry. In some instances, that boundary might even evaporate. In a book written in 2009, but which still retains its punch, Whittle sought to capture the atmosphere that can exist during the grand tours – Le Tour de France, Giro d'Italia and Vuelta a Espana – and a host of other events on the annual cycling circuit:

> Many journalists live and travel in this bubble with the teams and their personnel. Slowly but surely, the lines become blurred. Journalists develop an intimacy with the riders that is rare in other sports. They catch the same flights as they shuttle from race to race; they stay in the same hotels; they bump into them in lifts or at breakfast buffets, exchanging greetings and a word or two of encouragement. They share their successes and failures, wince at their injuries, develop friendships with their families and – in one case I know – transport their drugs for them.
>
> (2009: 5)

Journalists-as-drug-mules is a pretty depressing state of affairs. But Whittle's book, *Bad Blood – The Secret Life of the Tour de France* (2009), is a principled, sympathetic and at times disorientating account of how sports journalists can get caught up in cycling's circus to the point of running away with it and losing touch with the real world. While most sports journalists would instinctively – and without hesitation – state that they would expose drug-taking if they knew it was occurring, Whittle presents the case for why some sit on that insight and turn a blind eye. Travelling in the bubble, watching the Herculean agonies that cyclists put themselves through, stage after stage,

> many of them (journalists) suspect and often know far more than they reveal. Soon the *omerta*, the law of silence, governs their existence, just like it governs that of the riders. It is a closed, self-serving culture, a secret society, with its own unspoken rules. These rules are not those of the outside world.
>
> (ibid.)

Whittle writes that out on the road in the Grand Tour bubble, the normal duties of life – families, mortgages, everyday morality – can lose their grip. Yet the presence of performance-enhancing drugs contaminates relationships just as it can contaminate a journalist's professional practice. In a passage of courageous professional honesty, Whittle writes:

> Because of doping, my dream job, a job that gave me such a sense of escape, gradually imprisoned me. For a long time I refused to choose sides: it was easier, far easier, not to. Like others, I wanted to write about the glory and heroism of sport, but instead I became lost in the moral maze, an accomplice to the *omerta*, an accessory to the Big Lie.
>
> Then, standing with my notebook and tape recorder, when a drugs ampoule fell at my feet, as a rider exhaustedly pulled his racing jersey over his head, my journey from fan to accomplice became complete.
>
> "You weren't supposed to see that, Jeremy," he smiled weakly.
>
> I stared at the floor. I didn't know what to say.
>
> Eventually, I lifted my head and said: "Don't worry."
>
> Even now, it is easier not to name that rider, partly because he is not a thoroughbred but an also-ran who has never won a major race; partly because he is a "good" guy with young children, who don't deserve to have their father labelled a cheat or to have abuse heaped on them when they arrive at school; and partly because I am still surprised at my own naivety in thinking that, for some reason, he was too nice a guy, *too good*, to be a doper.
>
> (ibid: 6–7; italics in original)

In other words, nice guys cheat too, and nice journalists can lose their grasp of professional distance. Given such a tale, it would seem that sports journalists' moral compass can quite easily go haywire. Distance, therefore, is a critical issue. It is not merely an academic issue to be pondered by final-year undergraduate journalism students in a manner removed from the real world. As Whittle's case illustrates, it is essential that sports journalists consider the circumstances that can foster a culture of complicity, not least because many sports journalists believe the issue remains very much a live one, particularly in road cycling. Nick Harris, the *Mail on Sunday*'s chief sports correspondent, believes that the muzzling of truth in cycling is still widespread, with journalists sitting on doping stories for fear of having their access to cyclists revoked. "The amount of cycling journalists who must have known about all kinds of things going on in cycling for many years and, let me tell you, still do, and still aren't writing it, is actually shocking" (The Media Show, BBC Radio 4, 2018).

Case study of a sports public relations expert

John Simpson is a sports public relations consultant. After heading the West Bromwich Albion media and communications department for over a decade, he now works with several leading sports PR and marketing agencies, including Macesport, Adrian Bevington Sport & PR and eightyone600, across a range of projects. Simpson acknowledges that sports reporters can face a challenge in terms of retaining their independence, while also retaining a good relationship with the media officers at clubs they are covering. However, he believes it can be done provided that both sides – the reporters and the club press officers – understand that each has their own job to do, and that that those differing roles will on occasion come into conflict.

"Ideally, there should be a respectful and mutually beneficial relationship so that both sides understand the job – the at times very different job – that the other is doing," says Simpson. "The sports journalist is trying to fill web pages, column inches and air time with interesting content, while the public relations officer is trying to protect and enhance the reputation of their organisation.

"But I believe they can work together. Of course, there are going to be times of conflict – for example, when a team is having a tough time on the pitch, or there are off-field issues relating to the business. It's about respecting each other's position and job. Working together during both the good times and the bad times for a sports club would definitely be the aim."

On occasions, a sports club might ask a journalist to hold off on publishing a story – perhaps because an imminent player signing could be compromised if the name of the player were made public. However, Simpson says the rise of social media has affected the dynamics around such requests.

"Firstly, if you're asking a journalist to sit on a story there has to be a very good relationship in place," he says. "Of course, there are never any guarantees journalists will adhere to that request and it's even trickier now than it used to be because there are so many different ways a story can break in the age of social media. Previously, journalists could be a bit more confident that if they sat on a story for a bit it wouldn't break anywhere else. Sports journalists may be less inclined to do that now because they know it could pop up on social media."

A common gripe among sports journalists, and football journalists in particular, is that access to players can be tightly restricted, with a club hand-picking which players will be put up for interview by journalists and only making them available for increasingly brief periods. However, during the 2018 FIFA World Cup, England manager Gareth Southgate and the FA's senior communications manager, Andy Walker, surprised a number of media outlets by taking a more relaxed approach, allowing sports journalists to mingle more freely with players. Simpson believes it was an impressive strategy but says it remains to be seen whether it will be universally applied.

"Conflict can arise when journalists feel they aren't getting enough access to players or to the manager, and it was terrific what England did and they were quite rightly lauded for it," he says. "What England did was a shift towards how things are done in American football, in the NFL. Would it be workable at English football clubs? Quite possibly, and I'm sure clubs up and down the country will have noted how well it worked. But each club will have its own way of running its media relations, with its own unique challenges. It's all about assessing your own PR/media landscape and implementing the best strategy that works for you."

Simpson has had to deal with the media fallout from a number of incidents during his career, including Lee Hughes' imprisonment for death by dangerous driving, Roman Bednar's "News of the World drug sting" and the controversy arising from striker Nicolas Anelka's use of the "quenelle" gesture after scoring for West Bromwich Albion in a match against West Ham in December 2013. The French player was subsequently fined £80,000 and banned for five matches after an enquiry by the Football Association found that he had used the gesture, which has been described as an "inverted Nazi salute." Anelka denied that the gesture was anti-Semitic, but the incident resulted in property company Zoopla, which was co-owned by Jewish businessman Alex Chesterman, ending its sponsorship deal with the club (BBC, 2014).

Simpson breaks down three key areas which can cause sports club media managers to have to enter a crisis-management mode. They are the following:

- results and performances well below par, leading to mass supporter discontent
- incidents of player gross misconduct, on or off the field
- club reputational threat (which can arise from, among other things, financial mismanagement, criminal allegations or poor handling of sensitive issues)

When a crisis emerges, Simpson believes that those handling the media reputation of a club should not seek to hide away from what is occurring. "It's important to be visible as a sports PR and contactable at all times, both good and bad. In fact, it's almost the case that you should be more contactable during the bad times so that you can manage developing stories. That's when you really earn your corn as a sports PR officer.

"Being available and honest, and having the journalist's trust so that the journalist knows you are not just spinning things is important. Journalists need to feel confident that you are giving them solid, truthful information."

Such confidence in one another can, believes Simpson, increase the chances of the relationship between club and reporter remaining cordial when a sports journalist feels obliged to report a less than positive story.

"You would hope that most journalists that have a negative story to write would have a sufficiently strong relationship with you that, at the very least, they'd tip you off that they're going to run the story," he says. "That gives you the chance to pour cold water on it if there's no truth in it, correct any inaccuracies and give your side of the story before it's published. Again, that's down to having a good relationship with the journalist.

"However, a journalist's relationship with a club is not just about his or her relationship with a public relations officer, although they should be the main conduit. It's also about the relationship with the chairman/ owner, the manager and other key stakeholders at the club."

An interesting perspective on the question of distance between sports journalists and the sports people they cover is provided by Sky Sports News executive editor Andy Cairns, a journalist who has lived through a shift in what is regarded as an appropriate distance between sports journalists and the sports people they report on. It is worth quoting his reflections at some length:

Maybe unfairly in the past, sports journalists were often accused of being fans with typewriters. There was a feeling they were too close to the players and officials they reported on. They had great access with some great insight and interviews. But were they asking the difficult questions? When news reporters, as opposed to specialist sports reporters, started covering sport they had a greater distance and were able to ask the more difficult questions without worrying about jeopardising relationships. Some of the greatest resistance to these news journalists covering sport came from old sports hacks. They called them "the rotters." But the media explosion since the 1990s has seen a huge change. Sports journalists now are far more rounded. They challenge more and ask tougher questions. But that close relationship has gone. Reporters now very rarely travel with teams. They no longer stay in the same hotels. There aren't the opportunities to go out for a few drinks with a star player, or even meet up for informal chats in hotel bars. Information and access are strictly controlled by teams of media officers. They dictate who will appear at press conferences. They coach and advise them what to answer and even try to control what questions journalists will ask. Even though I've lived through this change I'm not sure what came first. Whether the closer journalistic scrutiny led to the more protective environment or whether the more pro-tective environment, and tougher access, meant sports reporters now had a greater distance that allowed them to take a step back, take a more critical view and probe more deeply into the broader issues.

(Cairns, 2018: 8–9)

It is interesting to note Cairns' choice of words. Media officers "dictate" who is put up for interview, and effectively stage-manage proceedings at press conferences. The sense is that genuine relationships between the reporters and the reported have gone, to be replaced by the information-management techniques of club media officers. The power dynamic between sports reporters and the communications managers who run the media departments at elite sports clubs is shifting, and it would be hard to argue that it is very much tilted in favour of the latter. A strong example of this is contained in a research paper into the Budesliga, the top division of German football. The research paper's hard-hitting title leaves no doubt as to the author's view on who holds the upper hand in the relationship: "Pressure on Printed Press – How soccer clubs determine journalism in the German Bundesliga." Interviews with the heads of media at 18 Budesliga sides and an online survey with 174 print sports journalists covering those clubs showed that both sides viewed journalists as more dependent on the spokespeople than the other way round. Ninety per cent of journalists asserted that clubs' spokespeople withheld information and did not constantly tell the truth, while 73 per cent regarded the authorisation of interview articles as a form of censorship (Grimmer, 2017).

It was once contended that sports clubs and the media both needed each other equally; that they fed off one another in a mutually beneficial and mutually sustaining manner. However, this symbiotic relationship between the media and the clubs they report on is arguably coming to an end (Sherwood et al., 2017). While journalists still need the clubs' PR departments, do the PR departments still need the journalists? Now that clubs have their own websites and social media platforms – platforms that enable them to bypass journalists and produce content that goes directly to supporters – the journalist is marginalised. Are we now moving – or have we already moved – to a situation where the relationship is now parasitical rather than symbiotic, with many piggybacking sports journalists now dependent on their more powerful host?

As Cairns' statement above suggests, the broader discourse around elite sport in Western culture is imbued with information management. The media departments of sports clubs and sports organisations seek to control the flow of information surrounding their club or organisation. Those clubs' athletes have often received media training so as to be able to bat away tricky questions in face-to-face and phone interviews, and are briefed on the messages that should be delivered within press conferences. It has been argued that one of the activities now undertaken by marginalised sports journalists is to lie in wait for such instances of media management going wrong, and then to pounce. The media departments of sports clubs may seek to deliver positive messages via social media platforms, but social media can also be fertile ground for stories when athletes temporarily shrug off the chains of media management and post their own sincerely held views on social media. In this context, Hutchins and Rowe (2012: 90) refer to an "almost ineradicable schism that exists between the individual right and ability of sportspeople to express themselves publicly, and the determination of leagues and clubs to exercise tight control over media comment and self-expression in order to keep unwanted stories out of the news." The final clause of this statement contains a powerful summary of the extent to which an environment of censorship – and self-censorship – pervades modern elite sport. This muzzling of the reported from the inside is an important factor to bear in mind when considering questions of self-censorship among reporters, which we first looked at in the preceding chapter.

However, the narrative of ever-increasing control over player access was disrupted by England football manager Gareth Southgate's approach to the media during the 2018 World Cup. Rather than holding the media at (at least) arm's length, Southgate instructed his England media management team to allow journalists greater access to players, on occasion making the entire squad available for interview at a time. In an effort to break down the sense of divide between players and media, England even introduced a light-hearted darts competition between journalists and players. In so doing, Southgate gave football journalists better access to international stars than those same journalists were getting to players at Premier League clubs. Reflecting on Southgate's approach, Nick Harris, *The Mail on Sunday*'s chief sports correspondent, told Radio 4's The Media Show:

I suspect it's because he probably sees that the approach before wasn't working, there was an adversarial mentality where the players were distrustful of the media, the media felt the players were always kept away and at arm's length [...] The message coming out is that he wants to be more open, to show that players don't have anything to hide and vice versa [...] The access that England have been giving during this World Cup is more akin to the access that American sports gives – get you into the locker room, give you access to all the players, whereas at Premier League clubs the players are in effect in metaphorical gated communities. There's very little interaction. You might get one player put up for a stilted 10 minutes once a week. Some clubs are much better than others but by and large the access is fairly limited and very controlled.

(The Media Show, BBC Radio 4, 2018)

Perhaps, then, the shift in power relationship between sports clubs and sports journalists is less clear-cut than described earlier in this chapter. What is certain, however, is that questions about the nature of sports journalists' interactions with sports media managers, and more general questions about journalistic distance from those they are reporting on, will remain central to understanding the dynamics and value of sports journalism.

Debate

"The sports media and the sports clubs they covered used to be equals. Now sports clubs hold all the aces and sports journalists operate from a position of weakness." Do you agree with this statement? Give reasons and examples in your answer.

Part II
Diversity

This section considers issues of inequality, discrimination and under-representation in contemporary sports journalism. Chapter 7 looks at issues connected to racism and ethnicity, while Chapter 8 considers sexual equality in sports newsrooms – both in terms of opportunities for women and the coverage of women's sport. The coverage of disability sport and issues connected to LGBT (lesbian, gay, bisexual and transgender) people in the sports media is evaluated in Chapter 9.

7
Racism, representation and sports journalism

Introduction

It is generally acknowledged that while the sports media in Britain celebrates successful black athletes and players, it also continues to perpetuate racial and ethnic stereotypes that circulate throughout wider society. Many industry critics suggest this is due to the fact that the "sports media is a long way away from being reflective of the communities we live in or the athletes we watch" (Mann, 2018). This chapter will highlight some of the key issues that sports journalists need to consider when they cover stories concerning "race," racism and cultural difference. In particular, we will examine Raheem Sterling's unprecedented criticism of the British media in 2018 and discuss industry guidelines on discrimination. We will also explore how the sports media is responding to demands to address cultural bias and make the profession more representative.

"Race" and the media: theoretical and critical perspectives

"Race" remains one of the most powerful, divisive and erroneous concepts in the world. As Farrington et al. (2012) argue, it exists as a "conceptual reality, but it is a lie – a myth which leads to the direct and indirect discrimination, abuse and suffering of billions of people on Earth" (Farrington et al., 2012: 12). Racism is generally understood to refer to a range of beliefs, actions and policies that lead to the subordination of people due to their "race," colour or culture (Hylton, 2009). In Britain, it has its origins in eighteenth- and nineteenth-century "race" thinking which came to dominate the political and popular culture that spread across the British Empire. This was based on the idea that every human being was a member of distinctive racial group and provided the necessary ideological justification for colonialism, slavery, exclusion, discrimination and inequality.

Unfortunately, "race" thinking is still prevalent in sport, which due to its popularity, influences audiences all over the globe. During the opening celebrations of the 1998 FIFA World Cup in France, the people of the world were characterised by four coloured giant dolls; Romeo, the European; Pablo, the Native American; Ho, the Asian; and Moussa, the African, supposedly representing the four "races" that populate the Earth. These crude and evidently embarrassing stereotypes, highlighted in the 2016 Netflix documentary *Les Blues: Une Autre Histoire de France, 1996–2016*, came to signify how a modern multicultural society still struggles to fully embrace footballers from minority ethnic and working-class backgrounds. More recently, the Australian newspaper *The Herald-Sun* published a cartoon of Serena Williams at the 2018 US Open, which was extensively criticised for reproducing an old-fashioned racist caricature of black women (Younge, 2018), although the Australian Press Council subsequently accepted the newspaper's argument that it had been drawn in response to Williams' on-court "outburst" during the US Open final and was not an ape-like depiction (Meade, 2019).

Another important dimension to "race" thinking is that it is not confined to skin colour. For example, the Victorian popular press in Britain depicted the Irish as simian caricatures. The Irish were routinely characterised as uncivilised, backward and untrustworthy, prone to drunkenness, crime, violence and terrorism (Curtis, 1996). Blatant anti-Irish racism virtually evaporated in the English media in the 1990s when the violent conflict in Northern Ireland came to an end, but some of these popular stereotypes persist today. Indeed, football manager Neil Lennon reminds us that racism can also mean different things to different people, and that "race" is closely entwined with ideas of ethnicity, national and religious identity. Following the abuse he received from Hearts fans during the Edinburgh derby in 2018, Lennon said:

> You call it sectarianism here in Scotland, I call it racism […] If a black man is abused, you are not just abusing the colour of his skin, you are abusing his culture, his heritage, his background. It's the exact same when I get called a Fenian, a pauper, a beggar, a tarrier.
>
> (*The Herald*, 2018)

Academic studies of racism in sports journalism

In the academic fields of communication, media and cultural studies, racism is usually broken down by type to illustrate that it is multifaceted. Racism can be overt, direct and intentional, but it can also be subtle, indirect, structural and unconscious. Jonathan Liew, chief sports writer for *The Independent*, argues:

> There's long been a fundamental problem with the racism debate in this country: a startling number of people don't really know what it is. Never

suffered it, never been affected by it, never really examined it in any great detail. And thus labouring under the first misconception of racism: that it is, essentially, all about incidents. That it must consist of a single, discrete act. That it has to be intentional. Put more simply: there's an extremely high proportion of the population who believe that racism is simply stuff like shouting the N-word, putting a brick through a window, desecrating a Jewish cemetery, throwing bananas, and nothing else.

(Liew, 2018)

Mark Knight's cartoon of Serena Williams illustrates many of the misconceptions surrounding media racism. He and his employers, News Corp, denied any racist intent and vigorously defended the cartoon (Davidson, 2018), but racism is often unconscious. Even if there was no "intent," the cartoon reproduces recognisable racist tropes. It was deemed offensive for not only demonising Williams but also for whitewashing Naomi Osaka, her Japanese-Haitian opponent. Then, there are so-called positive racial stereotypes. In 2017, a Manchester United fan chant about the size of Romelu Lukaku's penis was justified on social media as an affectionate celebration of their star striker. In football fan culture, these songs are considered by many to be inoffensive, but by definition, they still reproduce racial stereotypes. As Marina Hyde argues in her weekly sports column, research demonstrates that positive stereotypes are usually "accompanied in the minds of those who hold them by distinctly less complimentary ones" (2017).

Racism and racial bias in the sports media has been studied extensively in the United States (see, for example, Eagleman, 2011; Frisby, 2015). This body of work shows that African-American and Hispanic athletes receive "significantly more negative coverage" than their white counterparts (Frisby, 2015: 400). In contrast, there is a paucity of research on the representation of "race" in the British sports media, and the few studies that do exist tend to focus on the tabloid press rather than the broadsheets and broadcasters (see Farrington et al., 2012; Cable and Mottershead, 2018b). Nevertheless, this work suggests that media narratives around "race" in sport follow somewhat similar patterns to the United States. The sports media in both countries will frequently locate athletes and players, often unconsciously, into racial or ethnic categories. The most common stereotypes are the naturally gifted, strong, black male athlete, compared to the intelligent, hard-working, white male athlete (Van Sterkenburg et al., 2010: 831). This is perhaps best illustrated in the media narratives around two of America's greatest basketball players, the "gifted" Magic Johnson and the "hardworking" Larry Bird (*Celtics/Lakers: Best of Enemies*, 2017). Nakrani observed that in the English press, the "pace and power" of black footballers such as Manchester United's French international Paul Pogba is a recurring theme, which "feeds into narrative that follows black athletes around, namely that their primary attributes are physical rather than creative or intellectual" (2019). Stories may seldom mention the racial or ethnic background of an athlete, but they may emphasise certain traits that signify racial difference, for example, the necessary leadership skills and intelligence required to be a successful NFL quarterback, coach or manager, who generally tend to be white. In this way, "unquestioned assumptions about race and ethnicity have been embedded in sports commentary" (Van Sterkenburg et al., 2010: 831).

These studies offer a useful introduction to an increasingly complex topic, where "race," class and identity intersect to create contested narratives in the media, but arguably the most insightful work on racism in the sports media in the United Kingdom in the last two decades has been produced by sportswriters and biographers (see, for example, Barnes, 1999; Oborne, 2005, Rees, 2014). However, there are no in-depth studies to fully explain why countless stories of racism in sport go unreported. On the other hand, the role that sports journalists in Britain have played in supporting anti-racist campaign groups such as Kick it Out and exposing racism in sport and the media also needs attention. For example, Henry Winter reported that English football reporters staged a sit-in protest in the foyer of Atletico Madrid in 2017 when the club refused entry to a black reporter (Winter, 2018). This incident highlights the importance of research seeking to understand the experience of British black, Asian and minority ethnic (BAME) sports journalists.

More recently, debates about racism in the sports media have turned their attention to the pervasive influence of online and social media in changing the dynamics between established news media outlets and online platforms. The agenda-setting role that social media now occupies in sports news cannot be denied. Twitter, Facebook and Instagram have become vital sources for newsgathering and comment. Research on these platforms is still in its infancy, but it does suggest that online racism in sport is fuelled by the absence of regulation, ignorance, "tribal" loyalties, fake news, clickbait and the "echo chamber" effect (Cleland, 2013; Farrington et al., 2017). This places the mainstream sports media in a tricky position. By reporting online racism in sports news bulletins, they can amplify and add credibility to the racist discourse on social media and also perpetuate the misconception that racism is primarily all about "incidents."

Raheem Sterling

In December 2018, Manchester City and England football star Raheem Sterling responded on Instagram to the alleged racist abuse he received from a group of Chelsea fans during a Premier League match at Stamford Bridge, arguing that "aggressive" fan behaviour is directly "fuelled" by the media with negative stories about black footballers (@Sterling7, *Instagram*, December 9, 2018). Described as a "watershed" moment by a number of commentators, including Kick it Out and the Black Collective of Media in Sport (BCOMS), Sterling's post provoked a huge reaction, not just in the United Kingdom but also around the world (Google Trends, 2018). He shared a story about his young Manchester City teammate, Tosin Adarabioyo (black), and contrasted it with a similar story about Phil Foden (white). Both teammates had bought a house for their mother. The story about Foden was in Sterling's view "positive," whereas the story about Adarabioyo was "negative." The overwhelming majority of sports journalists did not disagree with this conclusion. Some went further to call time on the relentless "negative" stories about Sterling. Henry Winter, chief football writer at *The Times*, tweeted:

> This is a big moment for the media and for football. It's a wake-up call. People have to listen to Raheem Sterling on the negative depicting of young black players in parts of the media and the knock-on effects.
>   (@HenryWinter, *Twitter*, December 9, 2018)

Paul McCarthy, former sports editor at *The News of World*, also took to Twitter to speak out against former colleagues. In a long thread, McCarthy concluded:

> We cannot ignore the fact elements of the newspaper industry propagate covert and overt racism. Not against ALL young, black footballers but against those who don't fit into an historic white, middle class view of "knowing their place."
>   (@PaulMcCarthy66, *Twitter*, December 9, 2018)

Sterling's intervention in the debate on racism in sport was timely. The previous week a Tottenham Hotspur supporter was arrested for throwing a banana skin at Pierre-Emerick Aubameyang. Two people were also arrested in Edinburgh for allegedly racially abusing Motherwell's Christian Mbulu, and *The Guardian* published a major survey that highlighted more than two-thirds of ethnic minorities believe Britain has a problem with racism (Booth and Mohdin, 2018). Jonathan Liew (2018) wrote: "What Sterling has done so skilfully, with such devastating wisdom and insight, is to take these two forms of discrimination – the violent public act and the insidious, unacknowledged bias – and bind them irrevocably together."

The relentless tabloid coverage of Sterling's lifestyle choices and alleged misdemeanours had already been the subject of critical scrutiny. Indeed, a few sports journalists had publicly expressed their disquiet about the number of negative stories about Sterling (see, for example, Barney Ronay, *The Guardian*, December 22, 2017). There are too many to list here, but over 30 of them can be viewed in a long Twitter thread curated by Adam Keyworth (@AdamKeyworth, *Twitter*, 2018). They include: "THE FALL OF STERLING: Life and times of Three Lions footie idiot Raheem" (*The Sun*, June 30, 2016) and "Obscene Raheem: England failure steps off plane and insults fans by showing off blinging house" (*The Sun*, June 29, 2016). On the eve of the 2018 FIFA World Cup, *The Sun* ran a front-page story entitled "Sterling shoots himself in the foot," which featured a picture of a gun tattoo on Sterling's right leg. Former *Sun* sports reporter Simon McEnnis criticised the story for failing to include relevant facts: that Sterling's father was shot dead in Jamaica, and that Sterling himself was assaulted in a violent racist attack in December 2017. Ultimately, the story failed to adhere to basic journalistic standards of balance. McEnnis argued that "journalists are expected to source both sides of the story, particularly around controversial or contentious issues." In this case, *The Sun* not only failed to represent Sterling's side of the story but also showed no evidence of attempting to contact him. Sterling did, however, respond to the story on Instagram:

> When I was 2 my father died from being gunned down to death. I made a promise to myself I would never touch a gun in my life time, I shoot with my right foot so it has a deeper meaning N still unfinished.
> (@Sterling7, *Instagram*, May 28, 2018)

His response may have given *The Sun* pause for thought, but as McEnnis notes, they doubled down on their theme that Sterling is a poor black role model, linking his tattoo to the "epidemic" of gun violence in black communities, concluding that their treatment of the story "inevitably leads to social media debates around the 'right and appropriate sort of person' to be playing football for England" (2018b).

Sterling's experience at the hands of sections of the press has been amplified across numerous online platforms, which have reproduced stories about him with a similar negative tone. Following England's exit from the European Championships in 2016, *LADbible* produced a typical example:

> People aren't happy with Raheem Sterling after his latest post on Snapchat. First an appalling display at the Euros, and now this.
> (LADbible.com, June 30, 2016)

Editorial decisions to run stories like these are largely determined by the "clickbait" economy, but it also reflects a much more disturbing feature about the Internet, where search engines, algorithms and AdWords are creating a market for prejudicial stories about minority groups (Noble, 2018). If newspapers and online platforms can make money from negative stories about black athletes and players, such items may well continue. Leon Mann (Sky Sports News, December 10, 2018) and Darren Lewis (*Daily Mirror*, December 11, 2018) that if the culture does not change, black sports stars could simply refuse to engage with the sports media, as Tyrone Mings demonstrated the day after Sterling's Instagram post when he cancelled his appearance on TalkSport in protest at one of their presenters saying black players "make themselves targets" (*The Independent*, 2018). Romelu Lukaku made a similar point, stating that he won't speak to journalists from certain newspapers (OTRO, 2019).

Writing about the American sports media, Andrew Lawrence (2018) expressed a similar sentiment:

> Given the fraught state of sports discourse, it's no wonder that so many athletes are retreating to their Instagram and Twitter feeds, or the sanitized world of the Players' Tribune. There at least, they're free to define themselves on their own terms; they can push back against the ugly tribalism in the arena or play past it. The more they post, the less they have need for the middle men in the press box. And while that's an unfortunate development for ink-stained wretches like me, ultimately it may be for the best. The surest way for athletes to change the conversation around them is by leading it themselves.

All these developments underline that the sports media landscape is changing, but the extent to which sports journalists can effectively challenge deeply embedded cultural and institutional belief systems that revolve around "race" and ethnicity remains to be seen.

Regulating racism and discrimination in the sports media

One of the few studies to explore racism in sports journalism highlights that the system of press regulation in Britain does not protect minority groups from discrimination and cultural bias (Farrington et al., 2012), an issue the National Union of Journalists has raised for many years. The main press regulatory body in the United Kingdom, the Independent Press Standards Organisation (IPSO) has clear guidelines on discrimination. Section 12 of the Editors' Code of Practice states that

i) the press must avoid prejudicial or pejorative reference to an individual's, race, colour, religion, sex, gender identity, sexual orientation or to any physical or mental illness or disability;
ii) details of an individual's race, colour, religion, gender identity, sexual orientation, physical or mental illness or disability must be avoided unless genuinely relevant to the story.

In 2017, IPSO received 8,000 complaints about press stories relating to Section 12. Only one complaint was upheld and only one was referred to the police. Not all of these related to racial discrimination, but speaking to the Home Affairs Select Committee on the topic of "hate" speech in February 2018, IPSO chairman Sir Alan Moses admitted: "You are allowed in the law of this country to attack groups and be abusive about them" (Mayhew, 2018).

Despite this, there is little appetite for reform. Opposition to tightening up the regulatory code is predicated on a strong commitment to freedom of speech and the freedom of the press, cherished principles that are staunchly defended by the industry, particularly in an era when the newspaper industry is under threat.

Broadcasting is more heavily regulated than the press. Ofcom's guidelines state that broadcasters "should take particular care in their portrayal of culturally diverse matters and should avoid stereotyping unless editorially justified." Ofcom also reminds broadcasters that

> research suggests that viewers and listeners appreciate programmes that are representative of the diverse society in which they live. If there is an under-representation, the use of stereotypes and caricatures or the discussion of difficult or controversial issues involving that community may be seen as offensive in that it is viewed as creating a false impression of that minority.
> (July 12, 2017)

Incidents of sports broadcasters breaking Ofcom rules on discrimination are rare. In 2004, Ofcom stated that a comment made by BBC Radio 5 Live football commentator Alan Green during a Premiership match between Arsenal and Manchester United broke its code on standards. United's Cameroon international midfielder Eric Djemba-Djemba was seen remonstrating with the referee. Green suggested to listeners the player was saying "me no cheat." The BBC was quick to apologise for the incident, stating the comment was "ill-judged," but noted it was made during a live broadcast and that Green has campaigned against racism. However, Ofcom ruled: "We considered that the suggestion that a black player was incapable of speaking grammatical English was inappropriate, particularly given the drive to eradicate racist attitudes in football" (*The Telegraph*, October 4, 2004). In this context, it would seem that the best strategy for addressing cultural bias in the sports media will most likely come from increasing BAME representation in the industry.

Equality and diversity in the sports media

Opening the DWord3 conference on diversity in the sports media in 2018, Simon Green, the head of BT Sport, described the industry as "institutionally racist" (October 8, 2018). It was a candid admission for someone in such a senior position and suggests that some leaders in the sports media are belatedly taking the issue seriously. Accurate information about ethnic diversity in sports journalism in the United Kingdom is unfortunately not readily available. Indeed, until very recently, sports media organisations were reluctant to reveal the ethnic profile of their staff, but as the sports media shows signs of embracing active policies to diversify its workforce, a picture, albeit an incomplete one, is beginning to emerge.

In 2018, BCOMS produced a snapshot of the industry which highlighted that there has never been a black sports editor at a mainstream national newspaper in the United Kingdom, and that there was only one black writer (out of 63) employed by the British press to cover the 2018 FIFA World Cup. In a survey of 338 newspaper and broadcast journalists who covered the FIFA World Cup, the Winter Olympics and Paralympics, Wimbledon, the Commonwealth Games and the European Championships, BCOMS found that there had been minimal change between 2016 and 2018, except for the notable increase in women working in the industry.

Women	98/338	29%	8.9% increase since 2016
BAME	32/338	9.5%	0.1% increase since 2016
BAME women	11/338	3.25%	1.95% increase since 2016

Source: BCOMS, 2018

BCOMS acknowledge the data presents only a partial picture of an industry that is changing rapidly. There are no figures available, for example, on freelancers, online writers and the various production roles behind the camera or indeed from some of the big content providers, such as IMG, Sunset + Vine, Perform Media Group, LiveWire Sport and SNTV.

A BBC report published in 2016 stated that 13.4 per cent of their staff is from a BAME background, but that figure includes cleaners, catering and security staff, and according to Hugh Woozencroft, one of their few black sports news presenters, masks a number of historic inequalities in the sports department:

> In over 50 years of *Match of The Day*, there has never been a black host […] None of the domestic sport correspondents for BBC News are black. None of the individual sports correspondents (cricket, football, athletics, etc) within BBC Sport are black. None of the staff writers on the BBC Sport website are black. If you saw the BBC's Wimbledon or Six Nations coverage this year you won't have seen a single black host and, if you watch Sports Personality of the Year this weekend, you will not see a black presenter out of the three hosts on the main show (although the red carpet show is an all-BAME presentation team).
>
> (2018)

Sport is one of the most ethnically diverse parts of British society, a fact that Woozencroft argues is conveniently ignored by the BBC, and he argues that it is a particularly relevant benchmark when it comes to football coverage. The number of BAME footballers in the English Premier League is approximately

33 per cent. Woozencroft says that senior staff at BBC Sport also complain about the lack of BAME talent: "That might have been an argument four or five years ago, but not now. The talent is there. BBC Sport is just not looking in the right places for it" (interview with authors, 2019).

The sports broadcasters will draw attention to the progress they have made in diversifying their on-screen talent by employing more BAME pundits and highlighting industry initiatives to encourage young people from BAME backgrounds into journalism, such as the Journalism Diversity Fund. The positive impact of sports pundits such as Rio Ferdinand, Jermaine Jenas, Ugo Monye, Alex Scott and Eniola Aluko undoubtedly represents an important step towards better on-screen diversity. We are also seeing more BAME sports journalists on screen, such as Jordan Jarrett-Bryan (Channel 4 News), Jessica Creighton (Sky Sports) and Reshmin Chowdhury (BT Sport), but they would all be the first to point out that this can easily give a false impression about the lack of real progress behind the camera, in newsrooms and especially at the editorial level (interviews, October 8, 2018).

The DWord3 conference also heard that the real progress may be taking place on social media, which has opened up new opportunities for BAME talent with online success stories such as Copa90 and AFTV (formerly Arsenal Fan TV). Robbie Lyle, founder of AFTV, currently the biggest football fan channel in the world with over 20 million monthly viewers, argues that the traditional institutional barriers do not exist in fan TV because it is fundamentally democratic and may offer the best opportunities for young BAME sports journalists (interview with authors, 2018). Their remarkable success has not gone unnoticed by the industry, which is clearly attempting to co-opt the fan revolution and adapt their programming to capture these new markets. Sports journalists in the United Kingdom often look to the United States for inspiration and ideas too. The example of the Rooney rule in American sports, where ethnic minority candidates are shortlisted for interviews for senior roles, led to a debate at the DWord3 conference about whether similar "positive action" initiatives could work in the United Kingdom, not just in sport but also the sports media. However, there was limited support for any kind of measures that were anything other than "colourblind." Chowdhury later summarised her views on the subject:

> In an industry as cut-throat as this you have to be there on merit. You've got to prove yourself on the job and it shouldn't be about your colour. I think there is a major talent pool out there, but the problem is the closed nature of the industry means they're not getting in. […] This industry can be so much about who you know, the culture is very "matey" and that is a massive barrier if sport, journalism or both are not part of your immediate world.
>
> (*Sports Gazette*, December 10, 2018)

Barriers to entry, such as the practice of extended unpaid work placements and low-paid internships, clearly discriminate against people from lower socio-economic backgrounds and illustrate that the sports media may have to do a lot more if it genuinely wants a more diverse workforce. Indeed, BCOMS and other networks in the sports media are actively campaigning for sports media employers to undertake internal audits, set recruitment targets and provide greater diversity on recruitment panels (BCOMS, 2019). This is a major challenge for the wider profession too. A study by the National Council for the Training of Journalists "found that while 26% of white candidates were able to secure newsroom jobs six months after graduation, only 8% of their black peers found jobs in the press" (*The Guardian*, December 22, 2018). Most of the big media organisations have diversity targets and a head of diversity, but their influence is limited (Woozencroft, interview with authors, 2019). Moreover, research in the United States suggests that greater diversity in journalism has not necessarily improved media coverage of minority communities and issues, suggesting that dominant values and the daily routines and practices of journalists tend to reinforce cultures of conformity (Nishikawa et al., 2009). The absence of similar research in sports journalism in the United Kingdom makes it impossible to draw too many conclusions on this particular point, but the anecdotal evidence gathered from interviews for this chapter suggests a much more complex picture, especially among younger sports journalists starting out in their careers. Many confirmed that they have had opportunities to book guests from more diverse backgrounds, cover more BAME issues in sport and run stories about discrimination. However, they also reported that they still lacked confidence about reporting incidents of racism among work colleagues and feared they would be accused of "playing the race card" (interviews, 2018).

Conclusion

Academics and professionals involved in sports journalism training are raising awareness around racism and discrimination in sport and the media, particularly around unconscious bias, the use of language and the stereotyping of minority groups. Stereotypes need to be understood, interrogated and in many cases, challenged. With so many influential sports stars, pundits and journalists calling for further change, the sports media does appear to be belatedly giving the issue more attention. Editors repeatedly state that diverse newsrooms are essential for quality journalism, and competition is clearly focusing minds too. This optimistic diagnosis is however tempered by the fact that sports journalism as a career has never been more popular among young, white, middle-class men, who possess the resources and qualifications to break into the industry. It is also unclear whether current recruitment strategies and policies are effective, which suggests more research on this topic is essential if progress is to be achieved. The broader political wind blowing across the Western world is another concern. The disturbing levels of racism, xenophobia and "hate speech," particularly on social media, could be having a polarising effect. The sports media cannot escape the social and political climate in which it operates, but it can inoculate itself by becoming more representative, adhering to sound journalistic principles and editorial practices that actively promote an anti-racist agenda.

Issues for debate

"Sports journalism in the Western world is institutionally racist." Does this statement have any merit? Give examples to justify your answer

Describe the steps you think sports desks should take to make the content they produce more representative of their audience and wider society.

8

Coverage of women's sport and female sports journalists

When Vikki Orvice – the first woman to work as a football writer on a UK tabloid newspaper – died in February 2019, she was hailed by a former colleague as "not just a pioneer but a suffragette on the slow, back-breaking march towards equality" (Howard, 2019). Sports journalism has not always been at the vanguard of equality, but the landscape is changing. Orvice's premature passing from cancer at 56 afforded a moment for the industry to reflect on how sports journalism has changed since *The Sun*'s then-sports editor, Paul Ridley, offered Orvice a job as a staff football writer in 1995. When Orvice first made an effort to enter the sports journalism industry, female sportswriters were called "fluffies" by some of their male counterparts (Khorsandi, 2019). Sexist attitudes existed among the reported as well as reporters, although acceptance from most of her peers did come once she had displayed her ability to do the job. Orvice recalled: "Some managers were inappropriate in post-match interviews but my colleagues – once I had convinced them I knew my stuff – slowly began to support me" (Howard, 2019). Orvice went on to become *The Sun*'s athletics correspondent and became vice-chair of the Football Writers' Association and the first woman to chair the British Athletics Writers' Association (Khorsandi, 2019), all the time helping change attitudes and shift expectations. One of her legacies is that *The Sun* launched a sports journalism scholarship in her memory so that it could find a "young woman who has all the qualities Vikki held so dearly" to join the paper's sports department (Mayhew, 2019), an initiative which – while positive – underlines the fact that women remain under-represented on sports desks.

Orvice was not the only pioneer. Before Orvice broke the mould at *The Sun*, Julie Welch had been a pioneering sports journalist at *The Observer* in the 1970s, having become Fleet Street's first female football reporter in 1969 (Welch, 1999). But in the 1990s, female sports journalists were still rare to the point of near-invisibility on national newspapers, with Hazel Irvine and Kate Battersby among the exceptions to the male-only rule (Howard, 2019). Some women, however, were to go on to establish their reputations as high-quality writers while working in sports departments. Lynne Truss' renowned comedic quirkiness as a writer, for example, was forged while working as a sports writer for the *Sunday Times* (Truss, 2010).

Slowly in the United Kingdom, women have broken down barriers to gain a foothold in previously male-only sports media environments. When Jacqui Oatley commentated on a match between Fulham and Blackburn Rovers in 2007, she became the first female commentator on the BBC's flagship football programme, *Match of the Day*. The appointment gave rise to misogynistic ranting from some of those involved in the game, with Dave Bassett, a former Sheffield United and Wimbledon manager, complaining: "I'm totally against it and everybody I know in football is totally against it. The problem is that everybody is too scared to admit it. I knew this would happen eventually. The world of football is so politically correct these days" (Reuters, 2007). Although the BBC's then-head of sport Roger Mosey had announced that Oatley had been appointed on merit, *Daily Mail* football reporter Steve Curry was having none of it. He moaned that Oatley's "excited voice sounds like a fire siren," adding: "I am from the old school when football press boxes and commentary positions were men-only locations and the thought of a female commenting on football was abhorrent" (ibid.). Such remarks now seem patronising and out of date to the point of embarrassment. However, pockets of resistance to female contributions to the coverage of men's football persist. During the 2018 FIFA World Cup, for example, the inclusion of professional female footballers Alex Scott and Eni Aluko on punditry panels was likened to "getting a netball player to discuss basketball" (Lott-Lavigna, 2018).

Some of the bastions of sporting conservatism are changing, and female sports journalists are arguably helping drive that change. Cricket, not a sport usually associated with the early adoption of social change, is one example. As recently as 1998, the sport's bible, *Wisden Cricket Monthly*, ran an issue that it called "The Women's Issue," thereby safely ghettoising the female version of the game from the male one. The issue was published to coincide with a vote by the Marylebone Cricket Club (MCC) – effectively the custodian of the game's laws – on whether to admit women. Since then, however, a number of women have received prominent roles covering Test and first-class cricket for both broadcast and written media. Alison Mitchell and Eleanor Oldroyd broadcast with distinction on cricket, while Elizabeth Ammon has earned praise for her cricket reporting for *The Times*. However, for some there persists the belief that female sports journalists have to do more than their male counterparts in order to get the same roles. In 2017, as she prepared to cover the Ashes in Australia for Radio 5live, Oldroyd said in an interview that a woman has "to be two and half times better than the men" to get an opportunity covering sport on the radio (Rudd, 2017).

"Invisible women"

In 1995, two researchers published an article entitled 'The Invisible Woman: Female Sports Journalists in the Workplace' (Miller and Miller, 1995). Their conclusion was that female sports journalists in the United States felt invisible to their colleagues, and also thought they were given less important assignments than their male counterparts. In other words, they were discriminated against. The question that arises now is how much things have changed on English-speaking sports desks. Continuing Miller and Miller's lexicon, how visible – or invisible – are women in sports journalism today?

The issue was presented in stark and depressing terms by Diana Moskovitz, senior editor at US sports news website *Deadspin.com*:

> How many women ditch sports journalism because they decide, and understandably so, that it's not worth all the bullshit? Being called "difficult" or "shrill" or "bitchy." The energy and time wasted turning down unwanted advances from athletes, fans, and fellow journalists (regardless of if you are single or not). The "get back in the kitchen" emails; the "shut up c***" tweets; the harassment that comes, daily, from all sides.
>
> (Moskovitz, 2017)

Mokovitz' depiction of an environment of trolling, sexual objectification and the use of patronising and pejorative adjectives by male colleagues is a troubling one. Her account is personal, but there is also research that suggests that discrimination on grounds of sex is significant in the wider sports industry. A survey by Women in Sport, which collated the experiences of more than 1,000 people working for sports organisations in the United Kingdom, found that 40 per cent of women felt they had to deal with discrimination because of their sex, yet 72 per cent of their male colleagues reported that they did not see any inequality (Kessel, 2018b). In the sports media itself, a study that included a survey of almost 300 sports journalists in English-speaking countries found that, while there was widespread acknowledgement of unequal treatment within the profession, male journalists were significantly less likely than their female counterparts to give their support to an increased role for women. The study concluded that female athletes could be "forgotten" and female reporters "tokens" (Schmidt, 2018). There have also been high-profile instances of women in the UK sports media being discriminated against and sexually harassed – although these cases have centred upon the behaviour of interviewees rather than colleagues. Broadcaster Helen Skelton revealed in 2018 that she had been groped live on air by an interviewee while covering a sporting event in 2014. She was pregnant at the time and had felt too intimidated to complain (Slawson, 2018). In 2017, football manager David Moyes was fined £30,000 by the Football Association after telling BBC reporter Vicki Sparks that she "might get a slap even though you're a woman." Moyes made the remarks following an interview in which Sparks had asked a challenging question, although Sparks herself did not make a complaint to the Football Association (BBC, 2017). This sense of women being marginalised or diminished in their role as sports journalists as a consequence of being female is captured in the title of one academic paper on the subject, "'Feeling Much Smaller Than You Know You Are': The Fragmented Professional Identity of Female Sports Journalists" (Hardin and Shain, 2006). Much of the academic literature on the topic focuses on the difficulties that women face in what is often termed the male and "masculine" universe of sports journalism (Schoch, 2013).

Broadly, there are two issues of potential gender bias in sports journalism. One concerns the proportion of women working in sports journalism and how they are treated. The second concerns the amount of coverage of women's sport by the sports media and whether such coverage is unduly sexualised, patronising or in some other way diminishing to its female participants. The two issues are, however, closely related. The prominence of women in sports journalism is likely to be correlated in some way to the amount of coverage given to women's sport, and also linked to the manner of such coverage. Anna Kessel, a sports journalist for the *Telegraph* and previously of the *Guardian* and the *Observer* in the United Kingdom, is concerned that much coverage remains stubbornly, if often unconsciously, sexist. Looks, she argues, are still too often placed above athletic prowess, even in articles that on first read appear to have a pro-equality angle. Such sexism might manifest itself in the photographs used to illustrate a story, or through the manipulation of words by the journalist to suit a certain story angle. Kessel is concerned by the amount of "media coverage operating under the guise of female empowerment" which is nevertheless "ultimately objectifying and denigrating. Meanwhile, sportswomen miss out once again when it comes to recognition of their sporting talent" (Kessel, 2018a). She cites the example of Formula One dropping its "grid girls" – scantily-clad women who stand beside cars before races – a decision which she says led to the sports media providing "many more column inches (and gratuitous photographs) than any actual coverage of women racing" (ibid.). It is perhaps worth noting at this point that the *Daily Star*, a tabloid newspaper in the United Kingdom, covered the story on its website with a photograph of four grid girls standing in a line holding each other's bottoms, under the headline "Formula 1 has AXED stunning grid girls and the babes are NOT happy about it" (Thrower, 2018). A slideshow of 32 images was also provided for readers.

Analysing journalists from the daily newspaper market in Switzerland, one – female – researcher concluded that female sports journalists made deliberate use of feminine stereotypes when they believed that doing so would enable them to gather stories from overwhelmingly male sources. In a paper entitled '"I Love to Play the Bimbo Sometimes with Athletes'," Lucie Schoch concluded that female reporters would conform to the stereotype of "woman as object of seduction" and "woman as weak and inoffensive" if they believed that doing so would enable them to elicit newsworthy information from contacts (Schoch, 2013).

Sexist attitudes among sports journalists can manifest themselves in the questions that are put to sportspeople. A study of post-match tennis interviews by researchers in the United States found that sports journalists were more likely to ask women non-game-related questions than men (Fu et al., 2016). Indeed, the recent history of tennis is one that abounds in flashpoints over allegedly sexist behaviour by interviewers and commentators. In 2015, Canadian Eugenie Bouchard was asked by television interviewer Ian Cohen to "give us a twirl" after winning a second-round match in the Australian Open, while in 2013 experienced BBC broadcaster John Inverdale said on radio following Marion Bartoli's Wimbledon victory, "Do you think Bartoli's dad told her when she was little 'You're never going to be a looker? You'll never be a Sharapova, so you have to be scrappy and fight'." The remark triggered more than 700 complaints and the BBC apologised (Sweney, 2016). Inverdale personally apologised to Bartoli and later blamed the remark on him having been suffering from hay fever. Inverdale and Bartoli subsequently worked together on ITV's coverage of the 2014 French Open (Edgar, 2014).

Profile: Anna Kessel

Campaigning sports journalist Anna Kessel believes that UK sports desks remain dominated by a white male bias – a bias that influences both which sports are covered and how those sports are covered.

Kessel, a writer for the *Guardian* and the *Observer* in the United Kingdom before being appointed the *Daily Telegraph's* first women's sport editor in March 2019, was awarded the MBE in 2016 for services to journalism and women's sport. Through her work with the organisation Women in Football, she has campaigned against sexism, and her journalism often challenges issues of inequality in sport and the sports media.

"If you look at the make-up of sports desks at national newspapers in the UK, I don't think anyone would argue with the assertion that they lack diversity," she says. Referring to research which found that bylines by female sports journalists accounted for just 1.8 per cent of bylines in the sports sections of national newspapers (Franks and O'Neill, 2016), Kessel adds: "Women are in a minority and women have a tiny proportion of by-lines in those outlets' output."

While cautioning against generalisation, Kessel believes there is a link between a lack of women sports journalists and the traditional lack of coverage of women's sport.

"I'd argue that there is a correlation there. It's difficult to be precise about causality, and you've got to be careful you are not too simplistic. I've come across female sports journalists in the past who have said that they don't want to be pigeon-holed as the women's sports correspondent. They've wanted to report on sport at the highest level and that has meant covering men's sport. I think that's changing but that has been the atti-tude in some cases – and you can understand it. Why should only women be held responsible for covering women's sport?"

The preponderance of men over women in sports editing and reporting roles has an impact – sometimes unconscious – on what stories organisations opt to cover. She gives the example of a story from 2015 involving the number one British tennis player at the time, Heather Watson. Watson caused a so-called "taboo" to be broken when she attributed her loss in the first round of the Australian Open to the low energy levels, dizziness and nausea caused by her menstrual cycle (Sanghani, 2015).

"There had to be a discussion on sports desks about whether readers would be ready for a story about a period," recalls Kessel. "If there was more of a female presence on sports desks then that wouldn't have been a discus-sion. That was just unconscious male bias. The matter of who is sitting at a sports desk as an editor greatly affects output. There is still a more narrow approach to what stories are covered on sports pages then I would like."

Kessel says her former colleague at *The Guardian*, Martha Kelner, who is now Sky News' sports correspondent, played a prominent role in addressing gender inequality during her stint as the organisation's chief sports reporter. Kelner ran stories that were often atypical of what the mainstream sports media covered, such as the availability of sanitary products at football clubs, and Crystal Palace Ladies' players being asked to pay in order to be able to keep playing.

"Martha is a good example of how different personnel can affect the nature of output," she says. "When she was at *The Guardian*, it was interesting to see the kind of stories she covered. She gave a platform to stories that would have previously been seen as niche women's stories but she didn't see them that way and they were given equal billing."

While women's sport is receiving an increasing amount of coverage in the United Kingdom, Kessel believes more work needs to be done in the industry to eliminate discrimination in its various guises. As well as more female sports journalists, Kessel wishes to see more ethnic diversity in the industry. Research by the Black Collective of Media in Sport (BCOMS) into the UK media's broadcast and written coverage of the four major sporting events of the summer of 2016 – the Olympics, Paralympics, European Football Championships and Wimbledon – found that there were just eight black journalists filling 456 roles (1.75 per cent), while black and ethnic minority women accounted for just six roles (1.3 per cent) (BCOMS, 2016).

"We have got a long way to go. Even in gender-equal sports where you have as many women as men competing, such as tennis for example, there is a limited variety of people covering them. With Serena Williams, it's tended to be white men, or white women, writing about these issues. There is bias in the way these sports are covered; who covers them has a knock-on effect on the content."

Ethics is a concept that is increasingly occupying sports editors' thoughts, she believes, particularly in the wake of major sporting events that have brought women's and Paralympic sport into the foreground.

"London 2012 was a massive watershed moment for women's sport," claims Kessel. "We had the general population seeing women's sport on this great stage, and people asking why they shouldn't be able to see more women's sport. Sports departments were being scrutinised from the outside about their coverage and I don't think that had happened before. Sports editors began to think about whether they had any women's coverage or not. Initially, it was a bit of a box-ticking process but it's become more of a natural, organic consideration, which is a good thing – previously they would have been blind-spots."

Kessel co-founded Women in Football, a group which was initially set up as a networking organisation in 2007 but which evolved into a campaigning group. A motivating factor in the group's formation was Kessel's own experiences as a football reporter.

"Going to matches, often as the only woman journalist, there were comments ranging from the mild and harmless to the offensive – offensive remarks which left me feeling pretty rubbish. We then became campaigning and public-facing out of necessity because no one else was doing it."

Kessel believes the FIFA 2018 World Cup provided evidence that the group's activities had helped effect change. For the first time there were female pundits and commentators on men's games, while the purveyors of media content with sexist undertones were called out.

Kessel's career has coincided with the increasing power and reach of digital media technology, and she believes the era of digital sport has created an environment of unrelenting scrutiny of sports journalists.

"There are new demands in the digital age, and not just for the tech-savvy writer who has more technology at their disposal. The digital age means sports journalists are more accountable. You are more exposed. You have a wider audience due to social media and digitisation. I think for the first time sports journalism is being scrutinised for its ethics. For years I was told the sports desk was the playroom of the news room but I think there is now greater scrutiny around it. Sports journalists are being called out over questionable things written around sex or race."

Kessel says there is another side to the greater transparency provided by social media, and that is the increased amount of criticism – sometimes offensive – that can be sent to sports journalists from their readers. In the comments section of articles posted on theguardian.com, she says she can be left saddened and frustrated by the amount of reactionary "stereo-typing" of women's sport that is posted.

She gives an example, again involving US tennis player Serena Williams. Following Williams' verbal outburst against umpire Carlos Ramos in the final of the 2018 US Open, Kessel wrote an opinion piece in which she argued that there was a double standard at play in tennis. Her contention was that women were not given the same latitude as men to express frus-tration on court. In her piece, Kessel asked "whether tennis has a problem with women – and with black women in particular. The frequency with which the sport seems to castigate the sex it took so long to equally rec-ognise and remunerate is alarming. Williams, more often than not, bears the brunt of that" (Kessel, 2018c).

The article gave rise to a volley of online abuse. "I did the piece on Serena and did some radio interviews around it and I got an avalanche of comments from around the world," she says. "Over the years I've had some offensive comments – people saying I should do my children a favour and kill myself, or calling me a Nazi when I am Jewish. It does get to you and you learn to get a thick skin. But I've not had what Jacqui Oatley had (in 2007) after she became the first female commentator on Match of the Day – there were letters to the BBC threatening to attack her. Of course, not everyone's going to agree with everyone else's views, but it's unacceptable to bring a person's race, gender or sexual orientation into it."

Despite her diagnosis of ongoing flaws in the sports journalism industry, Kessel is an ardent believer that sport – and the sports media that transmits and reports on it – can be a powerful agent for positive change in the world.

"Sport is such an engaging arena for so many people, if you can use it as a vehicle to have important discussions it is a great way for the public to get to grips with those issues."

The issue of the gender imbalance in the sports departments of UK newsrooms has received critical scrutiny (Boyle, 2006a; Franks and O'Neill, 2016), with these studies giving consideration to the extent to which sports journalism remains a male "specialism" and the way in which gender disparity can affect media representation.

It has been contended that while the "visibility" of female sports broadcasters has increased in the United Kingdom during the twenty-first century, the same cannot be said for women sports journalists working in the print media (Franks and O'Neill, 2016). In their quantitative content analysis of gendered bylined articles in the national UK press around the time of the London 2012 Olympics, they concluded that "the damning conclusion of this research is that opportunities for women to write about sports in the United Kingdom are severely restricted" (ibid: 489). Moreover, according to their research, the problem of gender imbalance would seem to be more acute in the United Kingdom than in other countries. With the number of female bylines in the United Kingdom below 2 per cent compared with a global average of 8 per cent, their findings indicate that "the proportion of female sports writers in the UK press is lower than in comparable countries, with little improvement over time" (ibid: 474). From the period of analysis in 2012 (two seven-day periods, one in October and one in December), 2.3 per cent of bylined articles had a female byline. While there were 2,514 articles with male bylines, there were 58 with female bylines, equating to a visibility ratio of male journalists to female journalists of 43:1 (ibid: 483). However, there is evidence of an acceleration in the pace of change since Franks and O'Neill's study. As noted in the preceding chapter, a survey by BCOMS found there had been an 8.9 per cent increase in women sports journalists between 2016 and 2018.

Another dimension to the issue is how the low proportion of female sports writers skews the sports news agenda. The potential link between the low number of female sports journalists and the paucity of coverage of women's sport has been investigated in the United States by Schmidt, whose content analysis of 30 years of sports articles in *The New York Times* found that only 5.2 per cent of articles focused on women's sports and female athletes, while almost 86.7 per cent of articles focused on men's sports and male athletes (Schmidt, 2016). Moreover, articles about women had a lower word count, and coverage of women's sport reached its highest level in 1999 – when 9.8 per cent of all articles were about women's sport or women athletes (Schmidt, 2016: 282) – suggesting that the issue is not one that is on a trajectory that will necessarily see it resolved swiftly. In a similar quantitative content analysis of gendered bylines to that done by Franks and O'Neill (although with analysis performed on a single newspaper), Schmidt found that 10.4 per cent of articles with named authors were written by women, compared with 89.6 per cent by men (2016: 285). However, in contrast to the data about UK newspapers gathered by Franks and O'Neill, Schmidt found evidence that the number of articles written by women had "increased significantly" with the passing of time (ibid.).

Schmidt, like Franklin and O'Neill, identifies a link between low numbers of female sports journalists and low levels of women's sport coverage.

> The limited and marginalized coverage of women's sports does not exist in isolation; similar challenges exist for women pursuing careers as sports journalists [...] women are dramatically underrepresented as sports media professionals [...] Yet, women remain marginalized in sports reporting despite the increasing number of female athletes, sports fans and professional journalists.
>
> (2016: 277)

Whereas Franks and O'Neill use an idiom of invisibility, Schmidt refers to marginalisation. They would appear to be related concepts, with both studies invoking masculine hegemony as a framework through which to understand the phenomenon of gender disparity in sports journalism. Schmidt states that the concept of hegemonic masculinity posits that "the norms and expected behaviors that are socially associated with men become a dominant cultural force that exercises control over others" (ibid: 277), and that this premise can be a useful perspective from which to understand both the dominance of men's sport and the paucity of female reporters. Franks and O'Neill refer to the "dominant and resistant male hegemony found in sports" (2016: 488), but suggest that it is not likely to be the case that there is a single reason for why there is a low number of female sports journalists. They write:

> A myriad of interlinked factors will be at play, from wider cultural and societal expectations that limit women's aspirations or pigeonholes them in a narrow range of stereotypes, to active choices by women to avoid working in male-dominated workplaces; male preserves can put women off trying to break in. But perhaps also the lack of role models means it does not occur

to some women to consider sports writing as a career option or encourages them to believe it would be too hard to succeed.

(ibid.)

Both studies strike a tone that is at times frustrated, even morose, around the situation of women in sports journalism and sports journalism coverage. Franks and O'Neill refer to their data painting a "bleak picture" (2016: 487), while Schmidt seemingly does little to conceal a sense of exasperation:

Coverage of women's sports has not improved over 30 years and female sports reporters continue to be a marginalized or token group lacking the institutional clout needed to challenge group norms, move beyond male dominated or patriarchal newsroom practices or advocate for greater equality of coverage.

(2016: 292)

Taken jointly, the studies suggest that the view of Chambers et al. in 2004 – that sports news contains one of the "most historically enduring gender divisions in journalism, in terms of who is permitted to cover which sports as journalists, how athletes are covered, as well as in terms of which genders are served as audiences" (2004: 98) – continues to hold some truth. Sports journalism has "traditionally been a male stronghold in many countries" (Franks and O'Neill, 2016: 477), and gender disparity therefore remains a central issue for the industry. However, there are signs of change. Traditional newspaper brands in the United Kingdom, such as *The Daily Telegraph* and *The Times*, now have an increasing number of women covering traditional "male" sports like cricket, rugby and football, and – as Anna Kessel outlines in her interview with the authors – female sports journalists are now shaping the sports news agenda by covering an increasing number of stories from an angle that speaks more deliberately to a female audience. The 2018 research by BCOMS also suggests that more women are being appointed to sports journalism roles. These factors indicate that the invisibility and marginalisation referred to above are on the wane, but there are still elements of the "male stronghold" that need to be dismantled. Some women sports reporters are optimistic about the future. Michelle Owen, of Sky Sports News, told us:

Now more than ever is a good time to be a female in sport. It's still the case that men outweigh women. Just because you're a women doesn't earn you a place on, say, the punditry panel – it's because you know what you're talking about. The biggest challenge is social media because anybody can just pick up a phone. I had a tweet last week that said "slag." Why? You wouldn't say that to Chris Kamara. I hadn't made a mistake or anything, he just tweeted that to me. You get a lot of stuff on social media and I think you have to have a bit of a thick skin and just know that anyone can pick up a phone and tweet something to you – you can't take it to heart. Being taken seriously isn't perhaps as much as a problem as it was in the past because there are a lot of women in prominent sports broadcasting roles, and that will go up and up over the next few years.

(interview with authors, 2019)

Case study: freelance broadcaster Laura Winter

Laura Winter is a British freelance broadcaster who works for outlets on both sides of the Atlantic. While primarily covering cycling, she also covers swimming, rowing, cricket and golf, and her clients include NBC in the United States and BT Sport in the UK.

She is convinced that her focused use of social media has helped her forge her career. By using it as a networking tool and a technique for developing her brand, Winter says Twitter has broadened her work opportunities.

"I wouldn't be where I am now without social media. I've met people through social media – people who went on to become clients, contacts and colleagues – who I would never have met without it," she says.

"In my line of work, I've found that Twitter in particular is essential. You've got to set rules for how you use it. For example, I don't say anything on Twitter that I wouldn't say to an athlete's face. You also need to decide whether you are going to mix some personal content into your tweets alongside the professional tweeting. This can be done but you've got to view yourself as a brand. So, on Instagram you've got to understand who you are and what you want to present. Some presenters sit entirely on the fence but I like to give opinion and show where I stand. I'm passionate about certain things and will stand up for them on social media."

Following spells working in the communications team of the International Rowing Federation and then as a regional newspaper journalist, Winter embarked on a broadcasting career that has seen her cover sport all over the globe, from Oman to California, working as a presenter and roving reporter.

Winter believes there is a difference between the approach adopted by sports writers and sports broadcasters.

"As a journalist you are seeking stories, you are looking for controversy. That's the role. You present those stories using the quotes that will generate the most attention. As a broadcaster, you're more on the side of the athlete and I think you've got to be. I feel I'm more on the side of the athlete than I perhaps was when I was a (press) journalist."

It is a controversial position and not a view that all broadcasters would share, but Winter expands on her position. "As a presenter, you are still looking to start debate. You need to be fair and objective and I always will be. But you're not doing it with a disregard to the consequences. Writers can be quite cut-throat. You want to have an impact but you always want to maintain a relationship. That for me has always been quite a tricky balance.

"If you're working with federations and teams you've got to maintain relationships and as a freelancer you've got to make sure you don't burn bridges.

"I want to talk about the problems (in a sport) but talk about them in a positive way. I love sport and I want people to see the reasons why they should love it too. Yes, sport has its problems, but I try to talk about them in a positive and constructive way."

Since 2014, Winter has helped establish Voxwomen, the first TV show that is focused on women's cycling. "We position ourselves as a friend of the peloton, and we've been well received by the peloton. We go behind the scenes and tell the stories. Cyclists have raised the issues that are important to them. It's a space for them to say what they think."

Winter, who swam competitively when younger, is dedicated to raising the profile of women's sport. Increasing the coverage of women's sport is, she believes, linked to the wider issue of increased investment in women's sport. "Visibility is crucial. If young girls can see female athletes on the television it becomes far more normalised and you invest more in those athletes and teams because you know about them.

"From what I see at events covering women's cycling there has been a vast improvement since 2015. The status quo has been challenged and continues to be. Sky have done a lot for women's sport but all channels and all outlets can do more.

"Sport is still viewed as a boys' club in certain aspects. It's written by men, produced by men, and for men. And if there is a woman it's to look good to a male audience. I think that's changing. More women are in sport and I'm aware about it being done for the right reason. People say to me afterwards sometimes, 'Do you like sport then?' or 'That was actually quite good.' I now laugh it off and you have to have a thick skin; sometimes people will view you in a certain way."

Winter is also concerned by the superficiality of some content that can emerge through the clickbait culture that has appeared on some online sports desks. More depth and detailed examination of sport issues is what is required in order for sport to be better understood by the public.

"What frustrates me is the sensationalist view that many journalists can take – there can be scant detail rather than nuance," she says. "Digital technology is a factor in it. People might now spend a brief 18 seconds on a web story rather than a considered read of a newspaper."

Topic for debate:

You are a sports reporter for a broadcasting company. The ratio of male sports newsreaders and female sports newsreaders is eight to two. The company's editor-in-chief calls a meeting that everyone in the sports department is required to attend. The editor says that the organisation's sports news output is currently "too male" and outlines a proposal to introduce a quota that would require a minimum of 50 per cent of the station's sports news presenters to be female. A senior male colleague objects, saying that the demographic data from viewing figures suggests that around 70 per cent of the viewers of the organisation's sports output are male. He tells the meeting: "If we are to have a quota – and I object to quotas anyway, because they are based on a presenter's sex and not on their ability – then the quota should be for three women, so that the split in the sex of our presenters mirrors the split in the sex of our audience." Do you agree with your colleague? What points would you wish to make to the meeting about the quota proposal?

9
LGBT, disability sport and inclusive sports journalism

Women's representation in sport journalism has been a significant talking point for the industry in the last decade, but much less attention has been given to other underrepresented groups, such as LGBT. Academic study on this topic is sparse, although research based on in-depth interviews with ten sports journalists working in the United States found that none of them had worked with an openly gay colleague, and that they felt sports journalism "would be a challenging career for openly gay men, particularly if those individuals also did not conform to gender-normative notions of masculinity" (Kian et al., 2013: 895).

The first survey of LGBT people working in the British sports media was carried out as recently as October 2018. It found that "over 45 per cent of LGBT people in the sports media are either in the closet at work or are only out to their close work friends and colleagues." This is a higher proportion than Stonewall's workplace survey, which revealed that 35 per cent of LGBT people felt "coming out at work is still a problem" (Stonewall, April 26, 2018). It could suggest that the workplace culture in the sports media is less inclusive than other working environments, but the relatively small sample size (67) makes it difficult to arrive at any firm conclusions. However, the Sports Media LGBT survey also found that 45.2 per cent of their respondents "have witnessed or have been personally subjected to anti-LGBT language or behaviour in the last two years" (Sports Media LGBT+ Survey Results, October 29, 2018).

The survey was carried out by Sports Media LGBT+ a relatively new network group for industry professionals who are members of the LGBT community. The network was launched in November 2017 by Jon Holmes, currently Home Page editor at Sky Sports, where he coordinates Sky's support for Stonewall's Rainbow Laces campaign. Sport Media LGBT+ has established itself as a valued social network and a voice for change in the industry. They already have a mailing list of 300 members and (at the time of writing) just over 3,000 followers on Twitter. The support they have received from the Sports

Journalists' Association and other organisations has "really helped the network gain acceptance in the industry" (interview with authors, 2019). It is also significant that there are more openly gay sports journalists working in the profession than ever before, and that the sports editor of a national newspaper in the United Kingdom is openly gay.

Beyond providing a social network for colleagues and support for people working in the sports industries, Sport Media LGBT+ also campaigns for "fair and accurate representation of LGBT+ people in the media" (https:// sportsmedialgbt.com/). This includes highlighting incidents of homophobia in sport as well as running positive stories of authenticity, inclusion, inspiration and pride. Holmes argues that there should be no fixed rules when it comes to covering LGBT issues in sports, but his advice for sports journalists includes having an understanding of "inappropriate language" and the harm stereotyping can have to the LGBT community. Tone and empathy are important too, but "building trust" with sources is essential (interview with authors, 2019). With only a small number of people working in sport who are "out and proud," sports journalists also need to recognise that many athletes regard their sexuality as irrelevant and/or private. This was highlighted in Holmes' exclusive interview with Ryan Atkin in August 2017, the first professional referee in English football to come out as gay. As Atkin explains: "Being gay doesn't matter in the context of refereeing a football match but if I'm speaking about equality and diversity, then I'm going to mention that I'm gay because it's relevant" (Holmes, 2017).

Stories relating to transgender women competing in women's sport are arguably much more sensitive (Friend, 2017; Magowan, 2018; Navratilova, 2019). They are often beset by identity politics, the assertion of competing rights between women and transwomen athletes and the increasingly controversial role that science plays in women's sport, as the case between South African middle-distance runner Caster Semenya and the International Association of Athletics Federations illustrates (Ingle, 2019). The International Olympic Committee has allowed transgender athletes to compete in the Olympics since 2004, but it remains a particularly complex and unresolved topic given the variation or absence of rules across different sports.

Holmes recognises that many news outlets still approach LGBT+ stories in sport in a sensationalist fashion, which was echoed by one respondent in his survey who argued that:

> Much of [the] football media focuses on "why aren't there any gay players?" The coverage needs more depth and nuance, discussing broader issues around inclusion, grassroots homophobia, etc. I think there needs to be a closer relationship between news and sports desks, because news desks

often put out harmful stories around LGBT issues, which damages LGBT inclusion in sport.

(Sports Media LGBT+ Survey Results, 2018)

Other respondents also expressed concern about how LGBT+ stories are still marginalised in the mainstream media. Holmes is however encouraged by the growing interest shown in the range of stories Sky Sports have been running in the last few years, which suggests a cultural shift towards greater inclusion and acceptance. For example, his interview with Atkin, published the day before the new English Premier League season kicked off in 2017, was the top Sky Sports story that day with more than 450,000 unique page views (interview with authors, 2019). He also notes that the Rainbow Laces campaign – a campaign which sees sportspeople express solidarity with LGBT people by playing with multicoloured laces – is attracting more page views on the Sky Sports website. In 2017, Rainbow Laces stories generated 850,000 page views. In 2018, traffic increased to 1.4 million pages views (interview with authors, 2019). Holmes thinks that football in particular has huge potential to change attitudes:

> The Premier League is broadcast in over 200 territories globally; its reach takes Rainbow Laces to a great many places where society, let alone sport, does not even indulge talk of LGBT inclusion […] To me, that will always be the most powerful function of the campaign – to provide visibility, which can be seen far beyond British shores. It's not the purpose of football to bring about political change […] but the fact it helps to grow cultural understanding between peoples is something that makes the game truly beautiful.
>
> (2018)

This is a remarkably upbeat assessment, given the virtual absence of openly gay men in professional football and the fact that homosexuality is still illegal in many countries around the world. It further underlines that sports journalists will play an increasingly important role in shaping attitudes towards LGBT issues in the years to come.

Disability and sports journalism

Sport provides a unique platform to change social attitudes about a range of issues. One of these issues is disability, and in recent years the British sports media has played an important role in bringing disability sport into the mainstream, with London 2012 proving to be a game-changing moment in the history of Paralympic sports coverage (Gibson, 2012b).

The proliferation of academic studies focusing on the representation of parasports since 2012 indicates that the coverage of disability sport has grown (Rees et al., 2018). This research broadly acknowledges that the quantity and quality has improved, but it is not without its shortcomings. Indeed, studies tend to highlight the differences between the representation of able-bodied sport and disability sport, the persistence of patronising narratives and a tendency to stereotype athletes with an impairment (see, for example, Silva and Howe, 2012; Brittain, 2017; Rees et al., 2018). The aim here is to sketch out some of the critical issues sports journalists should be aware of when they cover disability sport and parasports.

During London 2012, disability sport provided one of the most compelling sports stories of the year as Oscar Pistorius made history by becoming the first amputee to compete on the track at both the Olympics and the Paralympic Games, but one of the more enduring legacies from the Paralympic Games was the media coverage. The International Paralympic Committee (IPC) heralded the global media coverage as the best the games had ever experienced, reserving some criticism for the American broadcasters, who failed to offer any live coverage of the event in the United States (Davies, 2012). Channel 4, the host broadcaster, however, produced 150 hours of "unprecedented rolling coverage" during the 12-day event, which included mobile apps and three dedicated streaming channels of additional coverage on Sky, Freesat, Virgin Media and Channel 4's website. Almost half of Channel 4's line-up of presenters, pundits and sports journalists had an impairment, which included eight new presenters drawn from a nationwide talent search. This included the discovery of sports journalist Alex Brooker, who established himself as one of the media stars of the games along with his two co-hosts on *The Last Leg*, comedians Adam Hills and Josh Widdicombe.

Channel 4 commissioned a weekly magazine programme, *That Paralympic Show*, which began broadcasting in 2010. This was followed up by a marketing campaign entitled "Freaks of Nature," with a weekend devoted to Paralympic sport in August 2011, including a groundbreaking documentary, *Incredible Athletes*. A two-minute trailer for its coverage, "Meet the Superhumans," was premiered simultaneously on over 70 commercial channels in the United Kingdom on July 17, 2012. The overall aim, according to Channel 4, was to "bring about a fundamental shift in perceptions of disability in the UK." Channel 4 argued that "Freaks of Nature" was "part of a bold campaign that portrays Paralympians as Channel 4 feels they should be seen – supremely talented athletes who, like their able bodied sporting counterparts, are set apart from the rest of us by their staggering ability, not their disability" (Channel 4, press release, August 9, 2010).

Channel 4's coverage of the opening ceremony was seen by an average of 7.6 million viewers and peaked at 11.2 million viewers, making it one of the most-watched programmes in the network's history (Plunkett, 2012). During its primetime coverage, an average of 3.3 million viewers tuned in each night, which peaked at 4.5 million viewers for the men's T44 200m final where Brazil's Alan Oliveira took the gold medal, beating Pistorius. The closing ceremony peaked at 7.7 million viewers.

Critical perspectives, terminology and controversy in disability sport

Amid the euphoria, there were some disability campaigners concerned about the tone of the coverage. Athletes with impairments being labelled "freaks" made some viewers uneasy, but it was the "superhuman" narrative where an athlete has "to fight against his/her disability" in order to overcome it and achieve unlikely "success" that received most criticism. These kinds of narratives can inadvertently perpetuate the idea that disability is a "problem." Studies show that social expectations are so low for disabled people that "any positive action may induce praise from others" (Silva and Howe, 2012: 178–179).

Many of the sports journalists who covered the Paralympics will argue that, of course, achievement should be praised and valued, but the IPC recommends that where disability is present, journalists should avoid the tendency to either "undervalue" or "overpraise" (See Silva and Howe, 2012: 178–179). Most disability campaign groups suggest that popular terms such as "brave" and "inspirational" are also rarely appropriate, for similar reasons, suggesting that low expectations lead to a prevalence of "inspiration porn" in advertising and the media (Young, 2012). In a celebrated TED Talks presentation, "I'm Not Your Inspiration Thank You Very Much," Australian comedian and journalist Stella Young says the word "porn" is deliberate to emphasise how one group of people (disabled) is objectified for the benefit of another group of people (able-bodied) (ibid.).

This criticism has informed the evolution of the IPC and British Paralympic Association media guides, which are now clearly shaped by the "social" model of disability rather than a "medical" one. For sports journalists the distinction is crucial to understand. Scope, the leading disability equality charity in the United Kingdom, describes the social model as "a way of viewing the world, developed by disabled people." It says that "people are disabled by barriers in society, not by their impairment or difference." Barriers can be physical, like sporting venues not having ramps or accessible toilets. "Or they can be caused by people's attitudes to difference, like assuming disabled people can't do certain things." Scope argues that the social model "helps us recognise barriers that make life harder for disabled people." Breaking down these barriers leads to equality and "offers disabled people more independence, choice and control." In contrast, the "medical model" of disability suggests that "people are disabled by their impairments or differences." The medical model looks at what is "wrong with the person, not what the person needs" and "creates low expectations and leads to people losing independence, choice and control in their lives" (Scope, 2018). Scope illustrates the difference between the two models with a disabled person approaching a building with steps at its entrance. The social model recognises that the problem rests with the building, not the person (Scope, 2018).

Not everyone subscribes to the social model of disability, but media guides emphasise the need to be careful to avoid using language that may be "inadvertently patronizing" and advises that athletes should be consulted on how they want their impairment or condition to be referenced (*English Federation of Disability Sports media guide*, 2016: 9). As the Activity Alliance notes, there are over 11.5 million registered disabled people in England. This is a diverse range of people and they don't identify themselves in the same way. The IPC guide goes so far as to suggest that "impairment" should be used instead of "disability" (October 2014: 2). Research conducted in 2016 highlighted that members of the Sports Journalists' Association identified a number of barriers to reporting on disability sport, including the lack of confidence around terminology and grappling with the complexities of the classification systems (*Sports media guide*, 2016: 4). There is no doubt that it can be a challenge to explain classification systems without employing language associated with medical models of disability.

However, recent allegations about abuse of the classification system have put disability sport under the spotlight for all the wrong reasons. Evidence given to the Digital, Media, Culture and Sport Select Committee in October 2017 suggested that "some athletes exaggerate their disability in order to be placed in a more disabled class giving them an unfair advantage." As Diane Taylor reported: "Sadly as the sport has increased in stature, so too have the allegations of corruption and foul play. The thorny issue of classification in Paralympic sport has been compared to doping in able-bodied sport" (2017). British parasports is in many ways a victim of its own success, and it can only expect much greater scrutiny from the sports media.

Another important parasport development since London 2012 has been the creation of the Invictus Games by Prince Harry, the Duke of Sussex – a four-day event launched in the Queen Elizabeth Olympic Park, London, in 2014 to celebrate the armed services and their wounded, injured or sick veterans. The combination of royal patronage, government funding, corporate sponsorship, plus multiple celebrity endorsements has resulted in the Games achieving a global following. Currently, it appears to be beyond criticism, but the BBC primetime coverage in 2018 suggests that the sport is secondary to the heroic personal stories of rehabilitation and recovery. Indeed, during the four days of coverage, more airtime was devoted to interviews, veteran stories, celebrity chat and Prince Harry and Meghan Markle than the actual sporting events taking place.

Profile: Gemma-Louise Stevenson, freelance sports reporter

Gemma Stevenson is a freelance sports reporter specialising in disability sport. She has covered wheelchair basketball, disability football, wheelchair rugby and para-powerlifting for Sky Sports, but it is on the wheelchair tennis circuit where she has developed her reputation as a sports reporter. Stevenson covers the wheelchair tennis draw at all four Grand Slams as well as the Masters and International Tennis Federation-level events for Sky Sports and has also contributed to their My Icon series on Paralympian sport. She has also written on disability affairs for the *Financial Times*.

Sports journalism was an unexpected career change for Stevenson. Her background was in musical theatre and dancing, but within a year of performing at the opening ceremony at the London 2012 Olympics, she was diagnosed with Ehlers-Danlos Syndrome (EDS) and now uses a wheelchair. After musical theatre, sport was Stevenson's other passion. With support from the Thomas Read Foundation, she completed a Master's degree in Sports Journalism at St Mary's University and started her journalism career at the BBC.

Stevenson believes that the remarkably positive impact of the Paralympics in 2012 is in danger of being squandered. "When I go to report on para-sport, alongside and separate to mainstream sporting events, I'm very often the only British journalist who bothers to turn up for them at press opportunities." Stevenson recalls that this was the case at the Australian Open in 2018 and 2019. "When I've questioned other reporters back at the press buildings about this I'm met with responses like, 'Well, even if the Brits win the whole thing they still won't necessarily be headline news'." Stevenson notes that the abled-bodied players on the tour take a very different view. "Djokovic in press conferences has even talked about the admiration he has for the players, calling them his 'heroes'. The ATP and WTA players in general have a massive amount of respect for what the wheelchair athletes do."

The quality of the wheelchair tennis coverage is, according to Stevenson, still "very hit and miss." Due to the lack of resources devoted to covering disability sport, a lot of outlets provide only a basic results service, and she has observed reporters do things they would never do in able-bodied sport. At the US Open in 2018, "there was an interview opportunity with one of the British players who had just won the wheelchair singles title and this was an actual question that was asked by a British reporter, 'Really sorry I didn't watch the match because Djokovic was on at the same time, can you tell me what happened?' Of course, the player was incredibly professional and obliged but I just sat with my mouth open thinking, dear god, Serena Williams and Rafa Nadal don't have to deal with this."

"When I report for Sky Sports I try to make sure they have analysis and some really interesting interview lines to go on. The focus is very much on the sport and athletic achievement." In the past, editors have asked Stevenson to lead stories with disability, but she refuses. Stevenson is adamant that the result, performance and sporting analysis come first, "just like you would with Roger Federer, Steph Curry or Usain Bolt. Of course if you're doing a background feature on a para-athlete, yes the disability needs to be mentioned and may be an important part of a life story but in the sporting arena, when you are reporting and analysing results, leave it out of the picture."

Stevenson believes that the British sports media can learn a lot from how the Australian media treat their para-athletes. "Look at Dylan Alcott, when you go to the Australian Open he is one of the most famous players there and he's on the wheelchair tennis tour not the ATP or WTA tours. There is as much focus on Dylan's progress through the tournament by the host broadcaster as there is on Ash Barty, Nick Kyrgios etc." Stevenson attributes much of this to Alcott himself and how he has worked hard to make himself a mainstream sporting celebrity, "but it's also required the media to have faith that he would bring them an audience, and he's done that in bucket loads."

Despite her success, Stevenson remains connected to grass-roots sport and the emerging talent she encounters. "It's where you'll find a lot of disabled media talent working. There are a number of great disabled reporters, commentators and analysts at the tour level events that aren't even touched by mainstream media. I have a lot of respect for them. It's where I started and I'll often suggest to colleagues to consider using some of them in their coverage. They have an encyclopaedic knowledge of their sport and are the real gems of the para-sports reporting world."

Stevenson also believes that disability sport is unlikely to make the breakthrough she would like to see until there is more diversity in the profession, particularly at the editorial level. She also thinks that the sports media need to do a lot more investigative work on barriers to participation in disability sport: "I think the biggest story the sports media aren't covering is how austerity and benefit reforms are stopping disability sport growing more at [the] grass-roots level." She believes disabled people who receive benefits are scared to get involved in sport because they fear that their Personal Independence Payments will be stopped by assessors who may equate being active with being able-bodied. Stevenson argues that "basically no matter what the health benefits, and the adaptations that have to be made to enable a person to play, they (the assessors) see people who play sport as no longer disabled. They can strip them of vital benefits to help with care and mobility."

Topic for debate

"Due to the powerful and positive impact that it can have on social attitudes, disability sport should be regarded as firmly belonging to the mainstream and should receive equal coverage as able-bodied sport." Is this wishful thinking or a necessary, ethical approach? Explain your position.

Part III
The crystal ball

This book has documented the evolution of sports journalism. We have examined both practices and journalists from the past and present, and in so doing we have highlighted the state of flux which the industry is almost perpetually in as it adjusts to new technologies, new audiences and shifting social attitudes. Over the past two decades, the reverberations of the digital revolution – the aftershocks of which are still being felt – have caused a major shakeup in sports journalism. Now, in this final section, we consider the directions that sports journalism might take in the future.

10

Extra time
A tentative look into the future
of sports journalism

It is a crisp autumn day in Switzerland and, amid the traditional baroque interior and high ceilings of the University of Zurich, various revolutionary routes for sports journalism are being mapped out. Over coffee and pastries, sports journalists are rubbing shoulders with data scientists, computer coders and academics from across the globe to discuss a brave new world in sports media. The currency that this brave new world deals in is data – and lots of it. Digital technology has heralded the era of so-called big data, and those who have flown into Zurich on this October day have done so out of a desire to explore just how such petabytes of data can be harvested to make for better sports stories, as well as how to improve sports performance.

Media company bosses from Germany chew over ideas with investigative journalists from the United Kingdom and the United States, while academics from universities across Europe share their research. It is a case of IBM meets BBC meets FIFA. "We have geeks here and we have storytellers here," says the keynote speaker, Chris Anderson, with a smile. Anderson embodies the spirit of the room. A man of many parts, he has taught all over the world as a distinguished social scientist, has been the managing director of an English Football League club, and in 2013 published a book that caused a minor detonation in the world of football: *The Numbers Game: Why Everything You Know about Football Is Wrong*. A grand piano sits in the corner of the main room of the Sports, Data and Journalism conference, pushed to one side and untouched. If Anderson were to roll up his sleeves and have a go at tinkling the ivories, it wouldn't come as much of a surprise. And if he did, it would almost certainly be a tune from the future rather than one from the repertoire of the past.

Sports journalism's repertoire from the past is a rich one, and a number of the perennial classics have been touched upon in this book already. From William Hazlitt's groundbreaking "The Fight" in 1822 to the magisterial use of Twitter by sports writers such as Henry Winter today, there are plenty of fine examples from the industry's past and present. We have considered examples of tenacious investigative reporters, such as David Walsh, whose fearless journalism for *The Sunday Times* helped expose Lance Armstrong as a fraud. And there have been sports journalists who have changed not only *how* a story is covered but also *what* stories are covered; in their different ways, George Plimpton and Martha Kelner deserve honourable mentions here. But there are changes afoot, largely driven by technology, which mean that the repertoire is about to be given a firm shake and augmented in ways which only a few years ago would have seemed unlikely. And, in many regards, this takes us back to the question that this book began with in Chapter 1: how is the role of the sports journalist changing?

Some things do not change. It is of course still important that sports journalists be engaging storytellers who can structure an attention-grabbing article or craft a slick broadcast package, as long as both can be successfully distributed on social platforms. And it is similarly important that sports journalists continue to have the ability to dig out stories through a nuanced interviewing technique. However, those things are no longer enough, assuming they were ever sufficient in the first place. To thrive in the twenty-first-century environment of big data and ever-faster communication we can now add supplementary attributes: an appetite to engage with algorithms and understand how they shape content distribution and audience engagement, a willingness to use computer programme languages such as Python, an ability not to run a mile at the mention of the word "spreadsheet" and the ability to comfortably apply some basic mathematics when working on certain stories. While these attributes might currently be regarded as somewhat niche, there is strong reason to think that they will rapidly begin to occupy the mainstream. Those sports journalists who declare themselves uninterested in such activities – or who regard the attributes as irrelevant to their practice – could find themselves marginalised and even obsolete.

That, anyway, is the gist of much of the conversation taking place close to the River Limmat. Big questions are on the table – questions which pose fundamental issues about the future roles, activities and identities of sports journalists. Predictions about the likely growth of automated (or robot-generated) content is one issue which is commanding a lot discussion, while how best to crunch data in the future in order to extract stories is another. But while there is a lot of crystal ball-gazing taking place, there are also examples being shared of how data investigation techniques have resulted in strong attention-grabbing exclusive stories being produced. Pressing ethical questions of the digital age are also being discussed. How, for example, can sports journalists – and all journalists for that matter – prevent their confidential sources from being traced in an ultra-networked society?

Some of the figures being thrown around as papers are presented and discussed are dizzying. The wall of big data that sports journalists can potentially tap into as the basis for stories and content is huge to the point of being potentially overwhelming. Costas Beckas, a researcher at IBM with expertise in artificial intelligence, states with a matter-of-fact expression that between Wimbledon 1990 and Wimbledon 2018 IBM captured a total of 58,252,751 points of tennis data from the championships.

Somebody who is comfortable with large amounts of data is Dirk Ifsen. Ifsen is the managing director of the German division of Perform, a company which owns the sport statistics business Opta. Perform is commercial proof that sports data – some of it gathered by GPS, some of it by employees watching sports events on monitors – is now big business. At the end of 2018, it had 3,000 employees in more than 30 countries. It collects, packages and distributes data to broadcasters, sports clubs and bookmakers, and has business partnerships with companies including Microsoft, Oracle and Amazon. Its list of media clients reads like a list of the biggest brands in sports media: NBC, BT Sport, *L'Equipe*, *Bild*, Fox, ESPN, the *Daily Mail*, Eurosport, Yahoo, BBC, beIn SPORTS, *The Guardian*. Ifsen tells the conference that the information his company gathers and distributes to media companies can enliven the sports journalism that is produced – although he is also mindful of how too much data can overload the audience and detract from their enjoyment. Instead, it is a case of relevant figures and information being woven into the live coverage so as to augment the commentary and content. "The viewer maybe gets bored if they have too much data. We can support journalists with our knowledge," he says, explaining that Perform doesn't just see itself as an information gatherer and disseminator, but regards itself as fulfilling an editorial function too. "Our expert team finds the story within the data to inform and power the client's content," he says. Opta is among the organisations that have pioneered the use of innovative statistics, such as the Expected Goals (xG) stat. Crunching data from every shot on goal, the statistic seeks to capture the likely number of goals that a specific team will score in a game. As Ifsen says, not every piece of data from a sporting encounter is itself news or of interest to the audience; it is how the data is mined for information – and how it is then presented (for example, through infographics) – that makes it a powerful part of the story-telling equation for sports journalists. Those who are able to gather the most revealing data and present it in the most digestible and compelling ways are likely to offer something that attracts audiences. It is a principle that it is hard to dissent from. In a digitally powered visual culture, audiences are becoming increasingly used to receiving information in bite-sized visual chunks. As the platforms and techniques used by sports journalists continue to evolve to reflect this culture, the smart use of strikingly presented stats is likely to continue to expand. This means that sports journalists will increasingly need to appreciate the power of data gathering and graphic design in the provision of content to their audiences.

Elsewhere at the conference, the phrase "automated sports journalism" is being uttered frequently and sending a chill down the spinal columns of some sports journalists, who sense a vague threat to their professional longevity. Discussions about automated sports journalism are essentially discussions about the extent to which artificial intelligence (AI) could affect the industry. Can machines write some types of sports journalism as effectively (or almost as effectively) as trained humans? To what extent can computer coding – or automation – replace the work of sports reporters? Can software and algorithms perform some types of sports reporting? Automated journalism is defined as "algorithmic processes that convert data into narrative news texts with limited to no human intervention beyond the initial programming" (Carlson, 2015: 417). To some journalistic traditionalists and purists, this concept may sound like a non-starter. It might be objected that journalism is all about *human intervention* in the sense of the application of distinctive and creative human faculties. However, automated journalism has been introduced in some fields of journalism, particularly in the United States, where it has been applied to comb through companies' financial statements and produce basic reports for business content.

While there are concerns that the use of automation could be akin to the opening of a journalistic Pandora's box, there are arguably some potential benefits to both sports audiences and media companies if automation can be successfully refined and applied. If the right codes can be written, then the software and algorithm could have production capabilities that far outstrip human journalists in terms of the speed at which huge amounts of data can be analysed and turned into templated articles. Automated journalism requires structured data which can be input into a code, with the code then translating the data into a story. Consequently, as more precise data becomes available through digital technology and companies such as Opta, it should in principle become more feasible for automated journalism to produce readable content. Moreover, provided data can be received from such games, automated production systems could open up the possibility of reports being generated about hyper-local amateur sports – sports which are often now overlooked by the mainstream media. In a related potential benefit, if automated journalism can take over time-consuming journalistic processes such as compiling basic match reports, or even converting the quotes from a press release into an article, then that could free up journalists to work on "deeper" forms of sports journalism, such as investigative work.

The downsides of automated journalism, at least as it is in its current state, are significant. The content produced by automation can be rigidly formulaic, dry and consequently unengaging. In a word, it can be robotic. Significantly, if the data is wrong or there is a glitch in the provision of the data, then reports will be either inaccurate, nonsensical or even non-existent. Errors of this nature could undermine outlets' – and even the entire industry's – reputation and credibility. Moreover, it is hard to grasp how an algorithm could possess news values – that somewhat elusive ability, as we saw earlier in the book, to have a "nose for news." It is impossible, too, to imagine an algorithm delivering the kind of flowing prose and human insight that a piece by a journalist of Hugh McIlvanney's calibre. On top of this, there are implications for journalists' labour opportunities. If AI increases in sophistication so that automated content becomes more readable and widespread, then jobs would almost inevitably be threatened.

However, this is possibly to overstate the potential reach of automated content. Perhaps what is needed is a more modest position on the type of sports content that automation could deliver. The introduction of elements of automation is not about a revolution in sports reporting but about the arrival of a potential supporting function that could take some of the strain off sports desks. AI is never going to usurp sports writers who detect the nuance of their interviewee's gestures, or who bring their years of experience to bear in powerfully capturing the emotion of a sporting occasion. Data itself is inadequate in these regards. In such instances, sports journalism is not just about the transmission of dry facts, and to attempt to reduce sports journalism to the collation and distribution of data is misguided. There is a need to go beyond the data when seeking to capture the magic of a great sporting moment, or to convey the import of a stressed manager's glance at his team. Where automation could be useful, however, is through the presentation of basic factual reports about sports matches which would otherwise receive little or no coverage. In this way, automation could supplement rather than supersede sports journalists' work.

Dr Jessica Kunert, a researcher at the Ludwig Maximilian University in Munich, has done research into how automation is perceived by the sports media industry in Germany. Her paper "The Phantom Menace or a New Hope? How German Sports Journalism Is Affected by Automation in the Newsroom" found that sports journalists regarded the quality of automated texts as quite low, with journalists still needed to provide atmosphere and contextualising information about the games where automation is deployed. The speed at which automated reports could be potentially produced was appealing, as speed of output was a significant business consideration. Those interviewed for the research were optimistic about automated journalism's scope to write a first draft of an article which could then be edited by a human journalist. However, one sports news outlet, *Sportbuzzer*, found that automation was not a time-saving tool for reporting on amateur football and so discontinued the technology.

Sitting in the late afternoon Swiss sunshine after delivering her paper, Kunert describes the challenges and future of automated sports journalism as she sees them. A key point for her is how automation could require some sports journalists to review how they perceive themselves and the industry they work in.

> Automated sports journalism shouldn't be dismissed out of hand because of ideological considerations of the profession and of what journalism is or has to be. You can still be a journalist when you are using data to help you out. I would say the use of it is definitely set to increase. It's still a young development. It's been adopted on other journalistic beats, such as finance, where speed is the thing that's needed. Speed is what it can give and speed matters in journalism. It can matter if you're first or fifth with the publication of a story. If you're fifth nobody will notice you.

Kunert acknowledges how potentially disruptive the technology could be. "With the arrival of automated journalism, long-standing traditions of reporting are under scrutiny – with an automated newsfeed, articles on all matches of that day may be created at once, without attending a single one." Kunert is far from being the only person at the conference interested in algorithmically generated sports journalism. Jure Štabuc, a self-confessed football and tech geek, has written his own code to produce match reports: Football Match Reporter. It is a title likely to strike fear into sports journalists who spend time doing just that – reporting on football matches. But Štabuc is quick to clarify that his mission is not to make a phalanx of sports writers redundant. "The idea is to help journalists, not to replace them," he tells the conference. "Journalists can expand on what the code gives them." Like Kunert, Štabuc sees automated sports journalism as a means of liberating reporters to pursue less "mechanical" stories. He also contends that a code-driven content producer could spot patterns in results that could be easily missed by human perception. However, it could – and should – be objected that match reporting should not be regarded as being a merely mechanical activity. The best match reports are infused with analysis, observation, intelligent analogy, wry humour and even sophisticated forms of figurative speech. Far from being algorithmic, they are creative. Štabuc admits his first attempts at writing the code for Football Match Reporter using the Python programming language resulted in stilted articles, but that subsequent iterations of the code have sought to ensure that the articles contain more contextualising information about what the result means as well as more natural language. The quality of automated sports writing generally is currently inferior to humans' writing, says Štabuc, but it will improve. And he sees algorithms as playing an important role in attracting page views. "With the ever-ongoing competition between news organisations over who will publish first, the algorithm plays a crucial role."

Computer coding using Python programming is not just for behind-the-scenes techies seeking to deliver automated content. John Templon, a US investigative data reporter for *BuzzFeed News*, has combined his nose for a story with a strong knowledge of computer programming to generate a number of exclusive articles. In one story, he sent shock waves through the world of figure skating by exposing widespread home-country bias by judges. He did this by translating PDFs into data which a piece of Python coding that he wrote was then able to analyse. "Code is important to me," says Templon. "It's really helped me in my work." Following the publication of Templon's investigative article, which was jointly written by Rosalind Adams, the International Skating Union added "national bias" to its constitution, and a fortnight later two Chinese judges were suspended for biased judging during the Olympics (Templon and Adams, 2018). Both those judges were among the 16 judges whose decisions the *BuzzFeed* article had highlighted. "Those were the most gratifying things to come out of the investigation," recalls Templon, who has also investigated match-fixing in tennis. The *BuzzFeed* analysis revealed that one-third of the judges chosen for the 2018 Winter Olympics had recently shown a consistent home-country preference, and that the odds of it happening by random chance were less than 1 in 100,000. Having crunched the data, Templon and Adams then spent three months interviewing prominent figures from the world of figure skating. Their interviews revealed that home-country bias was an issue that the International Skating Union had been well aware of but had done little to address.

The smart use of data to generate hard-hitting sports news stories has been deployed on the other side of the Atlantic, too. During 2017, Alex Homer and Paul Bradshaw led an ambitious sports data project that was run by the BBC Data Unit. Their goal was to provide an analysis of the financial health of all clubs in the Premier League and English Football League. During that year, they trawled through three years of accounts belonging to teams from all four English leagues, transferring the data from PDFs onto a master spreadsheet which enabled them to compare the accounts in a more sophisticated and detailed manner. The finished mastersheet eventually contained about 17,000 discrete pieces of data, and from it they were able to construct and publish a story that laid bare the extent of the financial chasm between Premier League and Championship clubs ("'Closed shop'" Premier League clubs £100m richer than EFL before bumper TV rights": www.bbc.co.uk/sport/football/40717176). One of their key findings that exposed the extent of financial recklessness within English football was that 16 out of 24 Championship clubs spent more than 100 per cent of their turnover on staff costs in 2016. The initial story from the project gained 2.3 million views on the BBC website. Paul Bradshaw says the story would never have been told unless he and his collaborators were prepared to patiently crunch the data and apply some maths. Indeed, he is at pains to stress the importance of sports journalists having a grasp of basic mathematics, of knowing their median average from their mean average. "There is a real ignorance and lack of financial literacy when it comes to football accounts," says Bradshaw, who points out to those gathered in the conference hall that half the clubs in English football have been in a period of administration since 1992. He is hopeful that the work he and Homer have begun will continue to be built on, so that the at times Kafkaesque and unsustainable nature of football finance can be laid open to public scrutiny. "It's more than a story – it's about creating an ongoing resource."

Python coding, spreadsheet analysis and algorithmic content are all technologies that are having an impact on the trajectory of sports journalism, changing the ways that stories are both gathered and consumed. However, attempting to second-guess the technologies that will come to the fore in sports media is a perilous activity, as the sports journalist and academic Roger Domeneghetti has wryly acknowledged:

> So, where next? Who knows; perhaps in a few years you'll be able to watch live coverage of games on the inside of your eyelids and download match reports direct to your brain without even having to bother reading them. Or perhaps I'm talking rubbish and the really smart ideas are being dreamt up by a bunch of 12-year-olds as I type.
>
> (2017: 371)

As well as questions about the technology, there are also questions about the nature of content. To what extent will analytics data about audience preferences influence what content is produced? And will the focus on celebrity and personality become entrenched in media coverage to such an extent that the brand that an athlete becomes eclipses their sporting prowess? Have we already reached that point? Some see the digital age as inevitably fuelling the sports celebrity culture further still in the future. "In a digital age where all sports – and publishers – are competing for media and public attention, and there is money to be made by selling controversy within a celebrity obsessed, expanding 24/7 media network, then one can expect the age of revelation to continue" (Boyle and Haynes, 2009: 181). On this understanding, the process begun by George Best in football, and handed down to David Beckham and then Cristiano Ronaldo (or CR7), will continue, with the media fixating on image and revelations about individuals rather than – or at least as much as – focusing on sporting excellence. Of course, the intersection of sport and celebrity is a long-established phenomenon, and the celebrity of certain stars has not inhibited superb journalism about them. One such example is the coverage of Muhammad Ali by one of the most decorated sports journalists ever, Hugh McIlvanney. Writing in 1974 for *The Observer*, McIlvanney drove to Ali's villa in Zaire just hours after the heavyweight's victory over George Foreman in the so-called Rumble in the Jungle. Granted an audience by Ali, McIlvanney wrote a piece that wove references to William Shakespeare's *Othello*, religious symbolism and gorgeous literary flourishes into one breathless piece (McIlvanney,

2016). Whatever the future shifts in sports journalism, the ability to enter-tain and offer insight through fine turns of phrase will hopefully not disappear. McIlvanney was himself an acknowledged master of such turns, as when he wrote in 1980 of a Welsh bantamweight boxer who died after being knocked out in a world title fight: "It was boxing that gave Johnny Owen his one posi-tive means of self-expression. It is his tragedy that he found himself articulate in such a dangerous language" (Shaw, 2019).

The Introduction to this book emphasised sport's eminent position – per-haps pre-eminent position – in global culture in these early decades of the twenty-first century. Such cultural dominance means the way in which sport is reported and refracted by sports journalists can have a profound impact on what it means to be human at this point in history. Major sporting events such as the Olympics, the Super Bowl, the football World Cup and the English Premier League help furnish countries, societies and even continents with a sense of identity, and the organisations that run those events wield significant power and influence in that process. The extent of identity formation is argu-ably accentuated in the digital age, with information and content circulating so quickly and visually. The task for sports journalists is to hold those organising bodies to account but also to make sense of human culture as it is manifested through sport. Sports journalists are therefore narrative builders themselves, as has been noted elsewhere:

> Sport continues to offer a range of compelling narratives for the 21st century and despite the rise of television sport, sports journalists remain one of the key narrators of that ongoing story. As sport remains a cen-tral aspect of contemporary popular culture, thus the commercial value of sports journalism, and selected sports journalists, will continue to escalate. The challenge for these journalists is to offer uncomplicit, informative and entertaining journalism against the backdrop of an increasingly commer-cial and privatised media system. In such an environment the need for some parts of sports journalism to question, investigate and call to account the powerful within sport and its attendant political and commercial cul-ture will become even more acute.
>
> (Boyle, 2006a: 182)

Boyle touches here on how high-profile sports journalism could potentially become an arena for just a privileged minority, with just a select few commanding decent salaries and genuine influence. Since he wrote those words, social media has in one sense highlighted the truth of them. As mentioned earlier, some sports journalists such as *The Times'* Henry Winter have vast and carefully developed Twitter followings and media profiles. Winter has well over one million Twitter followers, and therefore huge reach. When *The Times* poached him from arch rival *The Daily Telegraph* in 2015, they knew they were effect-ively buying that reach. Winter has a commercial value that has increased due to the growing prominence of social media, and *The Times'* own standing is raised by having him as its chief football writer. The question then arises of whether sports journalism could become a divided profession, with a few "rock star" journalists (with their horde of social media followers) having the vast majority of influence and income, and a growing band of poorly paid freelancers scratching around for commissions. Alternatively, Winter's case can be seen as a liberating and exhilarating one for aspiring sports journalists, illustrating the power of sports journalists in their own right. No longer tied to an outlet or media company, sports journalists can be brands in and of themselves. They can build and project these brands on free-to-use social platforms, and the door is therefore open for talented and tenacious sports journalists to forge their own credibility and status.

The jobs market in sports journalism is shifting in other ways, too. Roles are emerging in new areas, propelled by new technologies and shifting audience interests. In response to the growth of computer games such as *FIFA* and *Football Manager*, for example, the sports division of Reach plc, the largest news publisher in the United Kingdom, created the role of eSports and Fantasy Football Writer in late 2018. Some traditional sports journalists might baulk at the notion of such a role constituting a "proper" sports journalism job. But it is not difficult to grasp the logic behind the creation of such roles. News outlets – and sports news outlets are no exception – are always competing to secure a young audience, and gaming is a major hobby for many sports-obsessed young people. Having a specialist gaming reporter whose work could dovetail with the reporting of real-life clubs is therefore one route by which sports news outlets can attract and then build an audience for the future. Similar roles could proliferate if sports gaming retains its place as a central social activity for young people. Far from being a fringe activity within a sports department, the coverage of eSports could become a significant focus and perhaps even a staple of outlets' output.

This book has placed a significant emphasis on diversity, both in the sense of the diversity of sports covered by sports journalists and the diversity of people working as sports journalists. The two are connected, and shifts in one are likely to be accompanied by shifts in the other. There are some signs that sports journalism is becoming more diverse in both senses, although previous chapters have shown how much work remains to be done. Indeed, there is a risk that in a digital sports media economy which measures success purely in terms of the number of clicks that an item generates, uniformity of content could become an increasing issue. On this model, outlets will gravitate towards established, tried and tested sources of hits (e.g. football) to the detriment of other sports, and content is therefore likely to be more uniform rather than more diverse. For so long a largely white, male and middle-class preserve, however, there are signs things are opening up. For example, Hugh McIlvanney's reference to sports journalists as the "unruly brotherhood of press-box scribblers" (Shaw, 2019) now seems slightly archaic given the use of the term "brotherhood." There are signs of optimism as sports journalism in the twenty-first century edges towards a more diverse, wide-ranging culture. As Michelle Owen, a broadcaster with Sky Sports News, told the authors, "I just can't wait until the time when I walk into a press room and it's 50:50." The tone underpinning this is *when* not *if*, and, similarly, the leap of imagination to envisage the Women's T20 World Cup or Women's FA Cup attracting equal interest to their long-established male equivalents is now much shorter than it was only a decade ago. Sports journalists and editors have a role to play in facilitating this potential equivalence – through their story selections, through their deployment of resources and through their treatment of stories. As we discussed above, it was just three decades ago when female sports reporters in the United Kingdom were referred to by some of their male counterparts as "fluffies" (Khorsandi, 2019). When Vikki Orvice was appointed the first female football writer on a UK tabloid, some of her colleagues thought she would not last a week in the job (Howard, 2019). But just as they have the power to patronise, sports journalists also have the power to promote the profile of both stories and causes. Like the technology that underpins its practice, the social composition of sports journalism is changing, as are the topics of coverage. Change is happening. It is an invigorating time to be working as a sports journalist or studying one of the most defining components of twenty-first-century culture.

Bibliography

Aluko, E. (2019), "Declan Rice's switch shows why dual nationalities should be respected," *The Guardian*, February 14. https://www.theguardian.com/football/blog/2019/feb/14/declan-rice-england-republic-of-ireland-identity. Last accessed: February 14, 2019.

Anderson, D. (1973) "Jimmy Cannon, columnist, dies: Sportswriter ranged far afield," *The New York Times*, December 6, p.50. Republished online: www.nytimes.com/1973/12/06/archives/jimmy-cannon-columnist-dies-sportswriter-ranged-far-afield-protege.html. Last accessed: March 19, 2018.

Andrews, P. (2014) *Sports journalism – a practical introduction*. 2nd edn. London: SAGE.

Arbuthnott, G., Calvert, J., Wills, T. and Goddard, L. (2018) "Blizzard of ski doping cheats." TheTimes.co.uk: www.thetimes.co.uk/article/blizzard-of-ski-doping-cheats-q3ltj2djm. Published: February 4. Last accessed: December 19, 2018.

Bailey, M. (2015) "David Walsh on Armstrong, Froome and making a movie." Cyclist.co.uk: www.cyclist.co.uk/news/551/david-walsh-on-armstrong-froome-and-making-a-movie. Published: October 28. Last accessed: March 19, 2019.

Bairner, A. (2001) *Sport, nationalism, and globalization: European and North American perspectives*. Albany: SUNY Press.

Bairner, A. (2015) "Assessing the sociology of sport: On national identity and nationalism," *International Review for the Sociology of Sport*, 50(4–5), pp.375–379.

Ball, J. (2017) *Post-truth – how bullshit conquered the world*. London: Biteback.

Barnes J. (1999) *John Barnes: The autobiography*. London: Headline.

Barshad, A. (2018) "What happens when athletes do the sportwriting?" NewYorkTimes.com: www.nytimes.com/2018/02/21/magazine/what-happens-when-athletes-do-the-sportswriting.html. Published: February 21. Last accessed: July 24, 2018.

Baym, G. (2010) "Real news/fake news: Beyond the news/entertainment divide" in Allan, S. (ed.) *The Routledge companion to news and journalism*. Abingdon: Routledge, pp.374–383.

BBC (2014) "Nicolas Anelka banned and fined £80,000 for 'quenelle' gesture." www.bbc.co.uk/sport/football/26326484. Published: February 27. Last accessed: August 31, 2018.

BBC (2017) "David Moyes: Former Sunderland manager fined £30,000 for 'slap' comment." www.bbc.co.uk/sport/football/40221090. Published: June 9. Last accessed: September 8, 2018.

BCOMS (2016) "Senior decision makers in sports media pledge to do more to increase diversity in the industry." bcoms.co: www.bcoms.co/senior-decision-makers-in-sports-media-pledge-to-do-more-to-increase-diversity-in-the-industry/. Published: October 25. Last accessed: September 20, 2018.

BCOMS (2018) "Facts and figures" from "The DWord 3: A Conference on Diversity in the Sports Media," BT Sport Studios, London, October 8.

BCOMS (2019) The DWord3: A guide on diversity in the sports media. Last accessed: October 8, 2018.

Bell, M. (1998) "The journalism of attachment" in Kieran, M. (ed.) Media ethics. 2nd edn. London: Routledge, pp.15–22.

Berkowitz, B., Alcantara, C., Ulmanu, M. and Esteban, C. (2018) "How foreign-born players put the 'world' in World Cup." WashingtonPost.com: www.washington post.com/graphics/2018/sports/world-cup-countries-of-birth/?utm_term= .c25acfdaec50. Published: June 18. Last accessed: March 20, 2019.

Binns, A. (2017a) "Fair game? Journalists' experiences of online abuse," Applied Journal of Journalism and Media Studies, 6(2), pp.183–206.

Binns, A. (2017b) "Online trolls mustn't be allowed to intimidate journalists." The Conversation.com: https://theconversation.com/online-trolls-mustnt-be-allowed-to-intimidate-journalists-80531. Published: July 5. Last accessed: March 12, 2019.

Booth, R. and Mohdin, A. (2018), "Revealed: The stark evidence of everyday racial bias in Britain," The Guardian. December 2. https://www.theguardian.com/uk-news/ 2018/dec/02/revealed-the-stark-evidence-of-everyday-racial-bias-in-britain

Bose, M. (2012) "But can medalists write?" British Journalism Review, 23(4), pp.8–11. Also available online: www.bjr.org.uk/data/2012/no4_bose. Last accessed: November 28, 2015.

Boyle, R. (2006a) Sports journalism: Context and issues. London: Sage.

Boyle, R. (2006b) "Running away from the circus," British Journalism Review, 17(3), pp.12–17. Also available online: www.bjr.org.uk/data/2006/no3_boyle. Last accessed: November 28, 2015.

Boyle, R. (2017) "Sports journalism – Changing journalism practice and digital media," Digital Journalism, 5(5), pp.493–495.

Boyle, R. and Haynes, R. (2009) *Power play: Sport, the media and popular culture.* 2nd edn. Edinburgh: Edinburgh University Press.

Boyle, R. and Haynes, R. (2013) "Sports journalism and social media – a new conversation?" in Hutchins, B. and Rowe, D. (eds) *Digital media sport – technology, power and culture in the network society.* Abingdon: Routledge, pp.204–218.

Boyle, R., Rowe, D. and Whannel, G. (2010) "'Delight in trivial controversy?' Questions for sports journalism" in Allan, S. (ed.) *The Routledge companion to news and journalism.* Abingdon: Routledge, pp.245–255.

Bradley, J.M., (2014) "Sectarianism, anti-sectarianism and Scottish football," *Sport in Society*, 18(5), pp.588–603.

Bradshaw, T. and Minogue, D. (2018) "Filling the ethical vacuum in sports journalism," *The International Journal of Communication Ethics*, 15(1/2), pp.3–6.

Brittain I. (2017) "Communicating and managing the message: Media and media representation of disability and paralympic sport" in Darcy, S., Frawley, S. and Adair, D. (eds) *Managing the Paralympics.* London: Palgrave Macmillan, pp.241–262.

Brown, D. (2012) "Do foreign footballers really dive more?" Deadspin.com: https://deadspin.com/do-foreign-footballers-really-dive-more-5957921. Published: November 13. Last accessed: March 20, 2019.

Bruce, S. (2011) "Scottish sectarianism? Let's lay this myth to rest." TheGuardian.com: www.theguardian.com/commentisfree/belief/2011/apr/24/scotland-sectarianism-research-data. Published: April 24. Last accessed: March 20, 2019.

Bryant, K. "Dear Basketball" (2015) ThePlayersTribune.com: https://www.theplayers tribune.com/en-us/articles/dear-basketball. Published: November 30. Last accessed: June 3, 2019.

Cable, J. and Mottershead, G. (2018a) "'Can I click it? Yes you can' – Football journalism, Twitter and clickbait," *The International Journal of Communication Ethics*, 15(1/2), pp.69–80.

Cable J. and Mottershead, G. (2018b) "He's one of our own: An exploration of the representation of footballers Harry Kane and Raheem Sterling," *The Football Collective Annual Conference*, Glasgow, November 29–30.

Cairns, A. (2018) "Ethical sports journalism – the challenges," *The International Journal of Communication Ethics*, 15(1/2), pp.7–14.

Carlson, M. (2015) "The robotic reporter," *Digital Journalism*, 3(3), pp.416–431.

Castells, M. (2000). *The rise of the network society.* 2nd edn. Oxford: Blackwell.

Castells, M. (2004) "Informationalism, networks, and the network society: A theoretical blueprint" in Castells, M. (ed.) *The network society: A cross-cultural perspective.* Cheltenham: Edward Elgar, pp.3–45.

Celtics/Lakers: Best of Enemies (2017) Podhoretz [Film], ESPN Films.

Chambers, D., Fleming, C. and Steiner, L. (2004) *Women and journalism*. London: Routledge.

Cleland, J. (2013) "Racism, football fans, and online message boards: How Social media has added a new dimension to racist discourse in English football," *Journal of Sport and Social Issues*, 38(5), pp.415–431.

CNN (2012) "UK newspaper may sue Armstrong over doping libel case." CNN. com: https://edition.cnn.com/2012/10/13/sport/armstrong-doping-sunday-times/index.html. Published: October 13. Last accessed: July 2, 2018.

Collins, T. (2013) *Sport in capitalist society: A short history*. Abingdon: Routledge.

Collins, T. (2015) *The oval world – a global history of rugby*. London: Bloomsbury Sport.

Collision, C. (2013) "Sucking on the '70s: 'Hey Rube' and Hunter S. Thompson as sports writer." LAReviewofBooks.org: https://lareviewofbooks.org/article/sucking-on-the-70s-hey-rube-and-hunter-s-thompson-as-sports-writer/#. Published: November 12. Last accessed: September 11, 2018.

Conn, D. (2019) "Revealed: the 'dire consequences' of football's relationship with gambling." TheGuardian.com: www.theguardian.com/football/2019/jan/10/football-gambling-dire-consequences-young-men-bet-new-study. Published: January 10. Last accessed: January 24, 2019.

Corcoran, K (2014) "Football enthusiast, 17, with 25,000 Twitter followers fooled the world with transfer rumours he 'made up in his living room'." DailyMail. co.uk: www.dailymail.co.uk/news/article-2545891/Football-enthusiast-17-25-000-Twitter-followers-fooled-world-transfer-rumours-LIVING-ROOM.html. Published: January 25. Last accessed: March 19, 2019.

Crook (2017) "Why Fleet Street is right to fight government-backed regulation of the press." TheConversation.com: https://theconversation.com/why-fleet-street-is-right-to-fight-government-backed-regulation-of-the-press-70874. Published: January 6. Last accessed: September 13, 2018.

Cunningham, S. (2018) "Some media outlets reported the Leicester City helicopter crash like it was a transfer story – and that is inexcusable." inews.co.uk: https://inews.co.uk/sport/football/claude-puel-leicester-city-helicopter-crash-vichai-srivaddhanaprabha/. Published: October 29. Last accessed: March 20, 2019.

Curtis, L.P. (1996), *Apes and angels: Irishman in Victorian caricature*. 2nd edn. Smithsonian Press.

Cycling News (2012) "Kimmage receives UCI subpoena." Cyclingnews.com: www.cyclingnews.com/news/kimmage-receives-uci-subpoena/. Published: September 20. Last accessed: July 2, 2018.

Daily Telegraph (2018) "Colombia try to rattle England by resorting to the dark arts." Telegraph.co.uk: https://www.telegraph.co.uk/world-cup/2018/07/03/colombia-try-rattle-england-resorting-dark-arts/. Published: July 3. Last accessed: July 6, 2018.

Davidson, H. (2018) "News Corp defiant after 'racist' Serena Williams cartoon sparks global furore." TheGuardian.com: https://www.theguardian.com/media/2018/sep/12/news-corp-defiant-after-racist-serena-williams-cartoon-sparks-global-furore. Published: September 12. Last accessed: March 10, 2019.

Davies, G. (2012). "Paralympics 2012: NBC to only screen five-and-a-half hours retrospective coverage of Games," *The Daily Telegraph*, August 24.

Davies, N. (2008) *Flat earth news*. London: Chatto & Windus.

Davies, R. and Sweney, M. (2018) "UK betting firms back live sports advertising ban." TheGuardian.com: https://www.theguardian.com/society/2018/dec/06/gambling-firms-back-live-sports-advertising-ban-bet365-william-hill-ladbrokes. Published: December 6. Last accessed: December 19, 2018.

De Montford University (2017) "Hidden history of women's rugby to be revealed for first time by DMU researchers." Dmu.ac.uk: https://www.dmu.ac.uk/research/research-news/2017/june/hidden-history-of-womens-rugby-to-be-revealed-by-dmu-researchers.aspx. Published: June 28. Last accessed: March 10, 2019.

The Debate (2019), "Sky Sports. The Debate podcast – Ian Holloway and Danny Higginbotham," [podcast] January 17. Available: www.skysports.com/football/news/35611/11610315/listen-the-debate-podcast-ian-holloway-and-danny-higginbotham.

Devine, T. (2018) "Tom Devine: Why sectarianism in Scotland is on its death bed," *The Herald*, April 1.

Digital, Culture, Media and Sport Committee (2018) "Combatting doping in sport." Parliament.uk: https://publications.parliament.uk/pa/cm201719/cmselect/cmcumeds/366/36602.htm. Published: March 2. Last accessed: March 19, 2019.

Dodd, M. and Hanna, M. (2018) *McNae's Essential Law for Journalists*. 24th edn. Oxford: Oxford University Press.

Domeneghetti, R. (2017) *From the back page to the front room – football's journey through the English media*. 2nd edn. Glasgow: Ockley Books.

Douglas, M. (2018) "The newsroom vs the football club: What happened next." Medium.com: https://medium.com/behind-local-news-uk/the-newsroom-vs-the-football-club-what-happened-next-2b07e6d577bc. Published: May 13. Last accessed: September 20, 2018.

Duncan, P., Davies, R. and Sweney, M. (2018) "Children 'bombarded' with betting adverts during World Cup." TheGuardian.com: https://www.theguardian.com/media/2018/jul/15/children-bombarded-with-betting-adverts-during-world-cup?CMP=Share_iOSApp_Other. Published: July 15. Last accessed: August 30, 2018.

Dunphy, E. (1987) *Only a game? The diary of a professional footballer*. London: Penguin.

Eagleman, A.M. (2011) "Stereotypes of race and nationality: A qualitative analysis of sport magazine coverage of MLB players," *Journal of Sport Management*, 25, pp.156–169.

Edgar, J. (2014) "John Inverdale blames hayfever after sexist comments about Marion Bartoli at Wimbeldon." Telegraph.co.uk: https://www.telegraph.co.uk/ sport/tennis/wimbledon/10841556/John-Inverdale-blames-hayfever-after-sexist-comments-about-Marion-Bartoli-at-Wimbledon.html. Published: May 20. Last accessed: September 9, 2018.

Edmondson, T. (2018) " 'Guess and go': The ethics of the mediatisation of professional sport in Australia," *The International Journal of Communication Ethics*, 15(1/2), pp.54–68.

English Federation of Disability Sports media guide: Reporting on disabled people in sport (2016), http://www.activityalliance.org.uk/assets/000/000/731/EFDS_Sports_Journalists_ Media_Guide_WEB_Accessible_original.pdf?1472500124. Last accessed: January 15, 2019.

English, P.A. (2014) "The same old stories: Exclusive news and uniformity of content in sports coverage," *International Journal of Sport Communication*, 2014(7), pp.477–494.

English, P. (2016) "Twitter's diffusion in sports journalism: Role models, laggards and followers of the social media innovation," *New Media and Society*, 18(3), pp.484–501.

Eurosport (2014), "On reflection: The proof that British players dive MORE than foreigners," October 15. Available online: www.eurosport.com/football/on-reflection-the-proof-that-british-players-dive-more-than-foreigners_sto4718490/story.shtml

Farrington, N., Kilvington, D., Price, J. and Saeed, A. (2012) *Race, Racism and Sports Journalism*. London: Routledge.

Farrington, N., Hall, L., Kilvington, D., Price, J. and Saeed, A., (2017), *Sport, racism and social media*. Abingdon: Routledge.

Fenton, N. and Witschge, T. (2011) " 'Comment is free, facts are sacred': journalistic ethics in a changing mediascape" in Meikle, G. and Redden, G. (eds) *News Online – transformations and* continuities. Basingstoke: Palgrave Macmillan, pp.148–177.

Flanagan, C., (2016) "Inside Premier League Productions: The company you know nothing about servicing 730m homes every match day." FourFourTwo.com: www.fourfourtwo.com/features/inside-premier-league-productions-company-you-know-nothing-about-servicing-730m-fans-every#U1yELLlo5kZc56mW.99. Published: January 19. Last accessed: March 19, 2019.

Fondevila-Gascon, J.F., Rom-Rodriguez, J. and Santana-Lopez, E. (2016) "International comparison of the use of digital resources in digital sports journalism: case studies from Spain and France," *Revista Latina de Comunicacion Social*, 71, pp.124–140.

Franks, S. and O'Neill, D. (2016) "Women reporting sport: Still a man's game?", *Journalism*, 17(4), pp.474–492.

Friend, N. (2017), "'I wasn't being judged on how well I could play': Jaiyah Saelua on being the first transgender international footballer," *Sports Gazette*, November 24. https://sportsgazette.co.uk/tag/jaiyah-saelua/.

Frisby, C.M. (2015) *How you see me, how you don't: Essays on stereotypes and representation of media and its effects on minorities, women, and adolescents.* London: Tate Publishing.

Fu, L., Danescu-Niculescu-Mizil, C. and Lee, L. (2016) "Tie-breaker: Using language models to quantify gender bias in sports journalism." Online: www.cs.cornell.edu/~cristian/papers/gender-tennis.pdf. Last accessed: September 8, 2018.

Gallagher, B. (2011) "Gloucester centre Eliota Fuimaono-Sapolu banned for three weeks by RFU for Twitter attack on Owen Farrell." Telegraph.co.uk: www.telegraph.co.uk/sport/rugbyunion/club/8875777/Gloucester-centre-Eliota-Fuimaono-Sapolu-banned-for-three-weeks-by-RFU-for-Twitter-attack-on-Owen-Farrell.html. Published: November 8. Last accessed: July 25, 2018.

Galtung, J. and Ruge, M. (1965) "The structure of foreign news: The presentation of the Congo, Cuba and Cyprus crises in four Norwegian newspapers," *Journal of International Peace Research* 2(1), pp.64–90.

German, K. (2011) "Citizen journalists and civic responsibility: decorum in an age of emerging media" in Druschel, B.E. and K. German, K. (eds) *The ethics of emerging media – information, social norms, and news media technology.* London: Continuum.

Gibbs, C. and Haynes, R. (2013) "A phenomenological investigation into how Twitter has changed the nature of sports media relations," *International Journal of Sport Communication* 6, pp.394–408.

Gibson, O. (2012a), "Plastic Brits row 'unpleasantly xenophobic', says UK Sport chief." The Guardian.com: https://www.theguardian.com/sport/2012/apr/17/plastic-brits-xenophobic-uk-sport. Published: April 17. Last accessed: March 19, 2019.

Gibson, O. (2012b), "Paralympics TV deals break new ground as ticket rush continues," *The Guardian*, August 27.

Grimmer, C.G. (2017) "Pressure on printed press – how soccer clubs determine journalism in the German Bundesliga," *Digital Journalism*, 5(5), pp.607–635.

Guardian (2006) "Armstrong wins settlement." TheGuardian.com: www.theguardian.com/sport/2006/jul/01/cycling.tourdefrance2006. Published: July 1. Last accessed: July 2, 2018.

Guardian Sport (2018) "The Guardian wins seven SJA awards with double honours for Daniel Taylor." TheGuardian.com: www.theguardian.com/sport/2018/feb/26/taylor-mcrae-kelner-ingle-sja-awards. Published: February 26. Last accessed: December 19, 2018.

Hajdari, U. (2018), "Croatia's real World Cup star? The president in the stands," *The Guardian*, July 16. https://www.theguardian.com/world/2018/jul/16/croatia-president-kolinda-grabar-kitarovic-world-cup. Last accessed: July 17, 2018.

Hall, S. (ed.) (2003) *Representation: Cultural representations and signifying practices*. London: Sage.

Harcup, T. (2007) *The ethical journalist*. London: Sage.

Harcup, T. (2015) *Journalism: Principles and practice*. 3rd edn. London: Sage.

Harcup, T. and O'Neill, D. (2001) "What is news?", *Journalism Studies*, 18(12), pp.1470–1488.

Harcup, T. and O'Neill, D. (2017) "What is news? Galtung and Ruge revisited," *Journalism Studies*, 2(2), pp.261–280.

Hardin, M. and Shain, S. (2006) "'Feeling much smaller than you know you are': The fragmented professional identity of female sports journalists," *Critical Studies in Media Communication*, 23(4), pp.322–338.

Hardin, M., B. Zhong and Whiteside, E. (2009) "Sports coverage: 'Toy department' or public-service journalism? The relationship between reporters' ethics and attitudes towards the profession" in *International Journal of Sport Communication*, 2, pp.319–339.

HARDtalk episode from February 20, 2017. Available as a podcast: www.bbc.co.uk/programmes/p04sqp3n. Accessed: August 1, 2018.

Henry, C. (2004) "French judge to hear Armstrong case." Cyclingnews.com: autobus. cyclingnews.com/news.php?id=news/2004/jun04/jun18news. Published June 18. Last accessed: July 2, 2018.

The Herald (2018), "Neil Lennon: You call it sectarianism here in Scotland, I call it racism," December 2, https://www.heraldscotland.com/sport/17197388.neil-lennon-you-call-it-sectarianism-here-in-scotland-i-call-it-racism/. Last accessed: December 10, 2018.

Hermida, A. (2016) "Trump and why emotion triumphs over fact when everyone is the media." TheConversations.com: http://theconversation.com/trump-and-why-emotion-triumphs-over-fact-when-everyone-is-the-media-68924. Published: November 16. Last accessed: March 19, 2019.

Holmes, J. (2017) "Professional referee Ryan Atkin says being openly gay in football should hold no fears." SkySports.com: www.skysports.com/football/news/11095/10946184/professional-referee-ryan-atkin-says-being-openly-gay-in-football-should-hold-no-fears. Published: August 21. Last accessed: March 20, 2019.

Holmes, J. (2018), "Rainbow Laces in review," *Sports Media LGBT+*, December 13. Available: https://sportsmedialgbt.com/rainbow-laces-in-review.

Holt, R. (1989) *Sport and the British – a modern history*. Oxford: Oxford University Press.

Homberger, E. (2003) "George Plimpton – fashionable American writer who founded the Paris Review and turned sports journalism into an art form," TheGuardian. com: https://www.theguardian.com/news/2003/sep/29/guardianobituaries.sport. Published: September 29. Last accessed: July 24, 2018.

Houlihan, B. (2015) "Political science, sociology and the study of sport" in Giulianotti, R. (ed.) *Routledge handbook of the sociology of sport*. Abingdon: Routledge, pp.184–193.

Howard, S. (2019) "Vikki Orvice dies of cancer aged 56: The Sun's trailblazing athletics correspondent had unquenchable spirit, style, class and a core of Sheffield steel." TheSun.co.uk: https://www.thesun.co.uk/sport/8363990/vikki-orvice-dies-aged-56-the-sun-tribute/. Published: February 7. Last accessed: March 10, 2019.

Huggins, M. (2004) *The Victorians and sport*. London: Hambledon Continuum.

Hughes, S. (2005) *Morning everyone – an ashes odyssey*. London: Orion.

Humphries, T. (2003) *Laptop dancing and the nanny goat mambo: A sportswriter's year*. London: Simon & Schuster.

Hutchins, B. and Rowe, D. (2012) *Sport beyond television – the internet, digital media and the rise of networked media sport*. Abingdon: Routledge.

Hutton, A. (2018) "The death of the local newspaper?" BBC: https://www.bbc.co.uk/news/uk-43106436. Published: February 20. Last accessed: March 10, 2019.

Hyde, M. (2017) "Attention (some) Manchester United fans: All racial stereotyping is racist." TheGuardian.com: https://www.theguardian.com/football/blog/2017/sep/19/manchester-united-racial-stereotyping-romelu-lukaku-song. Published: September 19. Last accessed: March 20, 2019.

Hylton, K. (2009), " 'Race' and sport: Critical race theory. Abingdon: Routledge.

The Independent (2018) "Raheem Sterling: Tyrone Mings refuses to appear on Talksport after Dave Kitson comments," December 11. https://www.independent.co.uk/sport/football/premier-league/raheem-sterling-chelsea-abuse-dave-kitson-talksport-tyrone-mings-video-a8677661.html. Last accessed: December 11, 2018.

Ingle, S. (2019), "Court has Semenya's career in its hands – and decision could affect all of sport," *The Guardian*, February 18. https://www.theguardian.com/sport/blog/2019/feb/18/caster-semenya-testosterone-levels-female-sport-court. Last accessed: February 20, 2019.

Ingle, S. and Kelner, M. (2017) "Chris Froome fights to save career after failed drugs test result." TheGuardian.com: www.theguardian.com/sport/2017/dec/13/chris-froome-team-sky-reputation-abnormal-drug-test. Published: December 13. Last accessed: March 5, 2019.

Jennings, A. (2012) "Journalists? They're media masseurs," *British Journalism Review*, 23(2). Available online at: www.bjr.org.uk/archive+journalists?_they're_media_masseurs. Last accessed: March 23, 2016.

Jennings, S. (2018) "The Squawker Talker's 2018 World Cup group stage review" podcast, featured in http://squawka.com/en/news/eight-predictions-for-the-world-cup-2018-round-of-16/1044961#bmZOuTXwy8yM8fGG.97. Published: June 29. Last accessed: June 30, 2018.

Keeble, R. (2009) *Ethics for journalists*. 2nd edn. Abingdon: Routledge.

Kelly, D. (2012), "Plastic Brits insult our Games. DailyMail.co.uk: www.dailymail.co.uk/sport/article-2112899/London-2012-Olympics-Plastic-Brits-insult-Games--Des-Kelly.html. Published: March 9. Last accessed: March 20, 2019.

Kessel, A. (2018a) "From surfing to tennis, sportswomen still face sexualised media coverage." Guardian.com: www.theguardian.com/lifeandstyle/2018/mar/26/sports women-sexualised-media-coverage-surfing-tennis. Published: March 26. Last accessed: September 8, 2018.

Kessel, A. (2018b) "Report finds 40% of women face discrimination in sport jobs." TheGuardian.com: www.theguardian.com/sport/2018/jun/20/report-prompts-women-in-sport-call-urgent-action-discrimination. Published: June 20. Last accessed: September 8, 2018.

Kessel, A. (2018c) "Serena Williams again bears brunt of double standards in tennis." TheGuardian.com: www.theguardian.com/sport/2018/sep/09/serena-williams-again-bears-brunt-double-standards-tennis. Published: September 9. Last accessed: September 19, 2018.

Khorsandi, P. (2019) "Vikki Orvice: Sun journalist who blazed a trail for women covering sports." Independent.co.uk: www.independent.co.uk/news/obituaries/vikki-orvice-dead-sportswriter-football-athletics-journalist-sports-the-sun-a8775746.html. Published: February 13. Last accessed: March 10, 2019.

Kian, E.M., Anderson, E., Vincent, J. and Murray, R. (2015) "Sport journalists' views on gay men in sport, society and within sport media," *International Review for the Sociology of Sport*, 50(8), pp.895–911.

Kieran, M. (1998) "Objectivity, impartiality and good journalism" in Kieran, M. (ed.) *Media ethics*. 2nd edn. London: Routledge, pp.23–36.

Kimmage, P. (2007) *Rough ride – behind the wheel with a pro cyclist*. London: Yellow Jersey Press.

Kozman, C. (2017) "Use of steroids in baseball primarily sports story," *Newspaper Research Journal*, 38(1), pp.46–61.

Knight, M. and Cook, C. (2015) *Social media for journalists: Principles and practice*. London: Sage.

Lacey, D. (1985), *The Guardian*, May 29. *https://www.lfchistory.net/Articles/Article/665*. Last accessed: April 15, 2015.

Lambert, C.M. (2018) *Digital sports journalism*. Abingdon: Routledge.

Lavric, E., Pisek, G., Skinner, A.C. and Stadler, W. (2008) *The linguistics of football.* Tübingen: Gunter Narr Verlag.

Lawrence, A. (2018), "How the 'natural talent' myth is used as a weapon against black athletes," *The Guardian*, October 2. https://www.theguardian.com/sport/2018/oct/02/athletes-racism-language-sports-cam-newton. Last accessed: December 10, 2018.

Liew, J. (2018) "If we're serious about football being a force for good then we need to talk about racism all the time," *The Independent*, December 14. https://www.independent.co.uk/sport/football/news-and-comment/racism-in-football-raheem-sterling-racist-abuse-premier-league-jonathan-liew-a8683526.html. Last accessed: December 14, 2018.

Linford, P. (2018) www.holdthefrontpage.co.uk/2018/news/brighton-daily-tops-circulation-league-table-as-latest-abcs-unveiled/. Published: August 30. Last accessed: August 30, 2018.

Lott-Lavigna, R. (2018) "Complaining about female World Cup commentators only exposes your real attitude to women." NewStatesman.com: www.newstatesman.com/politics/sport/2018/06/female-world-cup-women-commentators-eni-aluko-alex-scott-simon-kelner-sexist-football. Published: June 22. Last accessed: March 10, 2019.

Luckhurst, T. and Phippen, L. (2014) "Good behaviour can be taught," *British Journalism Review*, 25, pp.56–61.

MacKenzie, K. (2016) "Sports mafia that's kept Big Sam's secrets safe for years," *The Sun*, September 30, p.13.

Magowan, A. (2018) "Transgender women in sport: Are they really a 'threat' to female sport?" BBC: www.bbc.co.uk/sport/46453958. Published: December 18. Last accessed: March 20, 2019.

Malone, E. (2013) "O'Neill has track record in law courts." IrishTimes.com: www.irishtimes.com/sport/soccer/international/o-neill-has-track-record-in-law-courts-1.1528182. Published: September 14. Last accessed: July 5, 2018.

Mann, L. (2018), https://www.connectsport.co.uk/news/journalists-organisations-support-connectsport. Last accessed: January 15, 2019.

Marsh, K. (2012) "Issues of impartiality in news and current affairs," *Journal of Applied Journalism and Media Studies*, 1(1) pp.69–78.

Mayhew, F. (2018), "IPSO has upheld one out of more than 8,000 discrimination complaints but its chairman says a 'balance has to be struck'," *Press Gazette*, February 26 https://www.pressgazette.co.uk/ipso-has-upheld-one-out-of-more-than-8000-discrimination-complaints-but-its-chairman-says-a-balance-has-to-be-struck/. Last accessed: February 27, 2018.

Mayhew, F. (2019) "Sun launches sports journalism scholarship in memory of 'trailblazer' Vikki Orvice." PressGazette.co.uk: https://pressgazette.co.uk/sun-launches-sports-journalism-scholarship-in-memory-of-trailblazer-vikki-orvice/. Published: February 6. Last accessed: March 10, 2019.

McEnnis, S. (2013) "Raising our game: Effects of citizen journalism on Twitter for professional identity and working practices of British sport journalists," *International Journal of Sport Communication*, 6, pp.423–433.

McEnnis, S. (2015) "Following the action: How live bloggers are reimagining the professional ideology of sports journalism," *Journalism Practice*, 10(8), pp.967–982.

McEnnis, S. (2017) "Playing on the same pitch – attitudes of sports journalists towards fan bloggers," *Digital Journalism*, 5(5), pp.549–566.

McEnnis, S. (2018a) "A comparative analysis of how regulatory codes inform broadcast and print sports journalists' work routines in the UK using *Sky Sports News* and the *Sun* as case studies," *The International Journal of Communication Ethics*, 15(1/2), pp.43–53.

McEnnis, S. (2018b) "The Sun's ethical failings over the Raheem Sterling gun tattoo story." TheConversation.com: https://theconversation.com/the-suns-ethical-failings-over-the-raheem-sterling-gun-tattoo-story-97469. Published: May 30. Last accessed: March 19, 2019.

McGuire, J. and Murray, R. (2016) "New work demands create inequity for sports journalists," *Newspaper Research Journal*, 37(1), pp.58–69.

McIlvanney, H. (2016) "From the vault: Hugh McIlvanney meets Muhammad Ali, hours after Rumble in the Juggle." TheGuardian.com: www.theguardian.com/sport/2016/mar/05/hugh-mcilvanney-muhammad-ali-rumble-in-the-jungle. Published: March 5. Last accessed: February 14, 2019.

McKay, F. (2010) "On doping and David Walsh": www.podiumcafe.com/2010/11/10/1805511/on-doping-and-david-walsh. Published: November 10. Last accessed: March 19, 2019.

McKie, J. (2005) *Daily Record*, January 1, quoted in Bradley, J.M. (2015) "Sectarianism, anti-sectarianism and Scottish football," *Sport in Society*, 18(5), pp.588–603.

Meade, A. (2019) "Serena Williams cartoon not racist, Australian media watchdog rules." TheGuardian.com: www.theguardian.com/sport/2019/feb/25/serena-williams-cartoon-not-racist-australian-media-watchdog-rules. Published: February 24. Last accessed: March 10, 2019.

The Media Show, BBC Radio 4. First broadcast July 4, 2018. Available online: www.bbc.co.uk/programmes/b0b85m94. Last accessed: July 7, 2018.

Miller, M.E. (2015) "How a curmudgeonly old reporter exposed the FIFA scandal that toppled Sepp Blatter." WashingtonPost.com: www.washingtonpost.com/news/morning-mix/wp/2015/06/03/how-a-curmudgeonly-old-reporter-exposed-the-fifa-scandal-that-toppled-sepp-blatter/. Published: June 3. Last accessed: March 23, 2017.

Miller, P. and Miller, R. (1995) "The invisible woman: Female sports journalists in the workplace," *Journalism & Mass Communication Quarterly*, 72(4), pp.883–889.

Mirror Football (2011) "Martin O'Neill: Apology." Mirror.co.uk: www.mirror.co.uk/sport/football/news/martin-oneill-apology-24-june-3318722. Published: August 8, updated March 31, 2014. Last accessed: July 5, 2018.

Mitchell, K. (2016) "Hugh McIlvanney has been the master craftsman of our magnificent triviality." TheGuardian.com: www.theguardian.com/sport/2016/mar/05/hugh-mcilvanney-sport-writer-retires-observer-sunday-times-boxing-horse-racing. Published: March 5. Last accessed: March 19, 2019.

mlb.com (n.d.) "Standard Stats": http://m.mlb.com/glossary/standard-stats. Last accessed: June 30, 2018.

Morrison, S. (2014) "The toy department shall lead us – why sports media have always been newsroom innovators" in *Columbia Journalism Review*, 53(2), pp.16–18. Also available at: http://www.cjr.org/reports/the_toy_department_shall_lead.php. Last accessed: August 25, 2016.

Moskovitz, D. (2017) "Women in sports journalism are still putting up with a lot of bullshit." Deadspin.com: https://deadspin.com/women-in-sports-journalism-are-still-putting-up-with-a-1821584038. Published: December 26. Last accessed: September 8, 2018.

Nakrani, S. (2019) "Paul Pogba's 'pace and power' stresses need for rethink over BAME coverage." The Guardian.com: https://www.theguardian.com/football/2019/jan/21/paul-pogba-pace-power-rethink-bame-coverage Published: January 21. Last accessed: March 20, 2019.

Navratilova, M. (2019) "The rules on trans athletes reward cheats and punish the innocent," *The Sunday Times*, February 17.

Nil by Mouth (2018) "What is sectarianism?" Online: https://nilbymouth.org/what-is-sectarianism/.

Nishikawa, K.A., Towner, T.L., Clawson, R.A. and Waltenburg, E.N. (2009) "Interviewing the interviewers: Journalistic norms and racial diversity in the newsroom," *Howard Journal of Communications*, 20(3), pp.242–259.

Noble, S., (2018), *Algorithms of oppression: How search engines reinforce racism*. New York: New York University Press.

Norris, B. (2000) "Media ethics at the sharp end" in Berry, D. (ed.) *Ethics and media culture: Practices and representations*. Oxford: Focal Press, pp.325–338.

"NUJ demands IPSO inquiry on press racism," (2017) Press Release, August 16 https://www.nuj.org.uk/news/nuj-demands-ipso-inquiry-on-press-racism/.   Last accessed: January 16, 2019.

Oborne, P. (2005) *Basil D'Oliveira: Cricket and controversy.* London: Sphere.

Orwell, G., (1945) "The sporting spirit," *Tribune,* London, reprinted in *The Collected Essays, Journalism and Letters of George Orwell* (1968).

OTRO (2019), "You all know who you are: Romelu Lukaku speaks out on racism in the media," [video], *The Guardian,* March 4. https://www.theguardian.com/football/video/2019/mar/04/you-all-know-who-you-are-romelu-lukaku-speaks-out-on-racism-in-the-media-video. Last accessed: March 4, 2019.

Plunkett, J. (2012). "Paralympics opening ceremony attracts almost 8m viewers." *The Guardian.* August 30. https://www.theguardian.com/media/2012/aug/30/paralympics-opening-ceremony-8m-viewers. Last accessed: September 15, 2012.

Ponsford, D. (2010) "Andrew Jennings: We have world's worst sport reporters." PressGazette.co.uk: www.pressgazette.co.uk/node/46398. Published: December 7. Last accessed: March 23, 2016.

Preston, P. (2009) *Making the News – Journalism and news cultures in Europe.* Abingdon : Routledge.

Pugh, A. (2012a) "David Walsh: 'It was obvious to me Lance Armstrong was doping'." PressGazette.co.uk: www.pressgazette.co.uk/david-walsh-it-was-obvious-me-lance-armstrong-was-doping/. Published: October 11. Last accessed: July 20, 2018.

Pugh, A. (2012b) "Twitter ban at Redknapp trial after reporter names juror." PressGazette.co.uk: www.pressgazette.co.uk/twitter-ban-at-redknapp-trial-after-reporter-names-juror/. Published: January 25. Last accessed: February 14, 2019.

Rada, J.A. (1996) "Color blind-sided: Racial bias in network television's coverage of professional football games," *Howard Journal of Communications,* 7(3), pp.231–239.

Rajan, A. (2018) *The Tortoise and the share.* Available online: www.bbc.co.uk/news/entertainment-arts-43230640. Published: March 5. Last accessed: April 5, 2018.

Ralston, G. (2019) "Steve Clarke in Rangers sectarian blast over 'sad f****n b*****d' fans' chants," *Daily Record,* February 21. https://www.dailyrecord.co.uk/sport/football/football-news/steve-clarke-rangers-sectarian-blast-14029236.   Last accessed: February 22, 2019.

Ramon-Vegas, X. and Rojas-Torrijos, J-L. (2018) "Accountable sports journalism. Building up a platform and a new specialised code in the field," *The International Journal of Communication Ethics,* 15(1/2), pp.15–28.

Rees, P. (2014) *The three degrees: The men who changed British football forever.* London: Constable.

Rees, L., Robinson, P. and Shields, N. (2018) "A major sporting event or an entertainment show? A content analysis of Australian television coverage of the 2016 Olympic and Paralympic Games," *Sport in Society*, 21(12), pp.1974–1989.

Reuters (2007) "'Match of the Day' gets first woman commentator." https://uk.reuters.com/article/uk-britain-match-commentator/match-of-the-day-gets-first-woman-commentator-idUKL198437520070419. Published: April 19. Last accessed: March 10, 2019.

Roberts, C. and Emmons, B. (2016) "Twitter in the press box: How a new technology affects game-day routines of print-focused sports journalists," *International Journal of Sport Communication*, 9, pp.97–115.

Ronay, B. (2017), "How Raheem Sterling was made into an easy target for gathered intangible rage," *The Guardian*, December 22. https://www.theguardian.com/football/blog/2017/dec/22/why-we-should-take-our-hats-off-to-raheem-sterling. Last accessed: December 10, 2018.

Rowe, D. (2005) "Fourth estate or fan club? Sports journalism engages the popular" in Allan, S. (ed.). *Journalism: Critical Issues*, Maidenhead: Open University Press, pp.125–136.

Rowe, D. (2007) "Sports journalism – Still the 'toy department' of the news media?", *Journalism*, 8(4), pp.384–405.

Rowe, D. and Hutchins, B. (2013) "Introduction – sport in the network society and why it matters" in Hutchins, B. and D. Rowe, D. (eds) *Digital media sport – technology, power and culture in the network society*. Abingdon: Routledge, pp.1–18.

Rowe, D. and Hutchins, B. (2014) "Globalization and online audiences" in Billings, A.C. and Hardin, M. (eds) *Routledge handbook of sport and new media*. Abingdon: Routledge, pp.7–18.

Rudd, A. (2017) "Eleanor Oldroyd: You have to be two and a half times better than the men." TheTimes.com: www.thetimes.co.uk/article/eleanor-oldroyd-you-have-to-be-two-and-a-half-times-better-than-the-men-vmzfgwjf9. Published: November 11. Last accessed: March 10, 2019.

Sambrook, R. (2012) "Delivering trust: Impartiality and objectivity in the digital age." Reuters Institute for the Study of Journalism. Published: July 2012. Available online: http://orca.cf.ac.uk/33772/1/Delivering_Trust_Impartiality_and_Objectivity_in_a_Digital_Age.pdf. Last accessed: March 21, 2018.

Samuel, M. (2018) "Sunday Supplement podcast," Sky Sports, September 9. Available: www.skysports.com/podcasts/sunday-supplement.

Samuel, M. (2019) "Republic of Ireland are the predators here ... Declan Rice is no turncoat for choosing to play for England," DailyMail.co.uk: www.dailymail.co.uk/sport/football/article-6706439/Ireland-predators-Rice-no-turncoat-choosing-England.html Published: February 15. Last accessed: March 20, 2019.

Sandomir, R. (2004) "Cycling; Armstrong is suing accuser." NYTimes.com: www.nytimes.com/2004/06/16/sports/cycling-armstrong-is-suing-accuser.html. Published: June 16. Last accessed: July 2, 2018.

Sanghani, R. (2015) "The last taboo in sport: 'I have nightmares about getting my period at Wimbledon'." Telegraph.co.uk: www.telegraph.co.uk/women/womens-life/11359785/Periods-in-sport-I-worry-about-getting-mine-at-Wimbledon..html. Published: January 21. Last accessed: September 19, 2018.

Schmidt, H.C. (2016) "Women's sports coverage remains largely marginalized," *Newspaper Research Journal*, 37(3), pp.275–298.

Schmidt, H.C. (2018) "Forgotten athletes and token reporters: Analyzing the gender bias in sports journalism," *Atlantic Journal of Communications*, 26(1) pp.59–74.

Schoch, L. (2013) "'I love to play the bimbo sometimes with athletes' – the role of professional interactions between female sports journalists and their male sources in the production of sports reports," *Journalism Practice*, 7(1) pp.96–111.

Schudson, M. (2001) "The objectivity norm in American journalism," *Journalism*, 2(2): pp.149–170.

Scope (2018), "Social model of disability," https://www.scope.org.uk/about-us/social-model-of-disability. Last accessed: November 5, 2018.

Scott-Elliot, R. (2013), "Jack Wilshere and Kevin Pietersen go head to head over definition of 'foreigners' in debate over Adnan Januzaj." TheIndependent.co.uk: www.independent.co.uk/sport/football/international/jack-wilshere-and-kevin-pietersen-go-head-to-head-over-definition-of-foreigners-in-debate-over-adnan-8869944.html Published: October 10. Last accessed: March 20, 2019.

Schultz, I. (2007) "The journalistic gut feeling – journalistic doxa, news habitus and orthodox news values," *Journalism Practice*, 1(2), pp.190–207.

Sefiha, O. (2010) "Now's when we throw him under the bus: Institutional and occupational identities and the coverage of doping in sport," *Sociology of Sport Journal*, 27, pp.200–218.

Shaw, P. (2019) "Hugh McIlvanney: A trailblazer whose dazzling imagery made him one of the greatest sports journalists." TheIndependent.co.uk: www.independent.co.uk/news/obituaries/hugh-mcilvanney-obituary-sports-journalism-george-best-muhammad-ali-pele-a8746056.html. Published: January 25. Last accessed: February 14, 2019.

Sheffer, M. and Schultz, B. (2010) "Paradigm shift or passing fad? Twitter and sports journalism," *International Journal of Sport Communication*, 3, pp.472–484.

Sherwood, M. and Nicholson, M. (2012) "Web 2.0 platforms and the work of newspaper sports journalists," *Journalism* 14(7), pp.942–959.

Sherwood, M., Nicholson, M. and Marjoribanks, T. (2017) "Controlling the message and the medium? – the impact of sports organisations' digital and social channels on media access," *Digital Journalism*, 5(5), pp.513–531.

Shoemaker, P.J. and Reese, S.D. (1996) *Mediating the message – theories of influences on mass media content.* 2nd edn. White Plains: Longman.

Silva, C.F. and Howe, D. (2012) "The (in)validity of supercrip representation of paralympian athletes," *Journal of Sport and Social Issues*, 36(2), pp.174–194.

Sims, D. (2014) "World Cup team stereotypes: Separating fact from fiction." TheAtlantic.com: www.theatlantic.com/entertainment/archive/2014/06/world-cup-team-stereotypes-separating-fact-from-fiction/372506/. Published: June 11. Last accessed: March 20, 2019.

Singh A. (2018) "BBC's Dan Roan reprimanded after claiming Leicester City boss 'died with his mistress'." Telegraph.co.uk: www.telegraph.co.uk/news/2018/10/30/bbcs-dan-roan-reprimanded-claiming-leicester-city-boss-died/. Published: October 30. Last accessed: March 20, 2019.

Sky Sports (2013), "Kevin Pietersen and Jack Wilshere in Twitter row over England eligibility," October 10. Available: www.skysports.com/cricket/news/12173/8965521.

Sky Sports (2018), "Mohamed Salah used for 'political propaganda' by Ramzan Kadyrov, say gay rights and equality campaigners," June 13. Available: www.skysports.com/football/news/12098/11404005/mohamed-salah-used-for-political-propaganda-by-ramzan-kadyrov-say-gay-rights-and-equality-campaigners.

Slawson, N. (2018) "TV presenter Helen Skelton reveals she was groped on air." TheGuardian.com. www.theguardian.com/world/2018/mar/15/tv-presenter-helen-skelton-reveals-she-was-groped-on-air. Published: March 15. Last accessed: September 8, 2018.

Smith, A. (2016) "The pedlars of fake news are corroding democracy." TheGuardian.com: www.theguardian.com/commentisfree/2016/nov/25/pedlars-fake-news-corroding-democracy-social-networks. Published: November 25. Last accessed: November 30, 2017.

Spiers, G. (2019), "Bigots will always be with us in Scottish football," *The Times*, Feb 23, https://www.thetimes.co.uk/article/bigots-will-always-be-with-us-in-scottish-football-xz9ktgjft. Last accessed: February 23, 2019.

Sports Journalists Association (2019) "Media release: Winners at the British Sports Journalism Awards," February 25. Available: www.sportsjournalists.co.uk/awards-news/media-release-winners-at-the-british-sports-journalism-awards/.

"Sports Media LGBT+ Survey results" (2018) *Sports Media LGBT+*, October 29. Available: https://sportsmedialgbt.com/sports-media-lgbt-survey-results.

Sportsmail Reporter, (2012), "Team GB have 61 'plastic Brits' taking part in London Olympics," MailOnline, July 11, https://www.dailymail.co.uk/sport/olympics/article-2171923/London-2012-Games-Team-GB-61-plastic-Brits.html. Last accessed: September 10, 2014.

Steen, R. (2014) *Sports journalism: A multimedia primer*. 2nd edn. Abingdon: Routledge.

Stonewall (2018) "LGBT in Britain Work Report," April 25. Available: www. stonewall.org.uk/lgbt-britain-work-report.

Sugden, J. and Tomlinson, A. (2007) "Stories from Planet Football and Sportsworld – source relations and collusion in sport journalism," *Journalism Practice*, 1(1), pp.44–61.

Sun Reporter (2016) "THE FALL OF STERLING: Life and times of Three Lions footie idiot Raheem," *The Sun*, June 30.

Sweney, M. (2016) "BBC stands by John Inverdale, saying Olympic tennis gaffe was 'simple error'." TheGuardian.com: www.theguardian.com/media/2016/aug/15/ bbc-john-inverdale-olympic-tennis-steve-redgrave. Published: August 15. Last accessed: September 9, 2018.

Sweney, M. and Duncan, P. (2018) "Watchdog reviews complaints about World Cup betting ads." TheGuardian.com: www.theguardian.com/media/2018/jul/17/ ad-watchdog-asa-reviews-complaints-world-cup-bet-now-offers-during-matches-problem-gambling. Published: July 18. Last accessed: September 11, 2018.

Sykes, A. (2018) "How to cover a football club when the fans are at war with the owners." Medium.com: https://medium.com/behind-local-news-uk/how-to-cover-a-football-club-when-the-fans-are-at-war-with-the-owners-c3380735002a. Published: May 13. Last accessed: October 3, 2018.

Taylor, D (2017), "Classification controversy marks terrible coming of age for Paralympic sport," *The Guardian*, October 31.

Templon, J. and Adams, R. (2018) "Two Chinese skating judges have been suspended for favoring their country's skaters." BuzzFeedNews.com: www.buzzfeednews.com/ article/johntemplon/figure-skating-authorities-suspend-two-chinese-judges-for. Published: June 20. Last accessed: November 1, 2018.

Thomas, R.J., and Antony, M.G. (2015) "Competing constructions of British national identity: British newspaper comment on the 2012 Olympics opening ceremony," *Media, Culture & Society*, 37(3), pp.493–503.

Thomsen, I. (1996), "Oh, Sorry: Tabloids Lose the Soccer War," *New York Times*, June 26, https://www.nytimes.com/1996/06/26/news/oh-sorry-tabloids-lose-the-soccer-war.html. Last accessed: March 20, 2019.

Thrower, A. (2018) "Formula 1 has AXED stunning grid girls and the babes are NOT happy about it." Dailystar.co.uk. www.dailystar.co.uk/news/latest-news/678618/ Formula-1-axes-grid-girls-furious. Published: February 1. Last accessed: September 8, 2018.

Tinley, S. (2012) "Covering Lance Armstrong was a wild ride, but the truth came out." Si.com: www.si.com/more-sports/2012/10/22/david-walsh-lance-armstrong. Published: October 22. Last accessed: July 20, 2017.

Truss, L. (2010) *Get her off the pitch! How sport took over my life*. London: Fourth Estate.

Turvill, W. (2015) "Andrew Jennings: Apart from Panorama and Sunday Times, UK coverage of wrongdoing at FIFA has been 'appalling'." PressGazette.com: www.pressgazette.co.uk/andrew-jennings-apart-panoroma-and-sunday-times-uk-coverage-wrongdoing-fifa-has-been-appalling. Published: June 5. Last accessed: March 23, 2016.

USA Today (2006) "Armstrong drops defamation lawsuits in France." USAToday.com: http://usatoday30.usatoday.com/sports/cycling/2006-07-06-armstrong-lawsuit-dropped_x.htm. Published: July 6. Last accessed: July 2, 2018.

Van Sterkenburg, J., Knoppers, A. and De Leeuw, S. (2010), "Race, ethnicity, and content analysis of the sports media: A critical reflection," *Media, Culture & Society*, 32(5), pp.819–839.

Vimieiro, A.C. (2017) "Sports journalism, supporters and new technologies – challenging the usual complicity between media and football institutions," *Digital Journalism*, 5(5), pp.567–586.

Viner, K. (2016) "How technology disrupted the truth." TheGuardian.com: www.theguardian.com/media/2016/jul/12/how-technology-disrupted-the-truth Published: July 12. Last accessed: November 2, 2016.

Walsh, D. (2012) *The program: Seven Deadly Sins – My pursuit of Lance Armstrong.* London: Simon & Schuster.

Walsh, D. (2013) *Inside Team Sky.* London: Simon & Schuster.

Ward, S. (2010) "Inventing objectivity: New philosophical foundations" in Meyers, C. (ed.) *Journalism ethics: A philosophical approach.* New York: Oxford University Press, pp.137–152.

Waterson, J. (2018) "Colombian ambassador complains about Sun's 'GO KANE!' front page." TheGuardian.com: www.theguardian.com/media/2018/jul/03/the-sun-go-kane-colombian-ambassador-complains-world-cup-england. Published: July 3. Last accessed: July 3, 2018.

"Weekly top 30 programmes". *Broadcasters' Audience Research Board.* Retrieved 1 August 2018.

Welch, J. (1999) "Indy Life." Independent.co.uk: www.independent.co.uk/life-style/the-secret-of-my-success-julie-welch-1091008.html. Published: May 2. Last accessed: March 10, 2019.

Whannel, G. (2002) *Media sports stars: Masculinities and moralities.* London: Routledge.

White, D. M. (1950) "The 'gatekeeper': A case study in the selection of news," *Journalism Quarterly*, 27(4), pp.383–390.

Whittle, J. (2009) *Bad blood – the secret life of the Tour de France.* London: Vintage.

Wilson, N., (2012), "There's no way I'll be standing for National Anthem when 'Plastic Brit' Porter wins gold." DailyMail.co.uk: www.dailymail.co.uk/sport/olympics/article-2112637/LONDON-2012-OLYMPICS-Plastic-Brits-wont-getting-support-says-Neil-Wilson.html Published: March 9. Last accessed: March 20, 2019.

Winter, H., (2018), "Raheem Sterling gets this level of abuse because he's black," *The Times*, December 10. https://www.thetimes.co.uk/article/raheem-sterling-gets-this-level-of-abuse-because-he-s-black-z2cv8dg36. Last accessed: December 10, 2019.

Wollaston, S. (2017) "When Football Banned Women review – Clare Balding recalls the beautiful game's ugliest decision." TheGuardian.com: www.theguardian.com/tv-and-radio/2017/jul/19/when-football-banned-women-clare-balding-fa. Published: July 19. Last accessed: March 10, 2019.

Woozencroft, H. (2018), "Why BBC Sport can't escape sports journalism's problem." BBC Sport: https://www.bbc.co.uk/sport/46571432. Published: December 14. Last accessed: March 20, 2019.

Yardley, J. (1978) "For better or worse, Jimmy Cannon influenced sportswriting," *Sports Illustrated*, August 14. Republished online: https://www.si.com/vault/1978/08/14/822869/booktalk-for-better-and-for-worse-jimmy-cannon-influenced-sportswriting. Last accessed: March 19, 2018.

Young, S. (2012) "We're not here for your inspiration." Australian Broadcasting Corporation: www.abc.net.au/news/2012-07-03/young-inspiration-porn/4107006. Published: July 3. Last accessed: March 20, 2019.

Younge, G. (2018) "The Serena cartoon debate: Calling out racism is not 'censorship'." TheGuardian.com: www.theguardian.com/commentisfree/2018/sep/13/serena-williams-cartoon-racism-censorship-mark-knight-herald-sun. Published: September 13. Last accessed: March 10, 2019.

Zirin, D. (2013) *Game over: How politics has turned the sports world upside down.* New York: The New Press.

Index

Printed in Great Britain
by Amazon

27870882R00112